ENDORSEME

"Alan first asked me if I could 'help the Osmonds toughen up their dance moves.' I taught them Tong Soo Do karate and created a karate fight routine set to music that they did on stage. Later when I appeared on *The Tonight Show*, I confirmed to Johnny Carson that I had taught the Osmond's karate to which Johnny made some wimpy hand gestures. I then said to Johnny, 'Hey, the Osmonds are tough.' Alan is tough in karate, but he is also tough in dealing with life's challenges. You are going to be inspired by his story."

> — CHUCK NORRIS, Champion, Celebrity, American Actor,
> Martial Artist with a Black Belt in Tang Soo D Karate

"Alan was our leader. I'm not sure he wanted to be, but the mantle fell on his shoulders at an early age. When we wrote songs together or creating inaugurals for presidents, the process was magical. Alan's creativity was extra special. He seemed to always receive inspiration when he was engaged in worthwhile causes. The album *The Plan*, in particular, is his greatest work. He heard it, he felt it, he saw it, and executed it with determination of heart and soul. One day the world will realize what a genius song writer my brother Alan really is. I'm truly honored to be his brother. He's one of the most creative people I've ever known. I love you for that. You will be a creator throughout eternity. I'll be watching you."

> — MERRILL OSMOND, Brother, Husband, Grandfather,
> and Lead Singer of The Osmonds

"Alan is a great leader! I know, because I had to take over the group as leader when he went to Fort Ord, California for boot camp in the military. I hated it. I just like to make people laugh by telling my jokes, and to play my guitar and musical instruments, like I did on 'Crazy Horses' and many other songs we wrote together. Alan is so creative, and I miss those times when we just jammed and performed LIVE in concerts. Alan, I love you forever my brother."

> — WAYNE OSMOND, Brother, Musician, Husband, Father, and Grandpa

"As a hyperactive bouncy young boy of two and a half years old, I learned very quickly that Alan was taking his job of being the leader of our little group very seriously. He was only eight but was expected to keep all four of us in line and make sure we were following instructions every day giving everything we had. From the very beginning Father let Alan know that he was in charge and the sergeant of our little platoon, and that we needed to listen to Alan and obey him. Alan took the charge and was very committed to the success of the Osmond Brothers. I can only imagine the pressure that was on Alan's shoulders at the age of eight. For quite some time, I felt that I held a grudge against Alan for all the years I missed being a normal child. But as I grew up and started to look back, I realized it was just the entire situation, not Alan. Not too long ago, Alan showed me his Heart when he said these words to me: *Jay, I want to tell you how much I love you. You and I have a very unique and long history together. As a young boy, I was put in a very difficult position and had to answer to Father. That was very demanding and overwhelming. You were a little kid and expected to do so much, which you did marvelously! I know there were many times that I was very hard on you, and I want to apologize. I felt so much pressure to meet Father's and the Andy William Show's demands. Nobody understands what we went through but us. I am sorry for any past offenses or hurt that I may have caused. I love you brother. – Alan*

I love you brother Alan and have finally appreciated your persistence and determination. I don't think we could have achieved everything we did without you at the lead."

– JAY OSMOND, Brother, Husband, Father, Grandpa,
Singer of The Osmonds, Drummer

"Our family has enjoyed remarkable success over the years, but it was the result of extraordinary hard work. How did a band made up of five young brothers achieve such harmony and synchronicity on stage? The answer is simple: we had a leader like Alan Osmond. I remember the countless hours Alan spent at the piano with each one of us as he meticulously played each of our complex, five-part harmony parts for us to learn. Alan was always there to help improve our dance routines in front of our rehearsal mirrors, and he spent days and days in recording studios writing and creating our albums. As entertainers, we had earned a reputation of being prepared for anything and everything. Wherever we performed—be it a TV studio, concert venue, or elsewhere—we delivered exciting flawless performances. That was achieved by dedicating nearly every waking hour of our youth to becoming what the industry called the 'One Take Osmonds.' That level of readiness requires discipline, commitment, and most importantly, leadership. We were not five soloists on stage; we were one cohesive unit, thanks to Alan's guidance. Every successful organization, whether it's a company or a boy band, needs a strong leader to achieve such success, and we were incredibly fortunate to have Alan as ours. But he was more than just a leader; he was my big brother. His demanding nature was equally matched by his loving spirit, which I believe is why everything worked so well. While the peak of the Osmond Brothers' success may now be part of musical history, future historians will certainly recognize that Alan Osmond was definitely the cornerstone of our achievements. Thank you, Alan, for being the leader of the band."

– Donny Osmond, Brother, Husband, Father, Grandpa, Singer of The Osmonds, Dancer, Actor, TV Host, and Former Teen Idol

"I was a boy on a bike the first time I encountered Alan Osmond. Alan had just married Suzanne, whose parents were customers on my newspaper route. Even at that young age I knew Alan wasn't ordinary. Decades later I unexpectedly inherited from Alan responsibility to carry on his production, *Stadium of Fire*. In the kindest way possible, Alan let me step into his giant shoes, and only then did I learn that Alan was more than a showman. Alan Osmond is a great human being, a loyal husband, father, patriot, and man of God. Yes, he is also one of the most creative people I know, a true showman, but that's because, like any good showman, he lives life to the fullest."

– Brad Pelo, President & Executive Producer, *The Chosen*

"I have known Alan Osmond for over 40 years and consider him to be a close personal friend. I have seen him at close range and in many pressure cooker situations as a performer, producer and world class creator but more importantly, I have seen his true character as a friend, father and husband. Alan is the quintessential family man to which anyone in his family would attest. His beautiful wife Suzanne and his eight sons are completely devoted to him. He is the most loyal of friends. I don't know anyone who speaks ill of Alan. This is an almost impossible feat when one has lived life publicly as Alan has. Most know him best for his key role as part of the Osmond's performing family. What they may or may not know is that because of that family's great power and influence during their so-called heyday, they trained a generation of music and television creatives at the famous Osmond Studios and essentially created the music, film and TV industry in the state of Utah. I, along with so many others, owe my career to this great family. The public may also not be aware of Alan's essential role in one of America's great national traditions— Provo's Freedom Festival. It was Alan's creative vision that sparked the sensation known as *Stadium of Fire* with its ubiquitous theme song that, try as you may, you can't forget! This festival has inspired a community tradition of service, pride and patriotism unrivaled anywhere in the USA. Alan has also been actively involved in efforts to benefit the victims of MS. His motto, 'I may have MS, but MS does not have me,' has been an inspiration to so many and he has lived by that credo. I have not been able to identify any ways in which his illness has slowed or deterred his activity. Lastly but foremost, Alan has a fierce and eternal commitment to his faith. He has never wavered or, like so many public figures, aired his doubts or grievances. His life has been an example of strength and consistency. His many years serving as a temple worker have softened him. This service has only made him sweeter, kinder and deeper. Once again, I thank Alan for everything he has contributed to my life and to the lives of so many. Few have lived life so large. The lessons he has learned are worth everyone's consideration."

— SAM CARDON, Musician, Writer Composer, Orchestrator,
Music Director of The Osmond Brothers

"Alan, you know our Lord like I do! Let's keep sharing Him and His wishes with others — I love you and the family."

— PAT (Pat Boone) Author, Entertainer

"Alan has always been the leader. If everybody could have the spirit and excitement for life and deal with life's circumstances as well as Alan Osmond, this would be a greater place to live."

— Elder M. Russell Ballard, American Businessman, Former Acting President of the Quorum of the Twelve Apostles of the Church of Jesus Christ of Latter-day Saints (2024)

"Having known Alan for many years, I am honored to call him my friend. Alan represents the values of God, family and country in everything he does and everyplace he serves, whether it be his church or in his service on the Freedom Festival board or speaking at a conference on families. Alan loves people and is excited to spread joy wherever he goes."

— Jeanette Herbert, Former First Lady of Utah

"I've known Alan for about 55 years. And over this brief period of time (ha!) I've come to be aware of many, many, things. He's super talented. Comes from a super talented family. Has an incredible life story. Is a spirit-filled child of God. And most importantly.....my friend. We've both been to the top of the mountain...and with God's guidance...learned how to kinda stay there. I truly look forward to reading his book!!"

— Michael Lloyd, American Record Producer

"I had the thrill of signing the Osmonds to their first major record contract, and Alan was an amazing leader who played such a major role in guiding the Osmonds to one of the most successful careers in the history of the music business. I treasure the many years that I have spent working with Alan and his incredible brothers."

— Mike Curb, Former Lieutenant Governor of California, American Musician, Record Company Executive, Motorsports Car Owner, Philanthropist

"For nearly 50 years, I've had the privilege of knowing and collaborating with this exceptional family. Without the Osmonds, Children's Miracle Network Hospitals would not exist today. Over the past 41 years, CMNH has raised an extraordinary $9 billion, benefiting 170 children's hospitals across North America and providing crucial support to millions of sick or injured children. That is a small part of what the Osmonds have contributed to the world. Their influential presence and enduring musical talent have enriched countless hearts and minds worldwide, leaving an unforgettable impact on both the industry and their adoring fans. Alan's book is a must-read for all Osmond fans, a cherished keepsake to pass down to future generations."

— JOSEPH G. LAKE, Co-Founder,
Children's Miracle Network Hospitals (retired)

"From time to time in the history of the world, there is a bright shiny star that shoots across the cosmos and lightens all of our lives. Alan Osmond is one of those bright shiny stars shooting across the sky. He makes our world better with his upbeat and joyful attitude. This comes through in everything that he does, and the end result is that I, and everybody else around him, wants to be better. Alan Osmond is a reminder of everything that is good. He gives us hope and encouragement. Thank you, Alan, for showing us an example of light and never giving up. It inspires us all and gives us hope."

— STEVEN R SHALLENBERGER, Chairman of
America's Freedom Festival, National Best-Selling Author,
Becoming Your Best, 12 Principles of Highly Successful Leaders

"If you are looking for inspiration of how to face challenges with courage, to lead by example, use your creativity to bless the world and your family, and live consistent with your values, then look to the life story of Alan Osmond. His life journey is filled with remarkable lessons to help us live a happier and more fulfilling life. He is a creative leader and, over the years, has used his writing, producing and musical talent to be a blessing to the world, his community, and friends. I have personally witnessed his love for people, generosity to those around him, and refusal to let multiple sclerosis or any other challenge stand in his way of doing good. His greatest achievement is being a wonderful partner to his wife Suzanne and father to his talented children. His life is a testament to the power of grace, humor, and an unbreakable spirit. I am excited for this book. Congratulations!"

– McKay Christensen, President and CEO
of Thanksgiving Point

"I met Alan in the early 1970's. He is five years younger than me. We were both young! Alan was the oldest of the performing Osmonds and they were on fire with success. Million selling records and sold-out arena tours. Alan was the leader on and off stage. I was a young personal manager in a major firm and had been assigned to guide the Osmonds logistically. A bit creatively but mostly hands on deck. In essence, Alan and I grew up professionally together. He had great ideas, and I had, somehow, a knack for putting them together. There were some ups and downs; mostly ups. There were a few classic sibling rivalries among his siblings, which his parents masterfully maneuvered. The Osmond's tenacity for 'family comes first' always won. It made a great impression on me. I went on to become a rather prominent personal manager having learned a lot from my Osmond experience. I once gave the commencement address at the University of Nebraska, and I referred to *family comes first.*"

– Jim Morey, Chairman, Morey Management Group

ALAN
OSMOND

ONE WAY TICKET

ALAN

ONE WAY TICKET

WITH

DEBBIE IHLER RASMUSSEN

NOIZ
MEDIA

For information contact:
alanosmondbooks@gmail.com

Published by:
NOIZ MEDIA, LLC

Cover design and interior book design by
Francine Platt, Eden Graphics, Inc.

Paperback ISBN 979-8-89454-020-7

eBook and Audio Book Published by:
Ascendt Publishing

eBook ISBN 979-8-89454-021-4
Audio ISBN 979-8-89454-022-1

Library of Congress Number: 2024945205

Second Edition

*To my parents, George and Olive Osmond,
who gave me life…my brothers and Marie who
'side-by-side' gave their all…Suzanne, my
wife and eternal love…my sons and their wives
for their constant support…my ever-increasing
posterity, that bring inexpressible joy.*

TABLE OF CONTENTS

BONUS MATERIAL

FOREWORD

ONE'S GIFT TO THE WORLD remains such not only by the accomplishments of a life well-lived, but by the attitude and sincere nature with which those accomplishments are made. So, it's been in the 67-year career of Alan Osmond. His accomplishments are countless, and the genuineness with which he has displayed them are as real as the man himself.

I asked this gifted entertainer one day, "If you had it to do all over again, would you?" His response surprised me. "Do what? Have fun? It's been hard, but I've had fun." He is quick to identify with the learning and understanding that has carried him throughout his journey. But indeed, the enjoyment he has garnered throughout these six-plus decades has not always been easy. There has been one mountain to climb after another, and he has tackled each path with determination and resolve. To Alan, his life story has been one with a foundational base of believing there is *purpose* in all things. Regardless of the degree each challenge may bring, there is a lesson to be learned—there is a reason in all things, and they provide for personal growth and understanding.

This book tells his story, and it does so in a profound, sincere, and raw manner. It has been in the making since first being assigned by his father, George, to take responsibility in leading the group to that which they were collectively seeking. That burden, placed upon the shoulders of an 8-year-old boy, was daunting.

But in him was placed the task of either making or breaking the Osmond Brother's Quartet. There was priority in getting them up each morning to do chores on the family farm, then gathering them for rehearsals during those early morning and evening hours. Largely by his maturing leadership and dedication to that which his siblings sought, the Osmond brand became one of history-making years spent perfecting that which they were so gifted to share. The "fun" came with intense and dedicated focus to a craft that would bring fame, fortune, then eventual heartache and renewal of a newly created life. But *determination* was his byword and *purpose* was his goal.

In reading the following pages, one will be overwhelmed by the countless stories so unselfishly shared. For the first time, Alan opens nearly every door of his life and career. And blessed with abundant talent in nearly every aspect of the entertainment industry, he has accomplished what few can or will do to bring joy and satisfaction to millions of fans the world over. He has mastered those multiple talents and has developed both a leadership style in directing his famous family and creating multiple entities that have built and blessed numerous lives.

This book has been in the making for those 67-years in show business. It is a vast collection of life's raw elements that have made Alan Osmond a household name—a show business personality and star who has given of himself freely before the eyes and hearts of those loyal followers from every corner of the globe.

What awaits you is the internal make up of Alan himself. He writes from the heart of those things that have made him a recognized leader, one who has met head-on with the challenges of a demanding profession, countless opportunities and privilege, and blessings beyond his ability to recognize and count. There is a fan base awaiting this biography, and Alan Osmond has been equally anxious to deliver it to them. One might say that it is still being written. He rarely sleeps through the night without churning over new ideas, lyrics to new songs, and considering and accepting the purpose behind his life adventures.

This writing contains emotional stories not only of years gone by, and of those being lived at the moment. It speaks of sheer determination and will power to give his very best to all things placed at his feet. From years of success in the recording studio, motion pictures, television, sound stage, and countless concert halls throughout the world. It's also a story of finding strength in such success to suddenly be turned upside down by the weakening disease that now robs his body of the physical nature of his creation. To the effects of MS, he refuses to allow its crippling outreach to stop him from doing so many other things he is yet capable of doing. But perhaps one of the most memorable aspects of this book is that in which he details the dating, falling in love with, and marriage to his sweetheart of fifty years, Suzanne. Their story speaks volumes in devotion, loyalty, and continued romance with a family of eight sons and numerous grandchildren.

I have known few like him. He is a man of exquisite faith and purpose—sustained by a belief in principles centered on family values and togetherness. He has gifted to the world tireless hours in all aspects of his life, ever trying to be an example of integrity and good will. It's to that world-wide fan base (that Alan refers to as friends and extended family) that this book has been written. He has shared so much of himself from stage after stage, tour after tour, decade after decade, that the more personal and intimate inside of his life be given in this manner.

He is a man of insight, aggressive thinking, perseverance and prospective, dedication and decisiveness, and his story now belongs to all who have been captivated by his multi-faceted life filled with that accomplishment and purpose which means so much to him.

His story now belongs to you...

– Ron Clark

Director of Public Affairs and Guest Relations, Brigham Young University; Director of Public Relations, Osmond Enterprises

PREFACE

by Debbie Ihler Rasmussen, Author

BESTSELLING AUTHOR Richard Paul Evans called me one afternoon. I had recently finished a research project with him, and he asked me if I had the bandwidth to write another book.

I heard *'brain width.'* "Maybe. What is it?"

"Not what, *who*. Would you be interested in writing Alan Osmond's life story?"

I'm not often speechless.

"Debbie?"

"Uh…yes. Yes."

"Good. Here's his number. Call him right away." Then he added, "Good luck."

After about fifteen minutes of deep breathing to calm my heart, I called, and Alan answered.

I introduced myself and told them that Richard Paul Evans had suggested I call.

"Debbie! Yes, we just got off the phone with Richard!"

Alan's enthusiasm caught me off guard. (I would soon come to learn that Alan's whole life was an exclamation point!)

He added, "Suzanne is here with me."

"Hi, Debbie."

I was immediately at ease.

So began my journey into the life of Alan Osmond. The only word that comes to mind is *unbelievable*. How could one person achieve so much in one lifetime? Because he never stops. To this day, Alan is up for just about anything, and Suzanne is right there by his side. They have the most dedicated fans on the planet, many who have remained faithful for fifty plus years.

With a creative mind that never rests (Suzanne will confirm this!) he and his siblings burst into the music world and took it by storm. But for the truly gifted, ever-talented Alan, that was just the beginning. This book was not without challenges, lots of them, and Alan was meticulous about its content. I have been in awe as I detailed on these pages Alan's never ending over the top achievements, crazy and sometimes scary experiences, his sincere faith in God, and a multitude of adventures that later included his and Suzanne's eight sons as the Osmonds Second Generation.

This book quickly became a labor of love as I tried to capture the true spirit of this extremely gifted, and delightful family. What a pleasure to co-author with such a talent as Alan, and what a privilege to be allowed into their life. Due to the mounds of information for research, I joked with them that I knew more about their life than they did.

I will be forever grateful for the call from Richard that day and feel sincerely blessed that Alan and Suzanne trusted me with a project that I consider sacred.

Debbie has written eight books; A paranormal mystery trilogy with two back stories, Two books in a superhero adventure series, and one children's book. After a forty-four year career in dance, she currently writes full time and is a content editor for Richard Paul Evans' Author Ready. She has six children, seventeen grandchildren, and has lived in Utah and California. She currently lives in Surprise, Arizona. She loves her family, life, writing, and the sun!

PROLOGUE

IF MY PARENTS had listened to the doctors, I wouldn't even be here.

George and Olive Osmond's first two boys, Virl and Tom were both born hearing impaired. Informed that the condition was hereditary, the doctor strongly encouraged them not to have any more children.

Another doctor, upon finding both boys had hearing problems, recommended putting them in an institution for the deaf where they would live the rest of their lives.

Had those doctors known much about George or Olive, they would not have given those suggestions. Strong faith, fortitude, and sheer determination would prove to have a huge impact on their future family and form the foundation of the Osmond legacy.

I was born June 22, 1949. Because the following came from my mother's journal, I want to include her words here:

> On June 22, 1949, our sweet little Alan Ralph Osmond was born at the Dee Hospital in Ogden.
>
> We had worried about the possibility of him having a hearing loss since we had recently learned about Virl's and Tommy's problem, but the doctor assured us that he was all right. He was healthy and strong and very active. We were relieved.
>
> I had a peculiar experience when Alan was born. Perhaps I was just partially unconscious but when I read about people

having 'out of body experiences' it makes me wonder if I weren't pretty close to that myself.

I could hear the doctor and nurses talking when one of the nurses became quite excited and called the doctor to come quickly. She said my blood pressure was dropping, and I wasn't responding to her trying to wake me. I felt nothing but seemed to be up in the ceiling — I wasn't aware of having a body — no pain — it seemed I was like a 'blinking light' (probably my heart beating). The doctor called my name, but I didn't answer. He called me again just a little louder and I thought, 'I wish they would just leave me alone.' The third time he called, I responded. I woke up — still on the table and the nurse was slapping my face. I was surely happy when they put my third little son in my arms and told me he was just fine.

– Olive Osmond

I would be followed by five more brothers and a sister. Not only were we all born with no hearing impairments, but the polar opposite. All seven younger siblings had impeccable hearing and an ear and gift for music. And our two hearing impaired brothers? Mother took it upon herself to teach them at home. Tom had the most severe hearing loss, and though he did attend a school for the deaf during regular school hours, neither of them ever spent one day in an institution.

All nine of us were blessed to be taught at our mother's knee and schooled by our military father in our humble home. There began an unexpected, unprecedented, and most incredible journey of the Osmond Family from Ogden, Utah.

Our philosophy: *"We Seek Higher Things."*

I'm Alan, the third son, and this is *my story.*

🙨 **1** 🙨

IT ALL STARTED
WITH GEORGE AND OLIVE

MY FATHER, George Osmond served in the military and left at the age of twenty-six as a retired Army Sergeant. Due to a chronically troublesome stomach, he had decided to remain a bachelor.

The day Father walked into the Ogden Army Depot looking for work, was the first time he saw Olive May Davis. She was typing and when she saw George, she turned to a co-worker and said, "Someday I'm going to marry that man."

It wasn't long after that when she was serving ice cream at the depot, she gave George an extra scoop and a smile.

Olive, a native of Malad, Idaho, who also had Star Valley, Wyoming roots, felt that someday, George would be important in her life. It was just a few days later when she and George talked about more than ice cream. Later Olive said, "My heart seemed to melt. I fell in love immediately."

She was surprised to learn that her mother knew the Osmond family. Her mother had lived in their house and carried George around when he was a toddler.

As they became better acquainted, George and Olive discovered that they both loved music. She was a gifted E flat alto saxophone player who had performed with big bands in the early 1940s, and

George sang with a rich baritone voice. She often accompanied him on the piano for hours.

It wasn't long before George asked nineteen-year-old Olive to marry him. Less than a year after they met, the two were married in the Salt Lake City LDS Temple on December 1, 1944.

Both were devoted members of the Church of Jesus Christ of Latter-day Saints and early in

George and Olive

their marriage when Virl and Tom were just toddlers, Father and Mother moved to Cedar City, Utah, and developed businesses in both real estate and insurance. After things didn't work out with a business partner, they decided to move to their hometown of Ogden, Utah, and start their own enterprises.

They lived in a twenty-seven-foot trailer until they found a modest, rundown house that they worked together to make livable. They loved the fenced backyard where their children could play in the sandbox they built for them.

They were blessed with two beautiful little boys, Virl and Tom. One day when the boys were playing and Mother called them to come in, only Virl answered. Tommy continued to play, seemingly oblivious to his mother. Startled and concerned, she wondered if Tommy might not be able to hear.

Father and Mother took both of them to the doctor only to learn that both boys were hearing impaired—Virl had forty percent hearing, but Tommy was ninety percent deaf.

The next thing the doctors offered in the way of suggestion to the young couple was to recommend putting the two boys in an institution where they would live the rest of their lives—a solution that was absolutely not an option for the young parents. Instead, they enrolled them in the local school for the deaf but afterward, the boys came home each day where Mother worked with them.

As time passed, Virl eventually was able to do quite well with ear plugs and a hearing device on his chest. When he was in junior high school, he attended regular public school, but Tom was never able to.

Mother took it upon herself to learn all that she could about hearing loss, and along with their studies at the Utah School for the Deaf, she read to her sons constantly, working with them tirelessly in an effort to help them learn to talk and communicate to the best of their ability.

Olive teaching Virl and Tom

While Father was on a hunting trip, Mother hired someone to build a stairway up to the attic of their house. When he came back from the trip, he finished her vision by turning the attic into a school room, where each of their children would have a different colored desk. They purchased special equipment to help Virl and Tom learn to speak; the machine would light up when the letters, S, T, M, and P were spoken correctly.

Father and Mother soon added six more boys to their ever-growing family. I was born in 1949, Wayne in 1951, Merrill in 1953, and Jay in 1955. Donny was born two years later in 1957, and then Jimmy in 1963. Between Donny and Jimmy, they were delighted to welcome their only daughter, Marie, in 1959.

FACT

Marie, our only sister, was born on our Father's Birthday. When she was born, we stood outside the Hospital window and sang, "I Want A Girl, Just Like The Girl, That Married Dear Old Dad"!

Our parents knew that hearing aids would be the best for their boys, but they lived a modest life, and the expense was beyond what they could afford. Father sold insurance and real estate, drove taxi, ran a small farm in Ogden, and was the North Ogden postmaster. During the holiday season when they had an overabundance of packages and letters, they would bring us boys in to help.

Due to their struggling young family and doing all they could to provide, at one time Merrill asked for a new bicycle. They did manage to get him one, and Merrill explains, "It was used, which was fine, but it was also pink, which was embarrassing."

Though the young family struggled financially they were happy and experienced what they felt were many miracles—one of those being the birth of me, their third son. Although they were advised by doctors not to have any more children, they felt strongly that they were to have more, and when I was born the first thing they wanted to know was if I could hear.

Father and Mother fostered their love of music in their children, especially when they discovered that four Osmond brothers, Wayne, Merrill, Jay, and I, could sing. These talents would prove to be the answer to the solution of hearing aids for Virl and Tom.

———— ✖ ————

Throughout the years of the Osmond family, Father was the disciplinarian and Mother the peacemaker. "Mother was an educator and a visionary, and Father an organizer who made things happen."

There were those that believed Father was too strict and too demanding; but guiding us in our singing career, would require precision and single mindedness toward the goal.

Marie had a different relationship with Father than her brothers. For example, she called him "Daddy" instead of Father. Marie says, "After Mother had a stroke, I spent hours by her side. So did Daddy, and we had a lot of conversations. I came to believe that sons need their fathers to help them become what they were meant to be. I believe that applies to mothers and daughters as well. Daughters need their mothers. I know that applies to me."

Father had a "do it right" mentality and helped us to accomplish this. He also insisted that whatever we did, we would do it as a family, no matter what it was. Father and Mother were always on hand to guide their children throughout our career, which proved to keep their family intact.

Mother liked to quote Jesuit priest Father Strickland from his 1863 diary, "There is no end to the good you can do if you don't care who gets the credit."

OSMOND FACT

Marie had her own bedroom. All seven brothers had to sleep on seven army cots in a dormitory!

Four Boys from Ogden, Utah

Our home, though full of love and fun, was run military style. Father built a dormitory or barracks in the back of our home with seven army cots, footlockers, and open closets that he inspected much like he did with his troops in his Army days.

Father had served as an Army sergeant during WW II and possessed a very strong work ethic. Our small home in Northern Utah provided plenty of opportunity for us kids to develop that same mindset. Chores were a regular part of our growing up experience. With a cow, chickens, horses, sheep, orchards, a huge garden, and pasture to take care of, those responsibilities fell on all of us.

Our daily routine also consisted of learning to play musical instruments. I played the bugle, and to the annoyance of my brothers, I was assigned the duty of waking everyone early by playing reveille. Once jolted out of our slumber, our chores began. Mother took it upon herself to teach Virl and Tom and we were all taught by her and by our hard-working military father in our humble home.

We each had our own assignments whether it be milking the cow, separating the cream, gathering the eggs, or hauling hay for the two horses and Shetland pony. We also had chickens and sheep. For the animals to have water in the winter, we often had to carry a five-gallon metal can of hot water to thaw the frozen water pipe. Our parents rented a two-and-a-half-acre field where they planted sugar beets and we were told, "hoe to the end of the row," then harvested every foot of them. We also bailed hay and hauled irrigation pipe. That was hard work. Once chores were completed, we gathered at the table for prayer and breakfast. Our family friend, Joe Deamer, picked Tom

My adult brother Tom next to our closets — kept open for inspection

up and drove him to the Utah school for the deaf. Both Virl and Tom went to that school, then Virl started Jr. High because he had new hearing aids and could hear well enough. The rest of us, including Virl, walked to school.

I remember being tired even before the first bell rang and more so when the school day ended, but relaxation was reserved for bedtime. We still had evening chores to do before gathering for dinner. Homework followed and then we would practice our music. When we went to bed at night, to help us learn new songs faster, Mother would play a recording she made of each of our harmony parts.

Hard work, talent, excellent secretarial skills, and their responsibility to provide for their growing family, Father and Mother ran successful business ventures in real estate and insurance, as well as running the North Ogden post office where our Grandma Davis worked at the front desk. We all worked in the Post Office, especially at Christmas time.

Mother also had a dress shop called LaVerna's Dress Shop. She ran it with our Grandma LaVerna Osmond.

Father's heritage was English. He had a rich baritone voice and loved to sing. Mother was of Welch descent. She read music and played a screaming saxophone in a band, as well as the piano; and she participated in her high school band. In their earlier years she performed for community events and church functions.

We didn't have much time for friends outside of our family; Father felt that school was the place for friends and socializing. We never had *birthday parties* like our friends had, ours were just for family. My brothers were my best friends and when there was time to play, we played games with each other. Otherwise, we were singing together.

more broken bottles. We had never experienced anything like that before. While the announcer thanked us, the crowd screamed that they wanted more fights. We hurried out of the ring.

Father had this habit of sniffing when he was nervous, and he was doing that when we reached him and Mother at the side of the ring. She was not happy and said, "If this is what show business is all about, we don't want anything to do with it."

They quickly ushered us out of the auditorium to our camper and Father said, "Good job boys." He told us he and Mother had decided to turn lemons into lemonade and asked if we wanted to go to Disneyland the next day. Thrilled at the idea, we began cheering and soon forgot about being booed off the stage. The next morning, we entered the "Magic Kingdom!"

———————— ✠ ————————

The story of how we were discovered at Disneyland has been told many times, but I still have to share it, because it is special to me. I remember seeing the Dapper Dans riding toward us down Main Street on a bicycle built for four. They were singing and I said to Wayne and Merrill, "Look, a quartet."

We got as close as we could to them. We were wearing matching outfits and one of them noticed, "You look like a quartet," and he chuckled.

"We are," I told him.

They asked us to sing for them, so, we did. The crowd grew so large it started blocking the pedestrians, the trolley car on Main Street, and other moving carts trying to pass by.

One of the Dapper Dan's said, "You need to meet our boss."

They took us to the office of Tommy Walker, the park manager. He was in charge of the fireworks shows at Disneyland as well as created the *Charge* routine used by the University of California Trojan's marching band.

They told Mr. Walker how they had asked us to sing for them, that the crowd loved us, and that he should listen to us. Tommy Walker thanked them and directed us to his office and he and

The Dapper Dans at Disneyland

Father went inside. After briefly talking with Father, he invited us kids to come into his office. "I heard you caused a little traffic jam out there and that our trolley car had to stop because of the crowd."

We thought we were in trouble, and we just nodded our heads.

Then he asked us to sing him a song. We sang two; "Hi There Folks" and "Side by Side."

He smiled at Father; I could tell he liked us. He asked us to sing a couple more songs and then he said, "How would you like to come back next summer and do just what you did today; sing on the streets for the patrons of Disneyland?"

Father said, "We would love to."

We were so excited! Father and Mr. Walker worked out the details, then Mr. Walker pulled out a bunch of Disneyland tickets from his desk drawer and said, "I'll bet you would like to go on some rides in the park." He was so nice and gave us plenty of tickets

On the set of Jamie McPheeters with Kurt Russell

night. Because we had to abide by the child labor laws, we would sometimes leave the studio, drive around the block, come back, and rehearse some more, and more, and more. We leaned heavily on our skills with musical instruments and our routines.

Dave Grusin helped us with our instrumental work; one of which was our swinging saxophone arrangement of a song called,

"Lester Leaps In," and during the later years of *The Andy Williams Show*, we worked with Earl Brown, a musical genius, who helped us work up some sophisticated and intricate vocal arrangements.

Andy was amazing—he offered us his best arrangers and production people that made us look and sound good. He gave us a great music education and even helped us with breathing and singing advice. One day he asked us if we knew how to ice skate. He said the whole stage was going to be an ice rink and that ice skating champion Peggy Fleming would be on the show.

Before I could answer "no," Father said, "We'll be ready."

That was one of those nights that we didn't go home after work. Instead, we went to the nearest ice rink with Jack Regas, our choreographer, who also didn't know how to ice skate. We bought skates and hired the manager to teach us. Within a week, we had

Seven Little Foys

us to branch out and try some appearances on our own. We had recorded a couple of albums; *Songs We Sang on the Andy Williams Show* and *More Songs We Sang on the Andy Williams Show*, and George Wyle produced a Hymn Album for us. None of those albums were pop music, which is what our friends liked, as well as what we listened to.

Andy was easy to work with, and though he expected professionalism, he was complimentary when we did well, and I can't honestly remember him ever getting angry when we were around. He helped make sure we were singing properly and gave us a few lessons on breathing while we sang.

I didn't want to let Andy down, and neither did my brothers, so we gave it our all for every rehearsal and performance. The only time I was concerned about upsetting Andy was when doing his TV shows he once said to me, "Alan, if you don't stoop over, you're off the show." I was taller than Andy and I took him seriously. So, from then on when singing with him you will notice that I somewhat slouched over.

Later, Donny did an imitation of one of Andy's hits, "You Are My Sunshine." Andy was so impressed that he had Donny perform the song on one of his shows with full orchestra accompaniment.

We were growing up in front of a nationwide and international audience. When Jay started losing his baby teeth, Father was a little upset seeing the gap in Jay's mouth and said, "Oh Jay, we've got this first big television show to do, and you're toothless."

But it turned out to work in our favor. The show's director, Bob Henry, had taught us to watch for the red lights on the television cameras. When we saw that light, it was the "hot" camera, and we were supposed to "play" to it. Father had also taught Jay to wink, capitalizing on that fact that he was a six-year-old natural ham. Jay would locate the steady red light, turn to it, and flash a toothless grin. The audiences loved it.

As the show progressed, Andy gave us more and bigger parts in the show. He even had his orchestra arrangers, Billy May, and Jack Elliott do some big band arrangements for us. By our second season we were doing full scale production numbers with six-or seven-minute medleys. We also did a dance number with Andy's wife, Claudine Longet, and sang with Julie Andrews and Cher.

Andy loved our high energy and versatility; along with ice skating, riding unicycles, juggling, etc., he had all of us perform a tap dance on top of five pianos, and that was after we played them. We later worked with one demanding choreographer, Jamie Rogers, on the *Jerry Lewis* and *Flip Wilson Shows*. He kept us on our feet for hours at a time, give us a quick break and then call us back to the dance floor. But through all of that exhausting work we learned a contemporary style of dance that served us well throughout our careers.

Father and Mother were careful in sorting out the offers for us, because they were definitely out there, but we did take a bold step forward with a new musical style and look. Pop star Bobby Darin and Terry Melcher were with Capitol Records. They approached us to record a single with them called, "I Can't Stop," but it didn't go very far. We also recorded a song I wrote called "Movin' Along." The song was pleasant enough, but it didn't say anything, and it didn't go anywhere. That experience caused me to really delve more into song lyrics and concept, as well as the music.

That song didn't excite me, but being in the studio did. It wasn't the first time I had been in a recording session, so I recognized immediately that it would require a different approach than what we were used to in singing to live audiences. I could see that in order to reach our goals, we would need to adapt the way we sang.

Andy was in the process of launching his new record company, I talked with him, and he seemed to agree that I had some valid points, and we left his show.

Leaving Andy Williams on good terms was a leap of faith and taking that step seemed like a big mistake. Nothing happened. No work at all. We tried to come up with our own creations and wrote our own songs. Though we learned a lot, we never got a hit.

We were regulars on *The Andy William's Show* from 1962–1969, the same time the Beatles were reveling in their greatest popularity. We loved their music and were influenced by it. We put together a parody of the Beatles music; I played rhythm guitar, Merrill was on bass, Wayne was lead guitar, and Jay played the drums, and Donny on keyboards. This moved us even further away from barbershop.

Besides the Beatles, we were influenced by other popular groups of the sixties, including Three Dog Night, Led Zepplin, Credence Clearwater, and later, the Bee Gees.

We knew we needed to find our own sound.

We wanted to keep our harmonies, but it was Rick Hall in Muscle Schoals, Alabama, who had us sing more guttural, soulful, and young. We had to be more hip, less barbershop. Through all of this I learned what it took to become a producer—this would prove to be valuable to me professionally.

Getting an Education Had Its Challenges

I was thirteen when we moved to California, and our grueling schedule caused me to miss much of the regular public-school experiences. I had to leave my friends in Utah. Once in a while we would return for a visit, but it was hard to pick back up with them. I didn't think I had changed, but my friends didn't seem to know how to relate to me anymore. I guess it was because I had been on television. It made me sad, and I regret not knowing what it was like to have school friends; to hang out, go to proms, cruise the boulevard, sign yearbooks, go steady, and hang out with the guys.

Being full-timed employed, regular attendance at school was an ongoing problem. We attended public school when we could, but most of the time we had private tutors. By law, the studio was required to provide that service, but it was often crammed in between rehearsals and performances. Finding balance wasn't easy. Mother and her parents, who were both schoolteachers, made sure we kept up on our studies. In my private studies, I earned mostly A's in the American School Correspondence courses. But when I went back to public school, they only gave me a C grade.

I enjoyed sports, but our work schedule didn't allow for participating in school sports. I played the stand-up bass violin in the Highland Jr. High School orchestra for a while when I was in the seventh grade. But when they had concerts, I couldn't be there for them because I was performing with my brothers. I was the only bass player and to hear the orchestra play without the bass, after practicing with me, made everyone mad. The music teacher asked me to drop out of the orchestra.

"If you can't play our concerts," he said, "Then quit."

So, I did.

During those years I attended Monroe High School through the eleventh grade. One day Mother forgot to pick me up from school, and while walking home I was attacked by a gang of boys who had been expelled from school. When they drove by me, one guy hit me hard in the back with a board, knocking me down. I landed on my face and was left with scars from it. I was in tears and a lot of pain when I got home, and Mother was done with public school. We were home schooled or tutored from then on.

I didn't participate in a high school graduation ceremony; however, I did graduate, earning two diplomas: one from the Ogden Utah School District and one for completing the American School with correspondence classes after taking the GED tests.

Headlining in Vegas

In 1965 we performed often in several hotels in Las Vegas where we were the opening act for such famous performers as Phil Harris, Nancy Sinatra, Jimmy Durante, Phyllis Diller, Roger Miller, and Shirley Bassey.

By the late sixties, we had our own main billing. By 1971 we were fortunate enough to be headlining at Caesar's Palace being the youngest group ever to headline in a major Las Vegas show.

When we did a Beatles medley on *The Andy Williams Show*, Fender gave us some new guitars and amplifiers. I was given a Telecaster, Wayne a Stratocaster, and Merrill a jazz bass guitar. Ludwig drums gave Jay a new set of drums, and we began experimenting with a new style.

Father got us a used three-track Ampex tape recorder—a multitrack recorder which allowed different tracks or channels of sound to record and playback all synchronized so we could start learning how to record our own music. Since there were only three tracks, we would record in mono and mix and "ping pong" back and forth among those three tracks when recording demo songs. We soon outgrew that and got into high tech sixteen and then twenty-four track recording studios. We learned quickly about the technical side of music, especially Wayne and Donny, giving us experience we would use later on.

OSMOND FACTS

Phyllis Diller rented a Restaurant and cooked dinner for all of us Osmonds.

While working in Las Vegas, I took Karen Carpenter out to dinner.

We experimented with some new sounds, hoping to attract some favorable national attention. Although none of those songs became hits, it set us on a path toward a more contemporary sound; and reaching young people our age.

That's when we met Mike Curb. Mother had followed him in industry trade papers and felt he could help us. So, in true Mother style, she reached out to him. They hit it off immediately and he became a trusted and long-time friend. Mike later became the president of MGM Records.

We Traveled the World – Sweden

During the summers of 1964–1966 we went to Sweden each year for three years, six weeks at a time, kicking off our international popularity. Now that Jimmy had joined us he was gaining his own fans and fame. We sang in their many folk parks and on TV and learned how to introduce ourselves in Swedish. We also recorded in Swedish and had a hit song, "Fem Smutsiga sma fingrar" ("Five Dirty Little Fingers.")

We started our tour in a fifteen-passenger van driven by Jaw

Elwing, and we pulled a trailer with all our instruments, sound system, and microphones.

We sang with a Swedish celebrity, Lasse Lindahl, and recorded some songs with him. We traveled to the folk parks in wooded areas, and we would do two or three parks a day. We set up the stage and sound system, rehearsed, did a sound check, and then performed. Swedish girls would often bring us bouquets of flowers and Swedish gifts.

One year, from August 1st to the 15th, Alice Babs and Lasse Londahl, famous Swedish entertainers, joined us on stage for a song at Berns Restaurant.

After each show, we would pack everything up and do the same thing over and over again for six weeks at a time in the summer months.

Per Alan's Journals—Our Swedish Tour:

July 4–9 Goteborg: Lisaberg
10 —
11 Lidkoping, and Skovde
12 Hunnebostrand, and Ellos
13 Vanersborg, and Bangtefors
14 Arvika, and Munkfors
15 Hallstahammar, and Koping
16 Eskilstuna, and Nykoping
17 —
18 Linkoping, and Mjolby
19 Kultsfred, and Gamleby
20 Huskvarna, and Vetlanda
21 Malmo, and Landskrona
22 Ahus, and Karlshamn
23 Kalmar, and Oskarahamn
24 —
25 Motala, and Tranas
26 Sala, and Vasteras

27 Rattvik, and Mora
28 Borlange, and Nas
29 Hedemora, and Hofora
30 Bollnae, and Gavle

We fell in love with these people. Of course we liked looking at the pretty girls, too. In fact, Hasselblad cameras knew that I liked photography, so they did a major magazine story about me and my brothers taking pictures of Swedish girls. It went over well, and the company gave me a free camera with an 80mm lens.

Journal Entry

December 14, 1965

We are in Las Vegas now and are working at the Desert Inn with Andy Williams. Andy is a wonderful guy, and the people love him. The show is going really well, and our part is going over super! Andy's father, Jay Williams, told us he didn't know what Andy would do without us! That was nice of him.

We finished Las Vegas with a huge success and G.A.C., (our booking agency) told us we got great reviews, and it was the best publicity we could have.

At the Sahara Tahoe Hotel, we worked with Jimmy Durante. His show was so loud and long show and ours was 'too sophisticated,' so we went early the next day and unpacked our drums, guitars, and saxes, reset the lighting, and worked up a new rock and roll show format. I called Al Tronte, the orchestra leader, to come over earlier and we added to our show rundown: 'Hang on Sloopy,' "I Can't Stop," "There's A Kind of Hush," "These Boots are made for walking" (Donny) and "Let's Hang On" with Jay's drum solo. We didn't get to rehearse it with the band, but I talked the run down thoroughly with Al Tronte and they did a pretty good job for the first time reading it. Everyone liked the show much better.

Mother took Marie and Jimmy up to Utah to see Tommy get out of the Mission home and take off to Canada on the jet to see brother Virl who is already serving there in Edmonton. Tommy did a great job as I understand at the mission home, and they said he's a leader and not a follower. Because of Tom's deafness, the General Authorities were questioning whether or not to send Tommy on the mission right before he entered the mission home, but through inspiration, they agreed for him to go and be Virl's Missionary companion in Edmonton, Canada. They are both the first deaf missionaries for our Church!

5

LEAVING THE SECURITY OF ANDY WILLIAMS

As a family, we prayed about what direction we should go with our music. Though Andy had offered to continue on with him, we told Andy we wanted to reach a younger teen market, so we felt we needed to pursue our own career path. We did not want to become to Andy Williams what the Lennon Sisters were to Lawrence Welk. We had signed a five-year contract with Andy Williams, but we ended up staying for seven years.

I began feeling concerned about where our careers were going. We were doing concerts all over the country at local fairs, and we were featured on several variety shows, but in my heart I knew we were better than that. I knew we could be bigger, and I wanted that for us. So, when I was eighteen I wrote the following letter to our manager Don Williams, on September 26, 1967.

Dear Don,

I don't know whether I should write this letter or not. (Mother and Father don't know that I'm writing it), but I have some problems that I have been worrying about.

We have managed to get a deferment from Uncle Sam (the draft board) to serve a mission, and before Wayne takes over the group (Osmond Brothers) and we have to reorganize the family's main source of income. I am not only concerned for myself but also for my brothers, sister, and Mother and Father.

My Mother and Father have devoted their lives to us and have given up their securities in their businesses so that we might have a chance to make and get our futures secure.

All I know is music, and I've got to either make it in this field or quit and go to college to learn some other trade so I can be secure in my future. Or do something! I don't know what it is.

You see you have a good job and income, have a nice family, and are pretty secure. I have these things yet to acquire and to be successful (to be able to be secure when we get older) is everyone's dreams and wishes. I know that our future is and can be big, Don, and I know you can make this for us, but it has got to be soon.

All our futures are in your hands, and it is a big responsibility whether you know it or not. I know the Lord is watching over us and guiding us, but you can't leave everything up to the Lord because He helps those who help themselves.

Here are a few of my questions:

1. You said we were in an awkward stage as far as our ages were concerned a few years ago, but the biggest things today are people within our age range, as far as pop music is concerned (which seems to be the way that we are leaning).

2. Don, why don't we stay home a little more and get records and TV appearances out and prove ourselves like others do instead of hitting the heavily scheduled road (tours) as we are, and pleasing thousands as compared to millions the other way?

3. Why don't we have a publicity agent like others have?

4. Why don't we have someone writing songs for us like others have?

5. Why don't we have articles in magazines and newspapers like others have? Even teen magazines: (After all, we are teenagers!)

6. Why don't we have a good variety of photographs to give papers and magazines like others have?

7. Why do we go into a town and not have advance publicity and people do not even know that we are coming or are there as others have?

8. Why doesn't someone see that our stage shows go smoothly instead of us working out the problems when we get there, which is very unprofessional?

9. Can't Universal do for us what MGM is doing for the Cowsills?

10. Why don't we try to be big when we get an opportunity instead of letting money be our first objective?

11. Why not make it big first and then demand the big money?

You know I kind of keep things within me and hold them back (especially when I come face to face with someone), but it isn't fair to my little brothers who have their questions but can't express themselves and are so innocent to other's discussions.

Don, let's be the biggest things in the business and I know we can!

We're going to let people know that we're still alive and that we are better than we were and that we are good!

We're going to be the biggest things in records, and we're going to have a TV series and have very good ratings and a strong following.

And Don, this next year is going to be the biggest that the Osmonds or the public has seen. People are going to say, "Look out, the Osmonds are coming!"

You know me better than to think that I am stuck up or something. I am thinking Big and Great. And people who think this way become Big and Great!

Sincerely,

Alan Osmond

I think my letter gave Don a wakeup call, and he was a little taken back. I mean, here we were, working our guts out at shows, fairs, and other venues. It was easy for our manager to sit back and collect his ten percent, but we wanted more.

Don responded to me that he had received my letter and would like to sit down and visit with me about it.

(*Note:* Everything I said in the letter would happen, did happen.)

Some Celebrities Could Be Unpredictable

The Andy Williams Show ended its first run in 1967, and we stayed in town and entertained on *The Jerry Lewis Show* for nearly two seasons. Working with Jerry could be unpredictable; for example, one afternoon the social worker who monitored how long we could work as minors, told us we had ten minutes before we had to stop working for the day.

Merrill tells about that day, "We were regulars with Jerry Lewis and were recording vocals and playing our saxophones of a complicated ten-page song. We had time for one take before quitting and the welfare teacher was watching her watch. We began singing when Jerry Lewis simply walked on the set. Someone put a hand over his mouth so he wouldn't make a sound. With his, "you can't tell me what to do" comedy school of thought, he walked over to us and lit our music on fire with his ten-inch flame cigarette lighter. Alan immediately raised his first finger. We all turned to him, and he directed us through the rest of the music. Fortunately, we had all memorized it, and we brothers performed it in one take."

Journal Entries

Tuesday, January 9, 1968 — Arleta, CA

I got ready to go to NBC with Donny who is doing a dancing skit with Jerry Lewis on his show. Donny and Jerry worked on dancing for a while I took a few pictures with Donny's new Pentax camera that Jerry Lewis gave to him. Jerry likes Donny and plays and teases him and bites him on the head. Donny did some schooling with his teacher/welfare worker and then did a run through of the whole show. Donny' part is going to be cute. Jerry Lewis enters as a child who is very, very awkward and whose mother sent him to as dancing school to be more graceful. Jerry shows the teacher what he knows (which is nothing) but he tries to dance—(funny!) Five or so years pass, and it is jerry's first stage appearance, and he dances with his teacher (Donny). Donny does all of the difficult stuff. Jerry then goes wild and does some adlib-bing tap-dancing and Donny follows and watches him. At the end, Jerry makes a motion to Donny asking, "How was I?" Donny gives a gesture saying, "Ehh, so, so." Rehearsal ended and I took Donny to the wardrobe department and had his tuxedo fit. He looks very nice.

Wednesday, January 10, 1968

I drove Donny to NBC in the Buick, and we stopped off at the wardrobe department leaving Donny's tap shoes with

Rhett Turner who is the head wardrobe designer. I took Donny to his school tutor and then after lunch worked with him on his dancing for the Jerry Lewis Show.

Jerry Lewis finally arrived at the studio, and he bit Donny on the head, as usual and had some comedic fun with him. We then rehearsed with Nick Castle (choreographer) and Alex Plachert (his assistant) to rehearse Donny's hand moves. We told all the family what we had done as they were curious.

Thursday, January 11, 1968

Father drove Donny to NBC for the taping of Jerry Lewis's Show. Our family all got dressed up and went later to support Donny. Mother really looked beautiful, and I took her picture with some fresh flowers. Father said, "Donny's hand moves to the dance needs some work," so I went out in the hallway with him and worked on his dance moves.

Jerry Lewis wasn't sure that he could remember the dance steps and was going to cut the number out of the show. But because Jerry really likes Donny so much, he kicked everyone out of the studio and worked privately with Nick and Alex on the dance routine for an hour or so. Donny and I then went in the studio and rehearsed the dance with Jerry once more. The Producer Bob Finkle and Director Bob Henry decided that Donny would wear his tap shoes to dance, but because Jerry couldn't think ahead, he would wear plain shoes and Alex Plachert, (assistant choreographer) would do Jerry's tapping on a microphone off stage, which sounds and looks like Jerry was doing it. Ha!

It came time for the dress rehearsal. The show announcer introduced Donny with equal billing as Ernest Borgnine. After, I took Donny to his dressing room to get out of his tuxedo. I had to settle him down and try to forget about dance routine for a while because if you worry too much, for too long before you go on stage, you won't do as well.

Later, when it came time for the taping of the show. Donny got his hair styled and his makeup done, then I helped him get into his tuxedo and I went over the tap-dancing routine with him once more.

At the taping, when the announcer introduced the stars of the show the audience applauded, but when they announced Donny, some fans that were in the audience all screamed as well! Donny's skit came up. I had been warming him up and talking over the points to remember. Jerry introduced him as his 'dance instructor' and called him 'Professor "KNUFBCLUOC,' or (some weird word). They almost got through the dance routine when the TV director hit the wrong button which playing the wrong prerecorded music, and they had to stop the taping. Jerry got a little mad though because he has a hard time remembering the routine. Boy was I glad though because Donny's arms were a little sloppy and so I reminded Donny to get his arms right, and the second take was at least twice as good! When the routine finished, the audience wouldn't stop clapping for a long time.

Jerry Lewis invited Donny, me and Mother and Father into his dressing room to watch the show on close circuit TV. Jerry really likes Donny a lot! He told one of his men, "It's awful to love this kid as much as my own, but I do." Jerry then gave Donny another attachment for the camera he had given him, and Mother and Father thanked Jerry Lewis for all of his kindness.

January 19, 1968 – Arleta, CA

Andy Williams and his brother Don Williams, our manager, met with us today and told us that Andy doesn't want anyone to influence our tastes in music, give their opinions about what we wanted to wear for personal appearances or on record covers, etc., but for us to pick them out ourselves. On the news tonight Andy Williams announced that he is forming a new record company, Barnaby Records, and that the Osmond Brothers will be his first recording artists to record for him! Andy said, 'I will give the Osmonds the best songs, musicians, orchestras, publicity, and encourage them to choose what they want to wear and what songs they record and how they want to record them without any out-side influence from me, my top recording producers, etc., and give them a change to let their personalities come out.' We are truly blessed. Thank heavens we kept Don Williams as our manager after we decided to leave the Andy Williams TV Series after seven years.

Letters to My Older Brothers

To Virl on his mission in Canada:

Mother probably told you that I took the G.E.D. test and the Ogden City Schools are going to get me my diploma! I have to finish Shorthand and Bookkeeping and then I'll get a diploma from the American School as well! I don't know what I'm going to do about College yet. I was plan-ning on going to Dixie College in Saint George this fall but that means I would have to quit the Osmond Brothers for a while, and I don't want that! I guess I'll just follow the inspi-ration of the Lord, and I know if I'm worthy and righteous He will guide and direct me to the path that I should take.

I really love photography and am still taking pictures. Mother and Father gave me an early birthday present for this year: a 250mm lens for my Haseblad camera! Boy, I love it!

I hope you like our new record. It might not be a #1 hit but we'll be doing some more recording and keep our fingers crossed! Ha!

Some good advice: Hold yourself responsible for a higher standard than anybody else expects of you. Never excuse yourself. Never pity yourself. Be a hard taskmaster to yourself and be lenient with everybody else." Be careful on your mission,

With Love,

Alan

To Tommy on his mission with Virl in Canada

How's my buddy? Our shows are going very well! Andy Williams is really nice to us and our shows are packed every night, and the other night our show was the only show with a packed house, so I guess it's the best one in town! Ha!

I love you very much and I know that you will be a very good Missionary!

With love, your little brother,

Alan

6

MY NEED TO FULFILL
A LIFELONG GOAL

My nineteenth birthday was approaching, and I knew there was one assignment that needed my serious consideration.

At that time, in the Church of Jesus Christ of Latter-day Saints, young men age nineteen (now they can serve starting at age eighteen) were asked to serve a two-year mission. Virl and Tom had each been on a mission, and I was excited for the opportunity to serve my own. The purpose of the mission is to share the message of Jesus Christ throughout the world and bring others to Him. The process begins by the prospective missionary submitting paperwork to the headquarters of the church, with the expectation of being assigned to one of the many areas around the world.

Not only do missionaries share the gospel of Jesus Christ, they do so at their own expense, and go wherever in the world they are assigned—with many learning a foreign language. These two years are a wonderful opportunity for growth and maturity for the missionary.

As I neared my nineteenth birthday, one of the leaders in our faith at that time was Elder John Longdon. My father told me that if I wanted to serve a mission, it was up to me. I wanted to, and so my mother contacted Elder Longdon and told him. He had a conversation with my parents about my mission and suggested I start the necessary paperwork. In preparation, I received from our church some missionary discussions and scriptures to memorize. I did, and proceeded to buy luggage, suits, shirts, some extra thick soled walking shoes, and other necessities I might need for my two years away from home and cut my hair.

I began preparing to leave the group and started re-voicing the vocal arrangements and restaging the choreography. I prepared Wayne to take over as group leader, so they could continue to perform as The Osmond Brothers during my two-year absence. The transition took some effort, but it was coming together nicely; I was excited and committed to serving as a missionary.

In January of 1968, I even sent a letter to my brothers Virl and Tom, who were serving missions in Canada at the time, about my anticipation for my mission call. I told them how proud I was of them, and how exciting it was that our family would have 'three missionaries out in the field at the same time!' I asked their advice about how I should prepare both spiritually and for the possibility of learning a new language. I explained the plans I was making for our other brothers to carry on in my absence, and that even though I was looking forward to doing the Lord's work, I would still miss show biz. I signed the letter, (Almost) Elder Osmond.

However, committed as I was, I felt that something was wrong. I knew that going on a mission was expected of me and was the right thing to do, but something was troubling my spirit, and I couldn't shake it.

The Vietnam war was raging, and the military was recruiting great numbers of men my age through the draft as well as volunteers, and I had been notified by the draft board to take my physical. Like other missionaries I had a religious deferment for two years which the military honors to allow those who chose to first serve a mission but I also had a strong patriotic desire to serve my country and was not trying to shy away from it. I hoped to do my mission first and then fulfill my duty to my country once I returned. Like my father who served in World War II, I was ready to serve in active military service if needed.

That too, became a matter of prayer. I notified the military of the deferment and felt confident that I would receive my mission call and that all would work out.

Still, something inside was still troubling me. Something I just couldn't put my finger on. I decided to seek the Lord's help and made it a matter of serious prayer. Over the next three days I remained isolated in our backyard trailer spending a considerable amount of time on my knees: praying, pondering, reading the scriptures, and fasting.

I was still trying to make sense of my feelings when the thought came that this was the adversary trying to discourage me from serving. A mission is a worthy cause, so, in the name of Jesus Christ, I cast him out. But, I was still filled with troubling feelings and questions.

It was then that I had the very distinct impression that I was doing it wrong. When asking for the Lord's help, I was doing all the talking. I needed to stop asking and start listening; to be still in order to know what He would have me do.

I was shocked when the question came to my mind, "What if I am not supposed to serve a mission right now?" So, I asked, "was I not supposed to serve a mission right now?"

The most warm, powerful, and emotional feeling came over me. It was an answer I never expected to receive, but it came with such a strong confirmation I couldn't deny it. I was *not* supposed to go on a mission. It scared me, and I thought, the Lord must have something else for me to do.

So, in a humble and honestly needy plea, I asked, "Heavenly Father, what do I do about the military?"

The spirit spoke to my mind and my heart, "Don't worry about it!" It brought tears to my eyes and a heavy tug on my heart.

I believe I was so set on serving a mission that the Lord gave me an answer in such a way that it was undeniable. But then, still questioning, the thought came again, "But what about the military?"

Almost immediately, the scripture from Proverbs 3:5-6 came to my mind, what I had been taught from my youth; "Trust in the Lord with all thine heart; and lean not unto thine own understanding. In all thy ways acknowledge Him and He shall direct thy path."

This was such a major decision in my life, and potentially life-threatening. I knew what I had felt, and heard within, and that He is in charge. So, I gave thanks to Him for the answer to my prayers, and then asked Him to bless me in the next steps I had to take. It was still early in the morning but I went to my parents' room and woke them up. I explained my experience and the answer I had received. I could see the worried look on my mother's face and the nervous sniffing started that my father does when under pressure.

After a few minutes, Father said, "We need to get the whole family together and confirm this decision with the Lord and make it a matter of family prayer, seeking His blessings."

We were never afraid to lay our challenges and troubles at the Lord's feet and this certainly warranted further request for more answers and direction.

My father offered the prayer. He wasn't finished giving thanks for further light and knowledge when the phone rang. The continual ring became irritating. Father cut his prayer short and answered the phone.

Even at this early hour it was Jim London, a friend and photographer for *LIFE* Magazine, who was currently serving in the military. He said, "I'm not even sure why I'm calling but I had a strong feeling that I should. I was concerned and wondering what your sons were doing about the military."

My father said, "Funny you should ask." He went on to explain about my decision not to go on a mission but was now facing the draft board. Jim asked to talk to me. He asked if I knew anything about the military and if there was a branch where I would like to serve. I told him I knew nothing about the military. He said, "Have you ever considered playing a musical instrument in a military band?"

I said, "No, I don't want to do that. I would rather serve as a soldier."

Then he said, "I have a friend who is a Lieutenant Colonel in a National Guard Unit near us in Van Nuys, California." He suggested that I go over and visit with him about my options. I said that I would.

That morning, my parents and I drove over to the National Guard Armory. Men my age were lining up, but I asked if I could speak to a Colonel. Several minutes later, Colonel Glass came out and asked what I wanted. I told him that Jim London suggested that I talk to him about getting into the guard.

It was obvious to me that the Colonel was trying not to laugh when he said, "Do you see those six hundred plus men in line? They want the same thing. There is no way you're getting into the guard right now."

I believe Colonel Glass noticed that his answer startled my parents and me; after a few seconds he said, "Well, Mr. Osmond, I have seen you and your brothers on *The Andy Williams Show*. Besides performing what other skills do you have?"

I swallowed before I said, "Well, Sir, I am a speed typist, I take shorthand, and I am a stenographer; a court reporter."

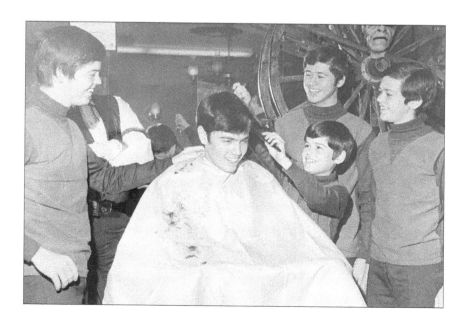

The Colonel was visibly surprised by my response—he thought for a minute then he said, "Could you give me just a minute?"

He went back into his office, then a few minutes later he waved me and my parents to come in.

Seeming a little uncomfortable, he said to Father and Mother, "I am almost embarrassed to tell you that, confidentially, we are in a mess here at the Armory. The head staff sergeant that does our paperwork is sick and near dying. We don't have anyone to take his place."

He turned to me. "Mr. Osmond, would you be willing to go to boot camp? Like tomorrow? You can then be trained as a clerk, come back here, and help get us out of this paperwork mess?"

I didn't hesitate. "Yes, Sir."

Colonel Glass said, "Great. Let's get you signed up immediately."

Right there, I signed a six-year commitment.

The next morning, I boarded a bus for Fort Ord, California.

Donny and Alan

I would begin boot camp training to prepare to fight in the Vietnam War if necessary and to be trained with the MOS of office clerk.

This was the first time I had been separated from my family for any length of time. I didn't know anyone; I was alone and honestly a little nervous about what was ahead of me. I have always considered myself "Mr. Friendly," but on this bus ride I was quiet. I felt lonely.

My little brother, Donny, who was eleven years old, was not at all excited about me going. He said, "I thought the world was coming to an end. I thought my leader and this brother I admired so much was going to be killed, and I cried and cried. I had a huge hole in my heart."

I knew in my heart that I could have coasted through with my musical talents, but I know how to work hard, and I wanted to serve my country like anyone else my age.

We were given shots, issued a M-14 rifle and equipment, fifteen-second short haircuts, and then orientation. I have to admit, I was taken back by the extent of profanity and chaos in the barracks.

The noncommissioned officers were less than courteous, and their vulgarity was hard to listen to. They seemed to be under the assumption that the new guys were a worthless lot and incapable of measuring up to the training.

That first night in the barracks my fellow recruits speculated about what we might expect the next day. Some were smoking and others told crude stories about women. It was a relief when the drill sergeant announced, "lights out."

But honestly, my most pressing concern now was that I was sharing a room with fifty other recruits, and I knew I wanted to say my evening prayers. My entire life I had knelt next to my bed to pray, but now I wondered if I would be ridiculed.

I considered praying while lying in bed because I didn't want to call attention to myself, I just wanted to fit in. But, I was having a hard time going against my lifelong choice of kneeling in prayer.

Finally, I thought, *Who do I fear? Do I fear man, or do I fear God?* So, I knelt by my bunk and quietly offered my prayer. The noise in the room quieted a little, but I did notice a few snickers and laughs.

As I climbed into bed, the noise started again, and someone said, "Hey Osmond, say one for me."

The next day we split up into formations, checked equipment, and generally got organized. At the end of the day, we ate dinner in the chow hall, and then headed back to our barracks for a much welcome rest. Many of the guys said to me, "I saw you praying, what happens if we die?" I briefly shared that God has a plan for us.

The next night I wasn't as nervous to pray because the previous night had gone okay, but right when I knelt down, I heard one of the soldiers say, "He's going to do it again."

The heckling continued each time I prayed until one night a voice from a bunk nearest the door yelled, "Shut up you guys. Osmond's going to say his prayers." The room quieted immediately; the toughest guy in the barracks had reprimanded them. His name was Private Rice; he had a foul mouth and would roust us out of bed in the mornings with crude language. I did, however, admire him for his toughness. He injured his leg on maneuvers but refused treatment and continued to march with the troops.

When it came time to return back to our various reserve and guard units, or to get our orders for Vietnam, Private Rice asked me if we could talk alone. We went into the barracks and my friend told me how when he was five years old, his father had made him start stealing. He was told if he didn't, he couldn't come home, that he had to work to help support the family.

My heart ached for this man when he said, "Oh, I wish I knew somebody loved me."

He asked me to teach him to pray. I did, and said a prayer to show him, and then he did. It was an emotional experience for both of us. We stood, and he hugged me and said, "I can go to 'Nam now." This exchange came at the end of my basic training, and I never saw him again.

I have often reflected that had I not had the courage to pray that first night, I might have missed out on that experience with Private Rice.

Many of these guys would be leaving for Vietnam, and because of the pressing war, our eight-week training cycle was shortened to six weeks. The drill sergeant pushed us hard, but I was okay with that. I was used to being under pressure and meeting deadlines, so I started to feel good about being on my own and where performance was easily measured.

Once I was acknowledged as a guy who prayed every night, I had some great experiences. I noticed a bunkmate praying; another guy who said he was a "Mormon" asked me to go to church with him on Sunday. He said he smoked a little, but otherwise was quite active. Another guy who called himself a "Jack Mormon," agreed to go to church on the Sunday coming up. I went to church the next week by myself. No one showed up at the building reserved for us, so I spent the time reading my scriptures and worshiped on my own.

My hope to remain anonymous didn't last long. In the fall of 1968, I was called into the sergeant major's office. He said, "I'm a song writer and I have a song I want you to get Andy Williams to record." Then he told me that he was as singer, too, and that he had booked us to sing at the officer's club the next weekend.

I had to think fast. *There is no way I'm going to do that.* So, I said that I had made a promise that I would never perform with anyone but my brothers. I ended up in KP! Later another sergeant asked me if I had a guitar, and if I did, everyone would sing along. He wanted me to play it around the barracks to get the guys singing and create an espirt decorps among the recruits; so, a few evenings I did play.

Also, one day when I was in the orderly room watching my brothers on *The Jerry Lewis Show* on TV, some of the guys saw me and asked, "Hey, are they your brothers?"

They caught me off guard and I said, "Yes."

I was told Andy Williams had written to my commanding officer to see if I could perform in uniform on his Christmas show. I was given permission, and I promised to run every day while I was gone. Some members of my platoon were serving dinner to some sergeants and overhead enough to realize who I was.

Home for Christmas

In order to get released to leave a day early to perform with my brothers, I had to do extra duty with another unit. I was sick with walking pneumonia at the time, making it even harder to do my training. But I was determined not to go to sick call for fear of being recycled or put in the hospital and losing the privilege of going on leave which would also have delayed my training.

But I had other skills that served me as well. I had gained exceptional skills throughout my life that served me well as a soldier. I was a top marksman in shooting a rifle, and used to choreography, so I quickly picked up how to fight using a bayonet. They made me demonstrate it on a high platform for all the company to see how to do it. I also had exceptional stamina and kicking skills.

After I went home during the Christmas break and did the *Andy Williams Show*, I returned to Fort Ord for active infantry training.

They told me I had some packages in the orderly room. I didn't realize that I had been awarded three individual trophies for my basic training skills and testing. I won the "Marksman Award" for the highest score in shooting, another one for having the highest graded test in overall knowledge. I was also voted by the drill sergeants that trained us as being "The Outstanding Trainee." They said I almost won another trophy and was in the top three for the top physical proficiency test.

I wrote home telling my father about winning the rifle marksman test.

"I shot thinking of what you taught me. Calm, cool, and squeeze gently."

Letter from My Mother

November 7, 1968

It was sure good to get your letter yesterday. We read them over and over. The kids kept saying over and over, Oh, Oh, Ah, Ah, poor Alan! Poor kid! They were really showing a little empathy and wishing you were back home with us.

Sure, like that haircut, too! Ha! Don't worry, it will grow. And I don't think you look bad anyway. "Ya always look good to yer maw." Andy Williams wants you to be on the Christmas Show pretty bad. They were going to try to contact your C.O. Said they wouldn't do anything to hurt your standing there though. Guess you'll hear about it. We'll be looking forward to the 18th of December (maybe sooner if you get to do a spot on the Christmas Show.)

Wish I could give you a big hug right now. I sure miss you! We all do! Wayne wouldn't mind a bit having you take over the responsibility of the "Group." Ha! (Father is a little rough on him—I think —"making a leader out of him." Ha!) We have our problems but—that's life! Keep your "chins" up. We're sure proud of you—your attitude—your character, etc. etc. We're proud to be the parents of such a choice spirit.

Remember when you're tired and discouraged, "this too shall pass"—You'll be home soon—and the future holds lots of happiness and pleasant surprises for you. Please be careful. Rest if—when you get the chance. Send any ideas or inspiration you get whether it's about songs, the act, the future, or whatever. I know you are inspired.

Love, Mother

My Reply

Don't worry about me! You've taught me well! I'm more fortunate than a lot of the guys because of the extra companionship of the Holy Ghost and the Lord's help and spirit. I have a lot of respect from all the guys, and they know I'm Mormon and I don't smoke, drink, or swear. It does make a couple of 'jack Mormons' feel a little embarrassed, I think.

Boys, I never did tell you how proud I was of you out on that stage in Reno, with Wayne in charge! What great brothers I have. You too, Marie!

Love, Private Alan R. Osmond
NG28309129
Co A, 5th BN, 1 Bde (Bct) 2d PLT, Fort Ord, California. 93941

Letters Home

November 17, 1968

The other day the sergeant called me forward and told me he was keeping his eye on me for a squad leader unless the present one shaped up. I hope he shapes up because they always have to do extra things and don't get much time to themselves. They lose a close friendship with the other guys, too. But I know if I do get chosen I'll do my best and tell him so.

Our platoon leader just got demoted so there are a lot of changes going on. Our platoon leader now is a high school dropout, construction worker, big mouth! Everyone hates him but I admire him because he gets the job done. The guys call him everything in the "book" behind his back, but he usually makes it up to them. He has a dirty mouth, too. That's one thing I'll be glad to get away from. I'm sure glad that I was raised up in a wholesome, religious atmosphere and can put myself above that junk.

My bunk bed got thrown on the floor yesterday. I guess one of the "hospital corners" wasn't right on the blankets. Oh well, mine was one of many.

Brothers, keep up the good work. I'm sure proud of you. I promise I won't yell at you when I come home. Ha! I can see that. It's not really necessary because I get so much and hear and see so much here. Give Wayne all you've got. I know he's a better boss than I was. We've got a lot of fun times ahead of us if we stick together, work hard remain religious and down to earth, and continue in the things our Father and Mother had taught us. Marie—you, too!

November 18, 1968

I guess you're busy with Andy's Special now. I'm sure glad that I'll get to be part of it. Even if I'm background. I sure miss the business. Can hardly wait to get back to the 'eat, sleep, sing bit again!

They sure ran us today! Almost everywhere! I was used as a bayonet demonstrator today and I had it down pretty well, I must admit. The D.I and the company clapped after I demonstrated the procedure. We do a series of *On guard, Perry Left, Thrust, Vertical Butt Stroke slam with the butt of the weapon, then slash!* Then you go back to the on-guard position again. I guess my dancing came in handy with routines, Ha! Another D.I. had me make corrections on the other guys, too. We then ran over to the hand-to-hand combat area and wrestled a little but mostly learned some defense moves which I want to show my brothers. Good to know!

I raised my P.T. (physical training) score from 406 to 425 yesterday. Every week we test and prepare for the final one. 500 is maximum.

Alan

December 1, 1968

Happy wedding anniversary! It's your twenty fourth isn't it? What wonderful parents I have! I hope I can be as good to my kids as you have been to me someday. Also, if I can make a good a choice as Father made! I sure love both of you. You're the perfect parents anyone could ever want.

We got paid Friday. They gave me $75.00 I'm sending a $40.00 money order home. Too much money to be carrying around. I get tired of sticking it in my boot when I have to go to priesthood meetings late Saturday nights. Ha. Mother, would you please pay my tithing with it and get you and Father something from me? I'd really like you to. I'm sending the receipt home, too. Let my bookkeeper take care of it. Ha.

Donny's birthday is coming up and I looked for a card for him. Can't find one. Will try again if I get a chance.

I had a 'song writing spell' a couple of nights ago. Started two. Don't know when I'll finish them.

Last night or the night before some guys that sleep near me said I started singing in my sleep and woke them up. I guess I still have show biz in my blood.

We had a so-called beer party at the PX yesterday. As you can see from the pictures, I had a 'rootin' tootin' time with my root beer.

Am going to church at 13:00 and taking about four guys with me. We were discussing religion the other night while shaving and one guy said, "Osmond isn't in the service. He's on a secret mission for his church." How about that! I don't know if I do much, but I mainly try to teach by example and stick up for my beliefs and try to live them.

Have you got a Christmas tree yet? I'm getting a little excited about Christmas. I'm sure glad I get to come home!

December 3, 1968

Got back from my Basic Rifle Marksman test and was so disappointed! Not really, I'm an expert! In fact, I got the highest record of the Company! Expert is 60 and I shot 67, the highest. Ha. I got expert on all but one of my practice tests. The targets will be a little camouflaged in with the background. Seeing them is one thing and hitting them another.

I shot them thinking of you Father, and what you told me. Calm cool and squeeze gently! We'll have to go hunting one of these days.

The first sergeant called me up after the class to talk to me. He said, Andy Williams wants the 14th and 15th and 16th, so I'll be leaving the 13th to make it and can probably just remain there and not have to return for graduation on the 17th! He said my P.T. (Physical Training) average is the highest in the company and besides getting a trophy for the best marksman (expert), I shouldn't do too badly on the GII testing, etc.

I'll be graduating and testing with another company. It will be a little harder because the cadre won't know me. But I'll sock it to em', huh Jimmy?

No one was taking charge of our group this morning, so I said, Well, somebody's got to do it and stepped up into the Platoon sergeant place and took charge myself. The S.D.I. (Senior Drill Instructor) admired the way I took over and got things in shape. I don't mean to brag or something, it's just that when I see something that needs doing and think I can do it as well as anyone else, I'll give it a try. Why not. Just like my father! Ha.

The Company was having a lecture on driving the other day and were telling us what alcohol does to people. He said, "If you've been drinking, let the Mormon drive!!"

Dear Family,

Well, I'm not behind a plow, and I ain't gonna get rich either. Ha! Today is Saturday the 26th. I'm in Barracks #18, bunk #2, in a platoon of 48 guys. There are some from Salt Lake and one attended BYU, but none are Mormons. I know all of the guys smoke except the guy in the bunk above me. I'm now sure about him. He's the one that attended BYU. I asked the Orderly Master about Church tomorrow, and he sent me to a sergeant Hernandez. Latter-day Saints was mentioned on the list of religions. He just looked at me and said, "Yea, it's tomorrow and don't miss it." He waved me out. A sergeant came, lined us all up, talked to us, marched us over to the Barbershop and in 10 minutes, 48 guys (including me) were ball headed. Ha! It feels weird. Although it doesn't feel too bad. Some guys say I look good with my hair short. Last night I had quite a decision to make. There are 22 guys in the bottom floor of the barracks where I sleep, and I wanted to say my prayers on my knees. I don't care how good of a Mormon you are, to have to do that is awfully hard. I talked to myself, prayed and thought. I said, "Do I fear God or man," and by golly I got down and said them. I felt much better and don't give a darn what anyone else thinks. I have much to improve on and find it a little hard to converse with some of the guys. Mainly because we don't speak the same "language" (cussing). I've talked to them all though and am one of them. Well, it's chow time again (4:30) and we have to line up. It's awfully cold! Sorry about the paper. (on the back of "Security and Valuables" Form). You'll have to send me some when I get the address.

I sure love my family,

Alan

By the way, They swear an awful lot! When we went into the supply room to get my bedding, the guy a couple of feet from me got cussed out for having his coat all buttoned up tight, so I quickly undid mine so I wouldn't get yelled at. Well, I got it for not having mine done up! They brought me to attention and were talking to each other that I looked like a 'goof off type,' 'a troublemaker,' 'doesn't want to obey orders,' and that they're 'going to remember my name and get me.' (All talk! Just trying to scare me.). One guy got paper wadded up and stuffed in his mouth, and they made him stand at attention with it for a while! After we got our M-14's issued, they made one guy walk around singing "Mary Had A Little Lamb"! I had to really work to keep from smiling! Another guy was caught having his hands in his pockets, so they filled his pockets with dirt so he couldn't put his hands in them. If any button is left undone, we have to do ten push-ups. Specialist Jones in barracks six runs around calling us all "magots," so we're all humble! Ha!

We run wherever we go, and our boots come off whenever we enter our barracks. We put them on and take them off like 20 times a day. We have to keep our floors and barracks spic and span clean. I just got finished buffing toilet and sink pipes. What a life! It's going to be rough because we are fitting an eight-week training schedule into six weeks, and we have to build physically and mentally in a shorter time because of an accelerated training schedule due to the Vietnam War. I do extra pushups and try to build up my muscles in the mornings as we lineup to go to chow, then we run back and forth on the horizontal ladder as many times as possible. We also have to carry a guy of the same weight up hill to the mess hall and run while doing it. We have to gulp our food down so we can get back to more P.T. training. After exercising and doing drills, we get supper before starting nighttime exercises, then clean the barracks and shave and shower for the next day. I also have spit shined shoes. It's hard, but we try to make it fun, and we all go through it together.

I couldn't hide my identity for very long. Most of the guys finally know me because some had recognized me. I wish I had my guitar, but I only have an 8" x 10" x 6" space for my personal belongings, and not much time anyway. Could you please send me some vitamin C's and a small bottle of Neosporin spray? I have had a couple of colds and had to borrow some C's from one of the guys. I don't want to go on sick call unless necessary because if I miss a couple of days, they will recycle me, and it will mess up my AIT (Active Infantry Training) schedule afterwards.

I made a lot of friends, and once borrowed a drill instructor's guitar and worked out a platoon song that he could call cadence to while we marched. We sang for a couple of hours before we ended up in the day room where a guy had a harmonica. We sang quite loudly and ended up serenading the officers.

I wasn't always praised, though. One day a commanding officer called me up and said, "I see we have a celebrity among us." He laughed, then he said, "Osmond, front and center! Sing us a song."

Well, I saw what this guy did to a fellow private whose last name was Byrd. He made Private Byrd run around making bird calls.

So, I said, 'Sir, I'm a soldier now."

Once again, Kitchen Patrol (KP duty) and this time included the most unpleasant job of cleaning grease traps.

This happened to me three times and eventually I made friends with the noncommissioned mess hall staff who made me "Alan, Chief Cook."

I had been the leader of my brothers since I was eight years old, so it wasn't hard for me to take control of a situation when the opportunity came up. One morning when no one seemed to be in charge, and the soldiers were complaining and doing nothing, I stepped up to the platoon sergeant's place and took over, just like Father would do. The senior drill instructor was impressed at the way I took charge and got things in shape.

I never preached to my fellow soldiers, but I didn't have any problem sharing my beliefs when I was asked. One night while shaving, we were discussing religion, when one of my buddies said, "Osmond isn't in the service. He's on a secret mission for his church." Honestly, that made me feel good and I wrote home and told my parents about it.

I had a hard time with the coarse language used by some of my fellow recruits but also from drill instructors. We were offered the chance to make candid, anonymous comments regarding our training cycle, so I wrote a complaint about the swearing and vulgarity. Some of the language had even been incorporated into our cadences while we marched. I simply said I felt it was excessive and unnecessary. I was happy to see an order issued for the noncoms (Non-commissioned officers) to clean up their language.

Before our unit completed our training cycle, word came that National Guard units would be activated for duty in Vietnam. The regular army draftees whooped it up. They laughed at us NG's (No Gooders) who had thought they were going to avoid active duty by joining the National Guard. Even so, I remembered what I had *felt* during my prayer when I was in the trailer in the backyard, and heard the voice, "Don't worry about it."

As it turned out, there had been a change in military policy of sending guard units to Vietnam, so my unit was not activated. Apparently some of those units had not done well in combat, there were many casualties, causing the government to reevaluate their policy.

I never did see combat in my military service, but I served for six years. During that entire time, I was on active alert and attended regular summer camps. I continued to organize and work on military records as a trained clerk. But typically, I would finish my work early, which allowed me to make up extra work time so I could be available to perform with my brothers, which the colonel authorized.

I was assigned six years of California military service and attended weekend drills. I was also called up when the earthquake hit in California and during the riots. When we relocated back to Utah, I was transferred into a Utah National Guard unit and completed my service obligation with a unit in Salt Lake. Though the officers tried to get me to go to officer's candidate school, and to be advanced to E5 Sergeant, I turned it down as I didn't want a military career. I was honorably discharged from the service with the rank of E4 Specialist.

When I was in my teens Mother encouraged me to become a speed typist and to do what my uncle Tom Davis had done; become a stenographer; a court reporter. Intriguingly she told me, "These kinds of skills are most needed and may save your life someday." (My mother was an inspired lady.)

Before going home early to do *The Andy Williams Christmas Show*, I did an interview that appeared January 10, 1969, in the *Panorama*, the Fort Ord newspaper, I was written up as an outstanding recruit; something I am proud of.

The article read:

According to the cadre in Company A, 5th Battalion, 1st Brigade, private Osmond is a fine soldier. On leave from his Nation Guard unit, he was nominated by the company for the American Spirit of Honor Medal, the highest award given a basic trainee, and he was named the Outstanding Trainee. He recorded the highest score for the company in basic rifle marksmanship, was among the top three on the final physical combat proficiency test and had a near perfect score on the graded test.

Oldest Osmond Brother, Alan, Completes Basic, Selected as Outstanding Trainee

By SP4 Fred Meyers

If you are among the millions who have watched Alan Osmond "grow up" during the past six years on the Andy Williams television series and numerous other shows, you know he is the oldest member of one of the brightest singing quartets to spring up in many years.

He is the lead guitar player, singer, and dancer for the famed Osmond Brothers who have become internationally acclaimed as performers and recording artists.

What you may not realize, however, is that the 19-year-old Osmond is also a fine soldier, according to the cadre in Company A, 5th Battalion, 1st Brigade.

On active duty from his National Guard unit, Private Osmond was nominated by the company for the American Spirit Honor Medal, the highest award given a basic trainee, and was named the Outstanding Trainee. He recorded the highest score for the company in basic rifle marksmanship, was among the top three on the final Physical Combat Proficiency Test, and had a near perfect score on the graded test.

Unlike many celebrities who have taken basic training with the 1st Brigade, Private Osmond came, "To work and become the best soldier I possibly could.

"I didn't want any special celebrity treatment," he recalls. "I just wanted to take everything like all the other guys and just be a typical trainee."

Private Osmond attempted this by letting his celebrity status go unknown for his first two weeks in the Army. He may have had it remain so even longer had not a phone call to the post from his agent revealed his true identity.

The call was a request that Osmond be granted an early Christmas leave so he might be able to tape the Andy Williams Christmas special with his brothers, which aired Dec. 20. The request was granted.

The ensuing weeks saw him leading his company on the practice PT tests, become high first on the rifle ranges with a 68, and display leadership qualities.

During breaks in training he would occasionally lead the group in song and he was often the center of attention. Perhaps one trainee summed it up best in saying, "You never would have known he was a star, he's just a real nice guy."

Osmond says he enjoyed the rigors of basic training. "I really liked almost everything we did. It was tough, but it's an experience I wouldn't trade for anything in the world."

Alan Osmond is above all a performer, and to hear him talk there is nothing more important than the work of the Osmond Brothers. "We're a group," he says, "and as far as all of us are concerned we are going to remain a group for as long as possible."

The quartet has been performing together for eight years, beginning when the youngest, Donnie, was only two. There is a two year age difference between each member beginning with Alan, then Wayne, 17; Merrill, 15; Jay, 13; and Donnie, who just turned 11.

One of their best memories, recalls Private Osmond, was a show outside the United States, in Sweden. "We played to a capacity audience of 29,-000," he explained, "and they were a great audience. They gave us a standing ovation and seven different curtain calls—and just wouldn't let us leave the stage."

Alan has begun writing and composing songs for the group and occasionally lends a hand in the choreography portion of their act. "I hope to delve into these areas very seriously when I begin singing with the group regularly again. I can't wait to get back into the swing of things. Once you get this show business in you you're hooked."

IN STAGE—In civilian life Alan Osmond, oldest of the performing Osmond Brothers, sings and dances for a living. The well-known group has been on many television shows and has played nightclubs across the country.

IN TRAINING—No longer singing or dancing, Private Alan Osmond still performed well. While going through basic training he was named Outstanding Trainee. (U.S. Army photo)

The article also noted that during breaks in training, I would sometimes lead the group in song. One of my fellow trainees was quoted saying, "You would never have known he was a star. He's just a real nice guy."

I am grateful for my military experience. It allowed me to become somewhat more independent than I otherwise might have been, and although I was known by my army and national guard friends as "Alan Osmond, the entertainer," I was accepted as a regular guy, which I enjoyed. At summer camp many of the guys would spend their time in the evenings drinking and partying, but I was content to stay alone in the barracks reading a good book and just drinking a can of root beer.

I had learned a lot—one of the most important things, "Dare to Stand Alone." I might not have learned that as well if not for my military experience.

7

GOING OUT ON OUR OWN

ANDY WILLIAMS understood that we were a bunch of restless teen-agers who wanted to make our mark with teen audiences, so he wished us well and we remained good friends with him.

He eventually started his own record label which he named after his dog, Barnaby. Andy told his brother Don, our manager, that, "He would love it if we were his first recording artists and record some original songs with some of the finest musicians." He knew we liked the Cowsills, a singing family group, so he got Bill Cowsill, who produced their songs, to produce a single release for us. The first time Bill came to our house he visited with us for a while, but then he got serious. He said, "Nobody is going to give you their hit records. You will need to compose your own music."

He pointed to our upright piano and challenged us to write a singable song in five minutes. We didn't have any warning, and my brothers were looking at me as if to say: 'what are we going to do?'

I quickly put together a pop version about Joseph Smith, Jr. The song talked about when Joseph was a teenager confused about religion; he went into a grove of trees to pray, then realized he was taking on a big thing. I titled the song 'Takin' On a Big, Big Thing.' Some of the lyrics were, *Hey, Joe, you're taking on a big, big thing. You said, there's people in the sky!*

Bill was blown away, and he helped us structure the song and give it more direction. He took us to the studio to produce it, and it became the B side to one that he wrote called, "Make the Music Flow."

The experience gave us the confidence to create lyrics, harmonies, and arrangements. We started to expand our thinking and our imaginations. We wrote from the heart in our writing to better communicate who we were.

Our producers found songs for us, and other top 40 hits followed: "The Proud One," "If Every Man Had a Woman Like You," "Yo-Yo," and "Love Me for a Reason." Some of those top hits Merrill, Wayne, and I wrote—"Down By the Lazy River," "Crazy Horses," and "Let Me In" from *The Plan* album, which were all original songs. I have written over two hundred songs by myself, and with my brothers, many that are on our albums.

It's hard to believe that collectively we earned forty-seven gold and platinum records and surpassed both Elvis and the Beatles with nine gold records in a single year, selling over a hundred million records.

Merrill, Wayne, and I composed most of the music. Merrill has a real knack for composing appealing music. He is remarkably talented, and we worked well together. Wayne on guitar, made solid contributions, as well. His instrumental and composing talents contributed substantially to the end result. Jay was also there on drums, and many times Donny would join in on the keyboards. Though we all solo'd, Merrill was our "lead singer," though I sang all of the hard to hit notes and harmonies. The four of us made a great team. And Donny made it even better.

Once in a while we would get a song submitted where the lyrics were not necessarily suitable for our standards. One came from an accomplished writer who had a history of hit material. The song was "Love Me For a Reason," and after we heard the demo and read the lyrics, there was one line that was inappropriate, and we knew we couldn't sing it. We didn't want to hurt the composer's feelings. We spoke to our parents about it, and Mother said she would talk to the composer. Mike Curb was afraid we would lose a hit song.

But Mother explained our standards, and the composer said, "If my mama were here she would slap my mouth. Now, let's go change those lyrics."

"Love Me For a Reason" became one of our top selling records.

We took our music and the message we gave seriously. Before every show we had a "meeting," (our code word for family prayer) asking that our music might influence someone in the audience for good. Over time, our philosophy of presenting uplifting and exemplary music stood out in the industry for good and bad. Interestingly enough our clean-cut image did not interfere with the friendships we made with other famous entertainers, such as Elton John, Paul McCartney, Elvis Presley, and Led Zeppelin.

After "One Bad Apple" was such a great success, we released an anti-pollution rock song we wrote in 1972 called, "Crazy Horses," that went gold and platinum. The crazy horses signified horse-power of engines and smoke, *A Message floatin' in the air,* and toxic fumes from thousands of vehicles crowding the freeways and smoking up the sky. I think it was the first song about anti-pollution in the Los Angeles area where we lived at the time.

Later, Donny told *Songfacts* that Ozzy Osbourne had said "Crazy Horses," was one of his favorite rock and roll songs. It was recorded and played by many other hard rock bands. The song was a minor hit in the United States, it peaked at number two in the United Kingdom and number one in many countries. Our rock songs were especially well-received in the UK and several rock groups did a cover record of our song "Crazy Horses."

One thing that was important was that our songs had meaning. Sometimes the meaning was misunderstood, such as in South Africa where they banned "Crazy Horses." Radio executives there mistakenly thought it was a song about drugs because in South Africa, "horse" is a slang term for heroin.

———————————— ✄ ————————————

By 1977, all of my brothers, except Jimmy, had reached the age to serve a mission for the Church of Jesus Christ of Latter-day Saints, but none of us had received traditional mission calls, except for Virl and Tom. We were now heavily involved with success as performers and like me, my brothers felt that we could "help open doors for the missionaries by singing more, rather than leaving the group to go on full time missions."

In 1974 with then President of the Church of Jesus Christ of Latter-day Saints, Spencer W. Kimball

U.S. President Jimmy Carter and our Church Prophet, President Spencer W. Kimball

Spencer W. Kimball, who was the president and prophet of the church in 1970, believed that the Osmonds were great messengers of the word by example and music. He also felt that we needed extra spiritual help while facing the press and doing missionary efforts with weekly firesides. In 1974, Paul H. Dunn suggested that each of us should be ordained and set apart as Seventies (a calling within the church) to do missionary work. He told us at that time that the missionary department referral system told President Kimball that the Osmond family had been responsible for twenty-eight thousand convert baptisms that past year alone.

8

MOTHER HAD OTHER PLANS

IN THE EARLY 1970s Father and Mother decided to move us back to Utah.

I was in my early twenties and had been thinking about dating and the possibility of marriage. After spending ten years in show business, our parents wanted to give us a better chance of meeting nice girls from our religion and to give us a more normal lifestyle away from Hollywood. They purchased the Riviera Apartments, a one hundred and thirty-seven room apartment complex located on Canyon Road in Provo, Utah, just west of the BYU campus. It already had a reputation of *the* place to live along with other nearby apartments that were home to many students. Living there would put us in touch with other young people and activities at the university. We also built a recording studio in the basement of the office building where our parents lived.

Some units were remodeled to accommodate our family and then we moved in. Our parents, along with Donny, Marie, and Jimmy, occupied the top floor of the main building, while Jay, Merrill, Wayne, and I each lived among other student apartments. By this time, Virl and Tom were both married and living on their own.

Living there was a great experience. We sponsored frequent dances for residents and guests and on some weekends, we had first-run movies flown in from Hollywood. The movies were projected onto white sheets draped on the side of the building, making it one of the reasons students would vie for the chance to live there. If students couldn't get home for Christmas, they were invited to spend the holidays with us.

While there we became acquainted with professional musician, Kenny Hodges. Mother had Kenny help her secure copyrights for the music that my brothers and I wrote. He also helped us select some of the music we were performing for our TV shows at the studio.

Dick Clark and A New Car

After growing up in modest circumstances in North Ogden, becoming famous and wealthy was something no one would have guessed about us. During the 1970's when we were at the height of our popularity, we were often compared to the Jackson Five. Our ages were close to the same as theirs and both groups' "booking agency" was Dick Clark Productions. Outside of appearing on television, playing to sold out audiences, and turning out popular recordings, our lifestyles were completely different.

Our parents didn't skimp on our careers; we had the best choreographer, vocal coaches, and managers, but not much in the way of frills. After we did a show, we typically rode home together and sat down to Mother's home cooked meals that would often include homemade apple pie and ice cream.

Father and Mother didn't believe we needed big cars and fancy stuff; the money, though we had it, was never the focus for them. The important thing was our family and the values we lived by.

Father had an analogy he used to describe our family—a bundle of sticks. An individual stick could be easily broken, but when tied together, the bundle becomes unbreakable.

Father looked at everything we did from the same lens. It didn't matter if we were working in the vegetable garden or performing on stage, we worked together, and all money was earned together

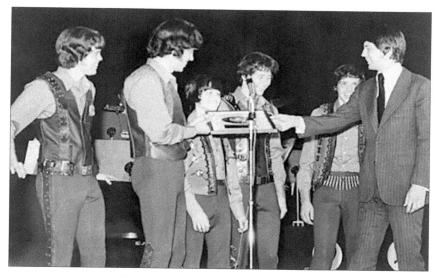

Receiving a Gold Record from Mike Curb

without salaries but given to us on an as needed basis.

Concerning money our parents' motto was, "Watch the pennies, and the dollars will take care of themselves." They had experienced times when money was scarce and even though things were going well today, there was always the possibility of the inevitable rainy day.

We did enjoy some of the perks of the rich and famous. While in Las Vegas, we were provided limousine service and stayed in luxury suites or penthouses of the hotels where we were performing, like Elvis' penthouse suite at the Hilton Hotel. We were living in Los Angeles in 1965. Since we were constantly on the go and because Mother was less than excited about me driving on the California freeways, I didn't get a license until I was seventeen.

I would drive my brothers to the studio in Father's Cadillac, so finally in 1973 when I got my first car, it was a big deal to me. Virl and Tom both owned their own cars, but I was the first of us younger brothers to get one. When we went to the Mercedes dealership, a light metallic blue car caught my eye, so Mother went ahead and got it for me.

With booking agent Dick Clark of American Bandstand

We were working in Las Vegas at the time, and I drove my Mercedes Benz, model 450SL, sports coupe off the showroom floor. I couldn't wait to see what it could do so I took it out on the freeway. I still don't talk about how fast I drove—there was no speed limit in Nevada—but it makes me happy just thinking about that fond memory.

Later, when I first met the love of my life, that cool car was the one I was driving.

9

OSMONDMANIA

OUR PARENTS had eleven mouths to feed, so after Andy Williams there was a period of concern as we looked for another break in show business. We considered moving back to Utah, but Father and Mother had sold our home in Ogden, and the one in Huntsville, as well, so there wasn't much waiting for us there.

Finally, we got a paying job, and Mother told us she had paid our tithing, which was no surprise because *we always did* no matter how little money we had.

I went to extremes to see the Osmonds. My friends and I would sit at a bus stop and go to the local convenience store to get a drink, and not so coincidentally, miss the bus. Later, we would walk over to a fast-food restaurant and again miss the bus. "I could make an order of fries, and a drink last all day." I often sat in my car behind the Riviera doing homework in the hopes I might see an Osmond.
– Linda Sosa

A strong management team was put in place with Ray Katz, Jim Morey, and Ed Leffler as managers. Eventually we were signed by Mike Curb with MGM Records and moved to Mike's new label, Curb Records. Mike recognized me and my brother's professionalism, our instrumental and vocal abilities, and knew we were a marketable package.

BEST DAY OF MY YOUNG LIFE. 8-11-1975 changed my life forever. So, there I was standing face to face with the group I admired most in life. But everything comes to an end....As we were leaving....there it was ...right in front of me... Alan's white Gibson double cut electric guitar. It was beautiful....gleaming... (my holy grail) so to speak. I ran my thumb across the strings a few times.... My HEAVENS, I was REALLY touching it!! Alan looked over and just smiled that Osmond smile at me....my life, at that time was complete!!!! – Lori Whitfield

Together, these three men quickly carved a niche for us that appealed to younger teens—it worked for us too because we were in their age groups, and we worked hard to make the chemistry work. And it did. With frequent number one records in our relatively new career, the ride was thrilling and energizing.

As our outside world of friends was shrinking, the closeness we developed as a family was something we never thought possible; we became each other's best friends.

In the meantime, Jimmy and Marie were enjoying their own recording success.

Jimmy hit the top charts in Japan when he was five years old. He recorded "My Little Darling" in Japanese, and another song

Commercial in Japan

OSMOND
FACTS

When Marie joined the group, we changed our name from 'The Osmond Brothers' to 'The Osmonds'!

of Jimmy's, "Long-Haired Lover From Liverpool," reached number one on the British charts. He was the first of our family to get a gold record with the hit song in Japan, "My Little Darling."

While we were touring in Japan as a family to promote Jimmy's song, he was walking through a revolving door when the door caught his arm and broke it. The news hit the press and newspapers, and the people felt so sorry for this little American boy, singing in Japanese, with a broken arm.

Our family also recorded songs in Japanese and did a series of commercials for a company called, *Calpis,* a non-carbonated soft drink. The drink was quite popular and gave us the chance to be

with Pat Boone

seen, and become well-known in Japan. We sang songs and learned to introduce ourselves in Japanese. Soon that country became a popular place for us to perform with very enthusiastic fans.

At twelve and a half years old, Marie was also enjoying success with her first song and number one country hit, "Paper Roses."

My responsibility as the leader of the Osmonds now exploded into overseeing all individual family careers. Fine-tuning my thinking on behalf of my siblings was not only a great responsibility, but it was also a privilege.

There were ups and downs as there are in any career, but we learned to deal with them. Father and Mother never raised us to be quitters. Looking back on it now, some of those difficult moments were of the greatest worth. We were bonded to each other and learned to rely on higher powers in every decision.

Briefly, I want to add my voice to the many, many other people whose lives were changed by the Osmond family. As a young teenager I was very depressed because of an abusive situation in my home directly affecting me. Eventually, I felt like the only way out was to die. I wanted to die. At fifteen, I was a very depressed, self-medicating alcoholic, shadow of a person. But the Osmonds' example of positivity and love kept me going. They gave me hope that someday it would get better. At 18, after attending a fireside where they all talked, I joined The Church of Jesus Christ of Latter-day Saints. I was able to quit drinking and life kept getting better and better. 47 years later, life is great! Is there any wonder I've been a fan since I was 5? I couldn't love them more. – Bonnie Bloomfield

Due to Virl and Tom's hearing impairments, our family learned to communicate in American Sign Language. Not only did it help us with our brothers but it became a way of speaking silently when the microphones were on during a recording session and backstage and across stage in the wings, when verbal communication was impossible. Though it may seem insignificant to the audience, it was a huge advantage when we had to alter a segment in the middle of a show or concert. After recording a few albums, Mike Curb had the idea of sending us to Muscle Shoals, Alabama, to work with hit record producer, Rick Hall. In 1970 Father took the five of us to Alabama where we moved into a house trailer and went daily to Hall's FAME Studios to experiment with different song styles.

at Rick Hall's FAME Studios (printed with permission)

We Each Had Our Own Color

When we were younger, Mother had painted each of our school desks our favorite color, and she designed our earlier clothes around those colors as well. These same colors became our trademark and followed us through our careers.

Mine was blue, Wayne's orange, Merrill's black, Jay's green, Donny's the famous purple, Marie in pink, and Jimmy in red. Costume designer Bill Belew, who designed Elvis Presley's famous embellished jumpsuits, also designed similar jumpsuits for us and accented with each of our specific colors.

I have been a fan of the second generation since 1981 and saw them in concert the first time in 1986. There's a lot more to tell, but I did cut it down. It all started on August 20, 1990, when I took the train back to St. Louis to meet up with a friend to drive to Wisconsin for the Wisconsin State Fair where the Osmond boys would perform for six days, three shows per day. I attended all three shows on all six days. – Jinafer Marie Sharp

"Then all of the brothers came out and sang 4 songs and then all of Alan's boys came out and put on a show. They were very talented and reminded me of New Kids on the Block and the Young Osmond Brothers." – Annette Blacknik

Donny and Alan

Alabama is where we got our first taste of what would later be called "Osmondmania." Young girls would hang around the studio hoping to see us. One day three of my brothers went on a bike ride and by the time they had gone around the block, several girls were chasing them.

In December 1970 we taped our first thirty-minute television program produced by Alan Blye and Chris Beard. It was billed as *He Ain't Heavy, He's My Brother* and aired on April 28, 1971. We didn't get to watch it though because we were on our way to Japan for a series of concerts. However, following the television show,

The Osmond Fan Club, at that time ran by Mother, along with Virl, and his wife, Chris, were swamped with responding to all the fan mail from adoring fans.

They're the closest family I've ever seen, I couldn't believe it that a family could be that close.

– Don Murphett, Head of Security, UK (also head security for The Beatles)

Brother Tom was involved in taking photographs of us as well as printing a monthly newsletter that our mother would write. She called it "MOM"—"Mother Osmond's Memo." She kept the fans up to date with the latest tour dates and some personal insights. Fans loved our mother and she was responsible for building a love and bond between us and our fans—many of whom still refer to her as Mother. She printed our Osmond Newsletters on our printing press run by Tom. In support of our growing fan club, we soon had photo buttons, T-shirts, scarves, photo books, etc.,

The Osmonds Cartoon Series

and eventually purple socks and caps for Donny. They were all a huge hit.

One day Rick Hall's song writing team was searching for a song for us when they found one called, "One Bad Apple." Rick had each one of us sing the solo, then for the lead he chose a mixture of Merrill and Donny. The legendary producer from Capitol Records agreed that Donny had all the makings of a legend, and was the total package, but Merrill had the voice. He said that I clearly was the leader, and that all of us had solo-quality vocal skills.

FACT

Marie and our mother ran our Fan Club answering tons of fan letters for us!

I think Alan would like to know that it is because of him and the group that I joined the Church of Jesus Christ of Latter-day Saints in March of 1975. Alan and I also had some brief email exchanges a few years back, when I learned that he and my older brother both suffered from MS. Thanks very much!
— Joseph C. Bernier

We recorded the song on October 26, 1970, and released it less than three weeks later, about two weeks before Donny's thirteenth birthday. It debuted on the Billboard Top 100 on January 2, 1971, climbing to the #1 spot.

Sometimes we were tagged as "the white Jackson Five" and some people in the media tried to peddle that there was some kind of rivalry between our families, but it wasn't true. We liked their music, and we were even told that Mr. Jackson sat his sons down to listen to us when we performed on *The Andy Williams Show*. The Jacksons told me he would say, "Now listen to them. They rehearse every day, and you need to do the same."

with Cher

Why I'm still an Osmond Fan after 53 years. I was 11 years old when I first became a fan of the Osmonds! I turn 65 end of year and still a fan like so many others that says a lot! I first heard the Osmonds on the radio as a preteen "One Bad Apple" and I loved it! Saw them in concert at only 11 years old at Madison Square Garden way back when! I want to thank them from the bottom of my heart for the music, the harmonies, and inspiration! I'm sixty-four years old, a wife, mom, and grandma, and my husband, my grown kids, and my grandchildren know about the Osmonds because they know how important the Osmonds were and still are to me! I'm an Osmond fan forever. – Barbara Stanisci

with Kurt Russell

with Nancy Sinatra

FACT

One time a woman approached me and said, "I love the Osmonds. You are my favorite! Now— which one are you?" I quickly responded, "I'm Donny." The woman said, "Oh, you are my favorite Osmond!" She asked for an autograph, and I signed it as 'Donny,' then whispered to the woman next to me, "She'll appreciate this one more."

Dick Clark of *American Bandstand* was both our agent and the Jackson Five's agent, so we often passed each other while on tour. Once in Las Vegas we challenged the Jackson Five to a friendly game of basketball, but we realized they would always win so we changed it to football. But we never did play that game. One of the major differences between our two groups while on tour; the Jackson Five rode in their own separate limousines, while we all rode together on one "big honkin' bus." We asked, "Father, we're making the same money that the Jackson Five are making, why can't we have our own limousines?"

Father simply said, "Someday you'll thank me."

I wasn't so sure about that. The bus we rode in was not a fancy celebrity vehicle with sleeping quarters or other frills. It was simply a nice bus and each of us was given a large beach towel and a pillow so we could sleep. Not even close to a limousine.

at Heathrow Airport

My sister Nancy and I volunteered to coordinate the helium balloon releases for the annual Fourth of July Stadium of Fire spectacular. We continued for many years to pass out programs at that event for many years. Nancy used to joke that she was sure she would marry Donny. She is three years younger than him, so naturally that made sense—to her.
– Sarah Carson

I like to think that I majored in Osmondmania, at Brigham Young University and in my opinion I would have earned a solid 4.0. I was eleven when I first experienced the Osmonds, but it was in the Haunted Mansion in Disneyland, and I was terrified. But I transferred my devotion from singer Bobby Sherman to Alan and his brothers. Now in my sixties, I'm still a devoted fan. – Linda Ann Sosa

While on that bus, Mother had an aluminum briefcase she called her "busy box," where she collected recipes, stored her needlepoint, kept her scriptures, her writing, and some things to teach all of us about faith and religion. Mother always said, "You need one book to read out of and one to write in." That's how we traveled.

We were told the Jacksons turned down "One Bad Apple" which became a number one hit for us and made the top charts on February 13, 1971, and stayed there for five weeks. An interesting note—we turned down a song offered to Donny called "Ben" which Michael Jackson recorded and became a hit for him.

OSMOND FACT

Marie helped us choose and coordinate our wardrobe.

KHJ Radio played a rundown of *American's top 40 Coast to Coast* with Kasey Kasem which was the foremost show of its kind.

I remember being at home one Sunday in Arleta, California; we hurried home from church to hear when Kasey Kasem announces on the radio, "And now, the number one record in America, "One Bad Apple and The Osmonds!"

We screamed like crazy, and Wayne ran outside and around our house. That was our goal, and we finally made it!

With the release of "One Bad Apple" and follow up records leading to our self-penned hits, "Down By the Lazy River" and "Crazy Horses," radio stations were overwhelmed with requests for our songs, and, as the saying goes, the rest is history.

> *I have been an Osmond Follower (I prefer this to fan) since I was 8 years old. Watching them on Andy Williams was me and my Grannies "thing." Many fond memories of that time. I remember the first time I met them in 1975 in Pittsburgh, I won a radio contest on WPEZ radio to "meet the Osmonds"....Well you know I was getting on that train...even with the old rotary phone to call in when they played an Osmond song my diligence paid off and I won my backstage pass.* – Lori Whitefield

Audience with the Queen

One of the highlights of our career was performing for and meeting Her Majesty, Queen Elizabeth, at the Royal Variety Performance at the London Palladium on May 22, 1972. A few incidents from that night have become part of a series of ongoing family jokes.

After the show, we were all anxious to meet her. There are rules about meeting Queen Elizabeth; you have to just stand there; you can't speak to her unless she first speaks to you or raise your hand to shake Her Majesty's hand, unless she first offers her hand to you. I mean, the protocol was out of this world.

Merrill was nervous and had cottonmouth. As he approached Her Royal Majesty, he licked his lips. Someone snapped a picture.

Audience with Queen Elizabeth II

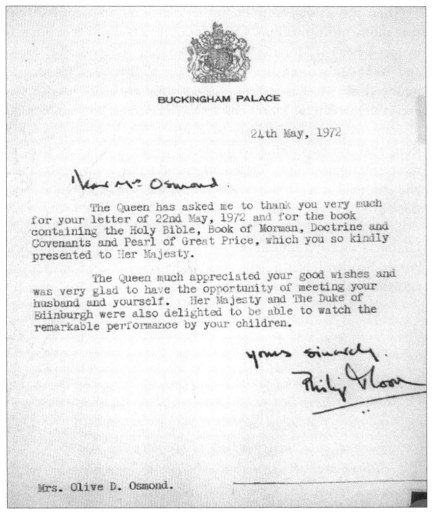

BUCKINGHAM PALACE

24th May, 1972

Dear Mr. Osmond.

    The Queen has asked me to thank you very much for your letter of 22nd May, 1972 and for the book containing the Holy Bible, Book of Mormon, Doctrine and Covenants and Pearl of Great Price, which you so kindly presented to Her Majesty.

    The Queen much appreciated your good wishes and was very glad to have the opportunity of meeting your husband and yourself. Her Majesty and The Duke of Edinburgh were also delighted to be able to watch the remarkable performance by your children.

Yours sincerely,

Philip Moore

Mrs. Olive D. Osmond.

Thank You letter from Queen Elizabeth II, Buckingham Palace

The next morning Merrill made the front page of the newspapers saying that he was sticking out his tongue at the queen.

In an interview with KSL radio, Jimmy explained that the code of behavior intimidated him. "I remember shaking Her Majesty's hand, and it was such a cool moment. She came to me first and I blurted, 'Hello, Mrs. Queen.'"

There was a notable moment that stands out in my mind from that momentous meeting. Our Mother reached into her purse to extract a *Book of Mormon* for the queen. She always carried copies and had handwritten her testimony in it. The Queen's security pounced on Mother, calming down only after the Queen said everything was fine. Mother had a lot of courage, and simply said, "I want to give Her Majesty my most prized possession; something that means so much to me and my family." Queen Elizabeth received it gracefully and said she would put it on her mantle. She also mailed my mother a registered letter of acceptance of the *Book of Mormon*.

Several decades later, on November 4, 2003, we met Her Royal Highness a second time at the Royal Variety Performance in Edinburgh, Scotland. She quietly told us she remembered our mother and still had her "Mormon Bible."

Alan and I met for the first time in 1984, at the OBIFC offices in Orem. Introduced by Jill Simmons. He was so gracious and welcoming, open to my thoughts and ideas on how to promote the fan club in the UK. It was a privilege to take these ideas forwards. – Kathy O'Connell

After our hit with "One Bad Apple," Dick Clark began testing the market to see if we were ready to start appearing in concerts.

It wasn't long after I wrote the letter to Don Williams, that we received a record offer from Capitol Records. Bobby Darrin and Terry Melcher owned and produced UNI, a Universal Record Label. We put out a single with "My Mom" on one side and "Mr. Sandman" on the flip side. Neither song did well, but it did push us further into the market. We also met and worked with record producer, Jerry Goldstein. He took an interest in us and even came to our home in Arleta. With Jerry we learned more about song structure and how to produce.

with Henry Fonda

Bill Sammeth was a young guy who was assistant to Jim Morey of our management team. He got us connected with teen magazines. Sharon Lee from *Tiger Beat* in Los Angles, and Nola Leon from *Sixteen Magazine* out of New York, both started doing interviews and photo sessions with us. They put pictures and articles about us in those monthly magazines, and we started to build a base of young teenage followers.

The heartland of America was considered a great testing ground for new artists, so after our return from Japan, Dick Clark and his assistant, Peggy Rogers, arranged two concerts for us in Cleveland, and Columbus, Ohio. On May 28th, ten thousand screaming fans attended our third *test* concert at Public Hall in Cleveland, Ohio. It was highly successful, and there was no riot.

Our concert in Cleveland was unforgettable. We packed the audience with ten thousand plus people at each performance. We needed big amplifiers to be heard over all the screaming and clapping from the audience. Our audience was mostly young girls who shrieked and rushed the stage. It was crazy and something we had never experienced; but we liked it and knew we were ready.

Wow! This was the show business we had dreamed about. We were finally singing for our peers and writing the music we liked. We had found a winning formula; a niche that would prove to pack audiences across the country and around the world. Believing that people want to see something, we also danced and created a moving and visual show.

> The Osmonds have exceptionally loyal fans. It's their talent, showmanship, and how real and authentic they are. I have no doubt that the availability of the Internet and fan groups play a big part. They are not only talented, but also dedicated, hard-working, honest, true, devoted, and family oriented. They are real-life people who have chosen to share their lives with us. – Kim Simcock

Hysteria!

When we arrived in Canada for a performance on August 30th, we had no way of knowing what kind of reception we would receive. The Canadian National Exhibition was sold out and the *Toronto Daily Star* reported the next day that it was the first time the outdoor grandstand stadium had ever been sold-out for a concert.

"I've never seen such a happy bunch of people in all my life as these, but security wise it's a different problem." – Rent-a-thugs (what we called these guys in England who were the original guards for The Beatles)

It was literally fan hysteria. We had planned to close with "Down By the Lazy River," but the audience seemed to sense the show was about to end and the young female crowd surged forward. They moved over the top of the protective barriers in front of the stage. It reminded me of the wave in the movie *The Poseidon Adventure.*

One of our managers, Ed Leffler, had worked as an agent for the Beatles and immediately recognized the potential danger to not only us, but our audience. He killed the lights and yelled for us to get off the stage. But we couldn't hear him, and we didn't know what was happening. When we realized what he was telling us, we ran for the exit.

It was pitch dark and I ran head on into a steal beam opening an ugly gash on my forehead. We were all running for our lives, and I was bleeding like crazy. Father was running ahead of me, puffing, and trying to get us to the limousine. I was the last one to get there and literally dove through the open rear door landing on top of my brothers. A wall of girls piled into the side of the car slamming the door on my guitar, snapping it right in half.

The mob of girls hit the car so hard they pushed it sideways a few feet. Screaming hysterically, the girls climbed on top of the car pounding on the windows. They broke off the antenna, side mirrors, and tore off the windshield wipers. It seemed as though they would break the windows, so we held our hands over our faces to shield our eyes. I was bleeding all over everybody, and we were yelling for the driver to get out of there, but we were surrounded and had he pulled forward, he would have run over someone. We didn't think they were trying to hurt us, but they were putting us, and themselves, in danger.

The security guards were dragging people off the car and trying to clear a path, but it was impossible. Finally, mounted police on horses were able to move the crowd back so the driver could move forward, but there were still girls clinging to the sides of the car. We finally got away, but it was scary for all of us. It was the first time we had experienced anything like that. It was so surreal; all of this for us? I still remember feeling overwhelmed when I first saw our name in lights in Las Vegas, but this was something else entirely. It was hard to process.

In 1973 we went back to England. We had been there two years earlier but were not well known and were able to walk the streets freely without being recognized. But this time back, we appeared on British television on a live program called "Royal Command Performance" attended by Queen Elizabeth herself. It was a gala, a national event staged in part to benefit the British Olympic team. The variety show included Liza Minnelli and the American comedy duo of Rowan and Martin. It was broadcast by the British Broadcasting Company (BBC) who dominates television and radio transmission in England, so the show was transmitted to the entire country.

A fan by the name of Bev Bowerman, who was only thirteen years old at the height of Osmandmania, later described her introduction to the Osmonds.

"I was at a friend's home watching the performance on television. Donny was just sixteen, and we young English girls immediately took him into our hearts. We loved his rendition of 'Puppy Love,' and other ballads, but we embraced all the Osmonds and their music. I was too young to have paid much attention to the Beatles or the Monkees, who had been popular for several years, but as a young teen, I found the Osmonds exciting."

That initial television exposure set off an explosion of interest in us all over Britain, as well as parts of Europe. The press began calling the hysteria "Osmondmania"—a frenzied, wide-eyed adulation of our music and what seemed like a mindless devotion to each of us.

The Osmond's represented what we were rapidly losing, the stability of a nuclear family. In the seventies, we had the sexual revolution, availability of the pill, and no-fault divorce, created changes never before seen in our nation and the world. Yes, there were other groups who sang together, but none like this fresh-faced group of gorgeous guys who were musicians, could harmonize, write music, and 'get down.' – Pamela Morgan Smith

It was incredible!

I don't know if I can paint an accurate picture of what it was like for us in England. It was the noise that stands out for me. Every time we appeared in public, the noise generated by these huge crowds of screaming young girls was deafening. Not just when we came on stage, but even when we waved to the crowd from the balcony of our hotel. I had never experienced anything like it; though exciting, it was also a little frightening. The frenzied girls soon became known as "teenyboppers," and their reckless behavior, destruction of hotels, vehicles, and performance venues became a concern of British officials, as well as the British citizens.

Wherever we went, fans pursued us. They would gather on street corners in the center of London, and if any fans saw us in a car, they would alert other fans that we were coming and then we would be tracked there.

There were times when some did make it into our rooms. One fan forced her way in by holding a knife to the back of a hotel security guard, and two other fans took a fire ax to an outside door of the building. Once they got in, they ran up several flights of stairs to our room, but just stood there staring at us until security removed them.

We were even banned from using some chauffeur-driven automobiles or staying in a few commercial hotels. A bit of anti-Osmond sentiment developed in England and a portion of the media criticized us for being too goody-goody or sugar sweet; that our wholesome image was simply a gimmick. We were even accused of looting the country of its money. The more we dominated the headlines, the more we were scrutinized by some critics, and even Ringo Starr ridiculed our music in the press.

Of course, our fans were mostly young women and girls, so we caused some jealousy among the young British males, and we even had some bomb threats. But during it all, Paul McCartney was quoted as saying, "I like the Osmonds."

Fleet Street tabloids pulled dirty tricks on us in order to sell papers. One time we attended a publicity party sponsored by Polydor Record company. When we were leaving, a scantily clad woman jumped from the bushes and grabbed my arm. Our manager Ed Leffler, and Roger Holdt of the record company, tried to intervene, but she had been hired for this purpose. Photographs were still taken of the scene and later published that I had been consorting with a stripper.

Once in a London airport, a reporter harassed me as I walked through. He obviously wanted a confrontation to cook up a story, but I just kept walking and smiling. That was always our best defense. The press constantly tried to cause controversy, but we worked hard to avoid it. We even turned it to our advantage when we could—kind of a contest or challenge for us. One time we led them on a chase to the "Mormon" LDS Temple Visitors Center located outside of London. There were pictures published with the temple in the background of us watching the Joseph Smith story on primetime TV.

One time the place where we were staying was overrun and seven policewomen were injured and ended up in the hospital.

And another time, two girls actually shipped themselves to our hotel where we were staying while others dressed as maids to sneak up to our rooms.

But we loved and appreciated our fans. They bought our records, attended our shows, and were forever trying to see or touch one of us. They genuinely loved us, and for that we were then, and we still are, very grateful. We were asked to host the popular weekly BBC music count-down show called "Top of the Pops," the first foreign group ever to host the widely broadcast show. For us, the popularity was great, but the security issues were horrendous.

Having been banned from some hotels, we stayed in an apartment made available to us by an international businessman, Adnan Khashoggi. It was supposed to be a secret, but fans found the location and laid siege on the apartment.

Most often when they did get to us, they would just stand there, crying. We might give them a hug, a T-shirt, or an autographed picture and then security would lead them away.

From my mom, "Your dad and I were so pleased that you were a fan of the Osmonds. We had seen them on the And Williams Show when we were in Singapore, and they were amazing. Such brilliant harmonies. We were worried that you were going to like other bands who were a bit on the "naughty side." Then you announced that you and your friendship group liked the Osmonds and David Cassidy." Two starry eyed teenagers singing all the way home in the car, partly deafened by the loudness of the concert. – Kim Wood , Whittington Staffordshire UK

We even had police bring dogs into the venues where we performed to find fans who had gotten in early or to search for bombs that had been reported. When our shows would sell out and there were no more tickets, someone would go out with a megaphone and announce to the crowd that there were no more seats; near riots followed those unwanted announcements.

Chuck Norris

While on tour, I had this idea of taking karate lessons to toughen up our dance moves. We asked our friend Chuck Norris, if he would teach us. I told him that we're in front of people who are three feet from us, and they would be able to tell if we were faking it. We were in Indianapolis with forty thousand people in the audience, and they were loving it. Jay and I were sparring and when I came to him with a punch, Jay was supposed to block it. But when I gave him a knee in the stomach just before that, he wasn't ready, and he didn't take the kick in the stomach very well, so he was a little slow coming back. When I came around with a roundhouse, I opened his nose up in front of everybody; from his broken nose and my cut knuckle, there was blood everywhere.

I didn't know what to do so I grabbed the mic and said, "We'll be right back we're going to have a word of prayer." I was surprised I said that, but we taped up his nose and we finished the fight.

Right after we took him to the hospital to have it set and then we came back and did our second show.

The show must go on.

We had to get creative to even get from our hotel to the venue where we were performing. Sometimes we hired impersonators dressed to look like us. We would create a diversion by the impersonators bolting out the door of the hotel to a waiting vehicle and we would escape through the hotel kitchen to a waiting bread truck. Still, we were often discovered, and fans would beat on the sides or violently rock the truck.

with Chuck Norris

I first met Alan in the mid-70s at the Osmond Studio. A friend's parents drove us to Utah for a few short days. Couldn't tell you much about that visit, but I was in my long hair and glasses age! Ugh! Alan and I would always tease each other on our birthdays, but him serenading happy birthday on a winding staircase in Ohio wearing a gorgeous blue suit is etched in my brain! Another time when i was loading the bus he surprised me by having all the fans sing happy birthday. If it wasn't for traveling and / or seeing the Osmonds, I wonder what my life would've been like. — Lori

> *Being around Alan and the other Osmonds fills you with light. The family used to end their concerts with the then popular song, "I Believe." They brought up the lights slowly, and much of the audience was so moved, they wept. This family could bring you to tears, but they would be tears of joy. You are a blessing beyond measure to those who know you. Love you, – Nancy Dyer*

Our popularity brought us mixed blessings. I think it would be hard for one to understand unless they had experienced something similar. Being internationally known was great, but sometimes we were literally captives of our own fame.

Our career was in full swing worldwide, but we found a huge audience of fans in England. A decade before we got there, the Beatles—John Lennon, Paul McCartney, George Harrison, and Ringo Starr—caused a worldwide phenomenon that became known as *Beatlemania*. Who would have ever thought that we would get screaming fans in the U.K. with popularity that soon became known as *Osmondmania*, and that we would hire the same bodyguards that the Beatles had. Except we called them "rent-a-thugs." They got us out of some very tight situations, and they told us all about the Beatles days but said ours was even worse, not only because the girls were doing anything they could to meet us, but with the Hells Angels in Germany who tried to stop our concert by egging us. When we came to the arena to perform, they took metal items from the gift shop and threw them at us on stage.

I remember one item flying through the air at me, so I ducked. It was a souvenir of metal letters spelling "LOVE" that barely missed my head, slamming into my marshal amplifier and took out my woofer speaker.

Our head of security, Don Murphet, hid behind me while we were performing. He told me that when he tapped my shoulder to jump to the side. I did, and he jumped into the audience taking out the ringleader in the third row where the main troublemaker was. He took him out as well as a couple of rows of fans and their seats.

When we made it to our limos, they started throwing eggs at us. They hit Father in the head so hard they knocked his toupee off.

Our managers Ray Katz, Ed Leffler, and Jim Morey were with us for the next few years. We were in for exciting, demanding, and even dangerous at times. Our fans were young and often took crazy chances to see us, even at the risk of their lives. We had stages collapse, airplane engines fail, and we escaped in a hotel fire in Memphis.

One of our guards, Patti, was chasing after fans who got backstage at another group's concert when he fell down an elevator shaft and died. His death shocked and saddened all of us. Another time one of our limousine drivers was trying to avoid hitting some girls, but they ran between our two limos and fell, and the limo ran over their hands.

I have been a fan of the Osmond's since seeing them on Andy Williams show. What started as being a fan grew into love for who they are. Loved the music the way they entertained us. They sang with passion and smiles, danced, played instruments and wrote songs. They are positive and honest people. Each one of them means so much to me and I feel like I grew up with them. I am thankful to each of them for giving me love and faith. For sharing themselves with us. I still listen to the Christmas Album every Christmas with joy. That is a small part of the big impact they made on me. – Dawn T.

By this time, we had started to expect crowds of screaming fans, but we were not prepared for what happened October 21, 1973, when we landed at Heathrow Airport.

We were traveling in our private jet that had "Osmonds" on the side. The airport had anticipated the challenge and had canceled leave for four hundred police officers and even added sixty more men to help. They estimated that more than ten thousand fans had broken through customs, shutting down the airport. Some of them crowded onto the roof gardens at the Queen's Building balcony, and the wall collapsed under the weight.

Hysteria broke out.

It was hard to tell who was crying because they were hurt or because they did not get a chance to see my brothers and me.

Seven girls were injured and four were taken by ambulance, so that night I went with Don Murphet to the hospital to offer comfort and prayers for them. When the site was cleared, officials found that a fifteen-foot section of railing weighing nearly a ton had collapsed twelve feet from an upper to a lower balcony. They suspected that injuries would likely have been much worse if fans had not been pressing forward against an outer rail.

After this happened, members of the British Airports Authority, along with police, considered a ban on certain pop groups traveling through Heathrow if their arrivals and departures were publicized in advance. Apparently about ten thousand fans had been notified that we were landing at Heathrow and the approximate arrival time. The fans had organized on every corner and screamed when they saw us, thus finding out where we were staying.

Heathrow Airport was closed to us because of the publicized instances where police and young girls were hurt.

Scotland Yard and British newspapers printed front-page headlines that read, "OSMONDS, GO HOME!" The story claimed the Osmonds were only there to make money and didn't care about our fans. That was absolutely not true, so we contacted BBC television and worked out a deal for the next year where we flew to England and performed every evening Monday through Saturday for half an hour shows in front of a live audience. Being on live TV, we were able to respond to critics by reading their review on live TV, then telling the truth about what really happened. That's how we shut down any rumors created by the press.

Then on Thursday, we did their popular "Top of the Pops" music hour, and everyone in the UK was able to see us this time for free. The BBC said they had never had such high ratings on their TV network.

At each show we would take a moment to hold up the newspapers and answer the press, refuting any misconceptions or lies with the truth, right from our own mouths. The reaction by the general public was so great that we set new TV viewing ratings records.

I remember being in Birmingham, at another sold out show, when I mentioned to one of the policemen that I wished I could go outside and see all the hysteria prior to our concert. He said, "Wait here." He soon returned with a Bobbie cap and coat and said, "Alan, do you wanna go take a look?" I did. It was so fun

I have been an avid fan of the Osmonds since 1973 when I was just 11 years old. I have now been a keen supporter of our lovely Osmonds for 51 years and this is how it all started. My brother Bradley took me to look at records for sale. Brad picked up an LP and said, 'they are a very nice family, Alison, I think you will like them.' Little did I realize then what a huge impact they would have on my life and still do all these years later. I'm now at 61 years of age! But a very special thank you to Alan for all that he stands for through his faith and influence!
– Alison Apasa

seeing what the scene was like prior to our concert with the fans lined up and banging on the front doors of the concert hall. They were yelling, "We want the Osmonds!" I will never forget it.

My sister, Tina, and I bumped into The Osmond's in Nashville. As a teen, they were our sound and looks, as a young adult, it was surreal; chances to travel to fan functions and meet them. As an adult, it has been the ability to continue to see them evolve and grow into even greater performers. Over fifty years and about some sixty concerts later—yeah, I'd say it's been a fun ride as a fan!"
– Tina Morgan and Donnajean Luciano

Another time when we came on tour to England, we performed at Earl's Court and used Led Zeppelin's sound system. We were told that we were the loudest rock band of the seventies. It wasn't because we turned our amplifiers up so loudly, it was because our fans screamed so loud no one could hear our music unless we pushed our voices out as loud as we could. Led Zeppelin's sound system was the only one big enough to do it.

The night before we rented their system, we attended Led Zeppelin's last concert. It was an awesome show. Different from ours, and an older audience. When the band finished, they went off to the back of the stage. The audience was going wild and clapping in tempo for them to do an encore.

I told their agent that accompanied us that we had better go before the crowd let out.

He said, "Oh no! The band wants to meet you."

"They're probably just being nice," I said. "No, they told me to bring you backstage," he said.

"Well then let's go!" I told my brothers to follow me.

When we opened the backstage door we were surprised to see what they were doing. They were playing frisbee with their kids. They saw us and we walked toward each other. We shook their hands and told them what a great show they had. We greeted them, and I could tell they liked our music. In fact, they said, "We really like you guys." I almost turned to my brothers to tell them to write that down, when the lead singer and guitarist, Robert Plant said, "Why don't you come up on stage with us for our last song, 'Stairway to Heaven'?"

I was about to say okay when their manager said, "No, not the Osmonds."

Robert turned to his manager and said, "Yes, the Osmonds."

He then called his stage manager over and told him to take us up the back stairs and onto stage right. We followed him up and onto the stage. Can you imagine what that audience must have thought as they continued clapping in tempo for Led Zeppelin to do an encore, only to see 'The Osmonds' coming up those stairs! Zeppelin came right up behind us and played an amazing rendition of "Stairway to Heaven." Jimmy Paige never played his guitar better than that night!

However, because of all the hotels who now would not let us stay because they were overrun by fans, we stayed at a private apartment building belonging to Khashoggi. We had been banned from the last hotel after it was overrun by fans. A few of them ran over four policewomen sending them to the hospital. One out of control teen threatened a hotel staff member with a knife against his back and attempted to get into the hotel through a back entrance. Other fans tried climbing up the outside walls to get to us. One fan broke into a firearms' box, grabbed the ax, and set off the alarm. It was crazy to say the least.

But it continued to get wilder. Once we received a delivery and Father called me. He said, "Alan, you need to see this to believe it." A special delivery crate showed up outside our hotel. From inside the four-by-four wooden container we could hear whimpering.

One of their friends had apparently helped them get in and literally shipped them to our hotel. They were inside the box for most of the afternoon until they were freed with a crowbar and the two girls climbed out of the box. They were as limp as spaghetti noodles. They ran toward me but stopped before they crashed into me. They just started crying and couldn't say anything. I put my arms around the girls and thanked them for going to such great lengths to see me and my brothers. I wanted to make sure they knew how complimented we were before security took them away.

> I'm a native of England, and I have a fabulous memory. I knocked on Alan and Suzanne's front door August 10th, 1979, to beg them to come to the United Kingdom and include Newcastle in their tour. I showed him signed letters from the fans in our region. I'm happy to say they obliged in April 1980 by doing back-to-back concerts. I will never forget how gracious Suzanne and Alan were to me that day." – Kathleen Ainsley

Because of vandalism by fans at some of the hotels where we stayed, other hotels closed their doors to us. We ended up renting an estate outside of the city near Ascot, next door to Rod Stewart.

Once we had a surprise visit from Paul McCartney. We were in France at the George Sank Hotel when I received a phone call from the hotel operator. She said, "There's a man down here who says he is Paul McCartney and who would like to see you."

"Are you talking about the *real* Paul McCartney?"

She said, "Yes!"

Wow. "Send him right up!"

That phone call woke up my brothers and me. When I told them who was coming up to see us, we all jumped like crazy cleaning up the place and combing our hair while we got dressed. A few minutes later there was a knock at the door.

I answered it and there stood Paul McCartney, the superstar, Paul the amazing entertainer, and Paul, the father. He had brought his little daughter to get Donny's autograph. It impressed me so much that later with our One Heart Charity and thefamily.com, our marketing site for 'Strengthening the Family,' I gave a tall marble award to Paul McCartney, the father, for being a good example to his daughter.

We visited for a short while, and after he left I reminded my brothers of the day they said we would "Never make it." They claimed we were, "Too Clean Cut; Too Goody Goody."

As a little girl, whenever I misbehaved, my mom would plop me in front of The Andy Williams Show to watch the Osmonds and ask why I couldn't be as respectful and polite as they were. They said, 'Yes sir,' and 'Yes, Ma'am' and were always smiling. It wasn't long before I was a die-hard Osmond fan. I have been an adult for a long time, but I'm still an avid believer in Osmondmania and have an assortment of Osmond memorabilia displayed at home. – Gina Facosi from Niles, Illinois

One day, Elton John had Mike Curb call us from MGM Records asking if he could meet the Osmonds. Mike called me and I had Merrill go with me to the MGM offices. Sure enough, it was Elton John. He had a pink flower behind his ear. We had a great conversation together. We talked about music, recording, tours, and entertaining and traveling to various concerts. He said he really liked us and wanted to invite us to a party he was having with many musicians and entertainers later that night. He gave us his phone number and directions to the party, and we said goodbye.

About fifteen minutes later, his manager called us and "un-invited us." He explained, "Elton was uneasy and felt that some of his guests might be a little uncomfortable having you there."

We loved England and the United Kingdom. Many of our father's ancestors came from England, and our mother's ancestors came from Wales. (osmondfamily.org) Both sides of our families are musical, so our gene pool was influenced by both sides. A lot of our music tendency and talent was probably inherited and passed on to us because of that.

More than thirty-five years ago I was traveling with three others to Gatwick Airport to see Donny leave the country. We had an accident, and the last thing I remember was someone asking for some form of ID. Alan gave me a blessing that day, and members of their family recorded audio tapes for my family to play for me while I was in a coma.
- Carol Sheardown

Elvis – Nicest Guy Ever

While performing one night at Caesar's Palace in Las Vegas, we were told that "The Boss" was upstairs. The legendary singer Elvis Presley was watching our show from the light booth. We were nervous to meet Elvis, because Bill Belew, who was Elvis's costume designer, had designed our five white jumpsuits, just like his rhinestone-studded jumpsuits. We also learned karate from Chuck Norris and knew that Elvis liked it also.

The first thing Elvis said to us was, "Hey man, I love the jump-suits!" *Wheww.* This initial meeting would be the beginning of a treasured friendship until his unfortunate passing.

The larger-than-life superstar also developed a special fondness for Mother because she reminded him of his own late mother. He gave Mother and our family a guitar-shaped floral arrangement as part of his Las Vegas welcome.

We were at the Hilton Hotel in Las Vegas in May of 1976 when Elvis Presley called Suzanne's and my room, and I had a great visit with him. Then I mentioned that my mother was in the room with us.

Elvis said, "Oh, could I talk with your mother?"

I handed the phone to Mother and she and Elvis had a nice discussion. She was never shy about sharing her belief about God. Father had arranged with security for our fans who wanted to meet us to go down by the kitchen into a hallway that led past our dressing rooms where fans could line up, and we could sign their autographs while we ate between shows.

Elvis Presley noticed that and made the comment, "If I could do it all over again, I would do just like the Osmonds and sign every autograph for every fan that wanted it."

In our phone conversation with Elvis, he told us that he had always wanted to be a preacher. That's when Elvis said to me, "I'd like to get to know your family better, so I'd like to invite your family to my home in California for a barbecue."

The meal never happened, because Elvis died from cardiac arrest before we could have that barbecue at his house. Mother considered Elvis a friend and missed him. Before she died more than twenty-five years later, she disclosed that when she passed away, she planned to check on her friend in heaven and see how he was doing. I'm sure that she and Elvis have had many discussions since then.

Elvis' drummer, Ronnie Tutt, was also a good friend of ours, and after Elvis passed, he performed on several of our shows and recordings.

I don't know why more people don't question why the Osmonds are not in the Rock and Roll Hall of Fame. What an honor it would be while all nine siblings are alive! – Cindy Robert

We Were Blessed to Meet Amazing People

We made many friends in the entertainment and music world, including legendary and contemporary performers, many who visited Osmond Studios. The diversity of personalities ranged from Lucille Ball, Frank Sinatra, Paul McCartney, Danny Thomas, Ann Margret, Edgar Bergen and Charlie McCarthy, Groucho Marx, Paul Lynde, Ricardo Montalban, Lorne Greene, Kris Kristofferson, Suzanne Sommers, Bob Hope, The Beach Boys, Wayne Newton, The Oak Ridge Boys, Toby Keith, Ruth Buzzi, Buddy Hackett, Tim Conway, Olivia Newton-John, Lionel Ritchie, Roy Clark, Crystal Gayle, John Candy, Loretta Swit, Pat Boone, Kate Smith, Lee Majors, Farrah Fawcett, Vincent Price, Monty Hall, Charlton Heston, Sally Struthers, Karen Valentine, Harlem Globetrotters, Ted Knight, The Were Brothers, Andy Williams, Jimmie Walker, Carl Bellentine, George Gobel, Charo, Raymond Burr, Esther Rollie, Peter Kastner, Sherman Hemsley, Pearl Bailey, Ann Meara, Milton Berle, Nipsy Russell, Tommy Eure, Jim Nabors, Jerry Lewis, Hal Lindon, Ron Palillo, Robert Hedgyes, Lawrence-Hilton Jacobs, Minnie Pearl, McLean Stevenson, Rick Hurst, Gabe Kaplan, Jack Albertson, Barbara Eden, The Great Tompsoni, Michael Landon, Don Knotts, Isabel Sanford, Little Richard, George Burns, Evil Knievel, Peggy Flemming, Chubby Checker, Gale Storm, Arthur Godfrey, Alan 'Elvis' Meyer, Desi Arnaz, Howdy Doody, Art Linkletter, Chad Everett, Florence Henderson, Brady Bunch, Patty Maloney, Rice Twins, Spike Jones, Jr., Billy Barty, Sonny Bono, Cher, Cindy Williams, Charley Pride, Raz Kelly & Pinkettes, Roy Rogers, Dale Evans, Georgia Engel, Rich Little, Andy Griffith, Bo Diddley, Fred Berry, Haywood Nelson, Ernest Thomas, Carl Reiner, Merle Haggard, Kaptain Kool & the Kongs, Gary Burghoff, Chuck Berry, Paul

OSMOND FACT

I went to Lucille Ball's home, and she was playing Scrabble™ with a friend in her kitchen.

Anka, Rip Taylor, Billy Preston, Tina Turner, Connie Stevens, Keely Smith, Pal Williams, Tony Martin, Cid Charisse, Fran Tarkenton, Ken Stabler, John Brascia, Bert Convy, Sonny James, The Silvers, Ray Bolger, Virginia Wood, Cheryl Ladd, Johnny Dark, Ben Vereen, Kristy McNichol, Billy Crystal, Big Bird, Glen Campbell, Bernadette Peters, Lucien Myer & His Chimps, Freddie Trenkler, Rod Gist, Mr. Frick, Red Foxx, Rita Coolidge, Lola Falana, Donny Most, Abe Vigoda, Anson Williams, Ken Barry, Mac Davis, Makenzie Phillips, Robert Young, Neil Sadaka, Susan Perkin, Desie Arnaz, Jr., Mormon Tabernacle Choir, Betty White, Andy Gibb, Tom Jones, Ron Howard, Englebert Humperdinck, Parker Stevenson, Mel Tillis, Joey Travolta, Dick Van Patten, Lassy, Robert Conrad, Lynn Hallowell, two Miss America's, Dirk Benedict, Harvey Korman, Cheryl Tiegs, Gavin MacLeod, Raquel Welch, Seals & Crofts, Debby Boone, David Copperfield, the 1979–80 U.S. Ski Team, Leif Garrett, Levar Burton, Joyce Dewitt, Moore's Mongrell Revue, King Arthur the Lion, Murray Hills elephants, Debbie Reynolds, Tanya Tucker, Larry Mahan, Boys Town Choir, Andrea McCardle, Adam Rich, Cathy Rigby, Wolfman Jack, Loretta Lynn, Grant Goodeve, Isaac Hayes, Hagar Twins, Tina Cole, Kurt Russell, Tony Orlando, Eric Estrada, Efrem Zimbalist, Jr., Lennon Sisters, Nel Carter, Commadores, Pointer Sisters, Scott Baio, Ronald Reagan, Led Zeppelin, and more.

Years later, these connections proved invaluable when I produced *Stadium of Fire*. I was able to tap into all this amazing talent and bring several of these stars to the Fourth of July celebration in Provo, Utah.

🌫 **10** 🌫

MY UNCONVENTIONAL DATING

GROWING UP in the entertainment world—I had plenty of opportunity to meet many girls. In fact, I collected a Rolodex full of names and numbers, but we were so busy traveling that I could hardly follow up, or go on a date with them. With all the touring and traveling I have done throughout the years. I wasn't shy about talking to or approaching girls. But when I met someone I liked, we would visit and maybe later I would call her but I wasn't looking for a relationship at that time, but friendship. I knew that when the time came to find a companion, I would want to find the 'one' that would be my best friend, the one I would want to be with forever. Once in Florida we were appearing at a theater across from the Miss Universe Pageant. I managed to get in, and when Miss Universe's military escort left her alone for a few minutes I took the opportunity to introduce myself. But there was never time to make a second contact because we were always off to the next show.

When we were working in Las Vegas, I took Karen Carpenter on a dinner date. Her brother, Richard, met me at the door with a serious look, but I assured him I would get her back home safe and sound. He was a really nice person, by the way.

We were raised by conservative parents who taught us to live by a strict moral code. We believed in a standard of morality that not only forbids premarital sex but also warns against putting ourselves in situations where we might be tempted.

The truth is, my brothers and I, just like other musicians, had a lot of female admirers. Had we not been committed to the strict standards we lived by it would have been easy to take advantage of those young women. So, we were careful to avoid any potentially awkward situations. We did hang around after our shows to sign autographs and talk to our female fans, it was fun. But we never invited any of them up to our rooms, or even to the floor we stayed on. We wanted to avoid the appearance of evil, and at the same time preventing any of our critics from accusing us being in any way hypocritical about what we professed to stand for.

I got to know some girls that I met through traveling and on tour, but I found most of them were focused on their careers and were interested in meeting people who could help them get ahead. I never considered myself to be a prude, but I did have certain standards I was looking for in a future wife, so if they dressed immodestly, drank, or smoked, I simply knew we didn't have much in common.

Moving to Provo, Utah, gave us more opportunity to meet friends that shared our same beliefs and values. For me personally, I loved dating girls who felt the same way about life as I did. I was glad to be living in a place where I could get to know women who shared those same beliefs.

I dated several girls and double dated as well in my quest to find "Miss Right." I never capitalized on my celebrity status to impress the girls I dated. I enjoyed going to movies or to a dance, in fact, I loved to dance. I never went steady with anyone, and I rarely had a second date. When I wasn't finding who I was looking for, I moved on.

By the time I was twenty-four, I was lonely and tired of dating. That's when I finally met someone who was a "real girl" with the same values as mine and who stole my heart; so, I married her in the house of the Lord, eternally. She has blessed my life forever. I was happy to get rid of the Rolodex.

The Girl of My Dreams I finally found her.

In 1973 I attended one of BYU's basketball games. I didn't go to the games very often, so looking back, I believe I was *supposed* to be at that game.

I couldn't take my eyes off one of the attractive cheerleaders. She was blonde, lively, and fun to watch. I suspected she didn't lack for dates. When she noticed I was looking at her, she would look away, but then I did the same when she looked at me.

Suzanne Pinegar

After the game I hustled out of the bleachers; walked directly up to this girl and introduced myself. Her name was Suzanne Pinegar, and among other things I learned that she had a boyfriend who had gone home for Christmas, so she had come to the game with her parents.

If she was interested at all, she didn't show it. She didn't know who I was, and when I told her, she didn't seem impressed. And after all, she was seeing someone else, so she didn't engage with me much. In fact, I spent more time talking with her mother than with her.

Because she was dating someone, I didn't press the issue much. Merrill was married and his wife, Mary, had been on the senior cheerleading squad when Suzanne was on the freshman squad.

I learned that Suzanne hadn't paid much attention to the Osmonds as performers and didn't know anything about me. She knew that Mary's husband was an entertainer with his brothers, and she had heard of Donny Osmond, but she wasn't very familiar with our music.

We were busy recording a new album, so Merrill had Mary help me reach out to Suzanne. She called her a few days later to ask if she wanted to go out on a Christmas date with me. But, she had already made other plans, and she declined. So, after working all day in our Orem recording studio and ending earlier than we had planned, Merrill had Mary ask again, this time on New Year's Eve to ask if she could go out with me—that very night. It was probably not the best idea to assume she was available, but since I had not yet met her, I asked Merrill to have Mary ask anyway.

Needless to say, she already had a date. I learned later that she couldn't decide if I was arrogant or just a thoughtless buffoon. Either way, she was insulted that I had someone else call on my behalf.

Following the holidays in 1974, our record producer, Mike Curb, was in Provo working with us on a project. One afternoon after finishing up at the recording studio, we all decided to go out to dinner. We wanted to invite some girls to join us, so while my brothers and I were finishing up, Merrill called his wife, Mary, and asked her to see if she could get each of us a date, including one for Mike, who was single.

I didn't mean any disrespect; Mary was just helping because we were so tied up at the recording studio that we didn't know if we would have time for a date. We found that we did, so I decided to make another attempt to go out with Suzanne, and asked Mary if she wouldn't mind asking Suzanne if she was available. Another cheerleader had agreed to go out with Jay that night, and she told Suzanne we would be double dating with them, but it didn't go over very well.

Apparently she was more than irritated to think I couldn't call myself, and Suzanne later said it confirmed her assumption that I was a conceited celebrity who couldn't take the time to make my own phone calls.

Obviously Suzanne wasn't wild about the idea of going out with me, but her girlfriend reminded her that they were two poor college students, and a free meal was exactly that. She agreed to go but with a chip on her shoulder. She expected me to be totally conceited, and she would just be one more girl on the list of "Alan Osmond's" girlfriends.

We double dated with Jay, so I couldn't take my Mercedes 450 SL, but borrowed Father's full size Mercedes sedan. I still think the car was one of the main reasons she agreed to go out with me. She hadn't ever ridden in one and was kind of giggly about it, but she has since made it clear that was not the case. She did ask me what kind of car it was. When I told her I guess it made her think of the Janis Joplin song, "Won't You Buy Me a Mercedes Benz?" since she said, "So this is what Janis Joplin is singing about."

She thought it was a nice car, but she didn't know cars well enough to be impressed.

We ended up having dinner in the Tree Room at the Sundance Ski Resort. That was Robert Redford's place and he and I were friends. When I got home I told Mother, "Tonight I went out with a real girl," that I liked Suzanne and wanted to see her again.

Alan's Mercedes

In fact, she seemed to be exactly what I had been looking for. I knew it when I first saw her, and my feelings were confirmed on that first date.

In May, after we had several dates, I left Provo for California to work and was gone for a few weeks. During that time away, I called her regularly. I knew she was dating other guys, which didn't thrill me, because I was really attracted to her, but I didn't ask her to go steady or make any commitments to me. I felt like if it was meant to be, it would happen, and in due time we would be together. Besides, it would hardly be fair to tie her down when I was away so much. But I missed her—a lot.

My family knew how much I had missed Suzanne, so that June when our family was planning to caravan from Los Angeles back to Provo by car, they suggested I fly home ahead of them. I didn't tell Suzanne I was coming home early, and I arrived in Provo on June 21st, the day before my twenty-fifth birthday.

I was anxious to see her and hoped she would be available to celebrate with me. However, when I asked her to go out that evening, she told me she already had a date. I asked her to cancel her date and go out with me instead. She was miffed and there was definitely friction between us when we hung up.

Obviously she was not on the same page in this relationship as I was.

I felt badly for putting pressure on her, so I called her back and apologized. I told her it was unfair of me to expect her to drop everything on such short notice and admitted she needed to keep her date.

I told her I knew her word was good, but then I added, "But don't have any fun." Apparently her date asked her out for the next Friday as well.

I stayed home alone pining over her. I played records and wrote in my journal. We had only been dating five months, but I really missed her when I was gone, and our telephone conversations meant so much to me during that time. So, I thought a lot and evaluated our relationship—but it still bugged me that she was out with another guy.

The next day Merrill said to me, "You really like her, don't you?"

I didn't hesitate, "Yeah, I think I'm going to marry her." I loved her. I was sure of that.

Days before our engagement in June, I saw a side of Suzanne that made me even more intrigued, and I developed even more admiration for her.

Our family owned a ranch near Logan, Utah, with a comfortable house, a beautiful view and two rivers running through it. We kept horses there and it was a favorite retreat for all of us. I invited Suzanne to go with me to the ranch for a family get together over a weekend. I was confused when she seemed reluctant to go. I thought she might be worried about us being alone there, even though Wayne, his date, Merrill and Mary were going along with us.

I tried to persuade her with all the fun we would have, horse-back riding and inner tubing down the river. I assured her that we had a trailer on the property the girls could stay in. But she still didn't say she would go. By that time, I thought she might have another date for the weekend. But that wasn't the case. She explained that she was teaching a class in Sunday School. She said she needed to be there for them.

I could see it was important to her, so I canceled the trip and instead I went to church with her. I was so surprised—she taught Junior Sunday School and there were only six children in her class. She simply reinforced everything I already thought—she was truly something special.

I was able to get a date with her the night of my birthday, and during the evening I mustered up the courage to tell her that I loved her. I had never said that to anyone outside of my family.

We were alone in the recording studio when I told her. I played some records for her and kissed her. She cried, so I knew it meant something to her. She gave me a quilt that night that had "Big Al" embossed on it. I was pretty sure she liked me too.

It was such a tender moment for me.

Mother had furnished a room in the living quarters in all white. Furniture, draperies, and carpet; everything was white. It was reserved for special occasions, family home evening, prayer, and quiet times. So, after swimming, I chose that room to declare my love for Suzanne and asked her to marry me.

I had prayed, fasted, and recorded my feelings and my answers to my prayers, on a sheet of paper. I read it to her. We knew we were right for each other. I remember it as a spiritual and tender experience. I told her to think about it, but we had a date for the next night, so I called her at work and then I asked if she had decided.

She said *no*.

Anxious to know her answer, I called two more times, only to get the same response. Still feeling anxious, I picked her up for our date and while we were driving, I asked her again.

This time, she nodded and said, "Yes."

I slammed the brakes, and the car screeched to a stop right in the middle of the road. We were at the stop sign on Center Street and 500 East.

I laid on the horn, whooped, jumped out, and ran around the car. I could hardly contain my excitement. The woman I loved said YES!

We were on our way to a wedding reception and in the guest book we wrote "Mr. & Mrs. Alan Osmond."

I proposed to Suzanne in June of 1974, at the very peak of our success and popularity. We were regularly making recordings, under contract to perform in Vegas, and were about to begin an international tour that would start in England.

I wanted Suzanne to go with me, but in order for that to happen, we would need to be married. We had very little time to plan, and there was something else.

The press is important to a performer's success, they are a necessary evil because they can also be a major annoyance. Reporters were often intrusive and downright rude. Along with great publicity, we had often been ridiculed for our squeaky-clean image, our large family, the whiteness of our teeth, and just about anything that could be imagined by reporters and their editors. So, I could just imagine where that would go if I took a girlfriend on tour with us.

Then there was the other scenario, if we suddenly got married, without any advance notice, negative press could be made of that as well. So, to avoid all of that, I decided that we needed to hold a press conference announcing our engagement.

Our publicist recommended that Dick Clark of American Bandstand, our booking agent, make the announcement in Hollywood where we would receive maximum press and exposure. So, the day after she accepted, we traveled by car with Merrill and

Mary from Provo to Los Angeles where we stayed at our Manning Apartment.

Our costume designers, Rhett Turner and Bob Mackie, treated us to a shopping spree to some exclusive Hollywood stores to purchase an outfit for the press conference. Together, we picked out a wedding ring from a guy named Mr. Glass.

We went outside the store and into an alley, which could have been dangerous. I put the ring on Suzanne's finger and asked her again if she would marry me. She said yes, and then, on July 3rd we made a formal announcement of our engagement and wedding planned for just thirteen days later.

We flew back to Provo, and applied for our marriage license. Then, something that was normal for me but new for Suzanne, I caught a plane to Las Vegas that same day where we were opening a new show at the Tropicana, while Suzanne drove with her family to Star Valley, Wyoming, for a Richardson Reunion.

For the next several days I communicated with Suzanne via long distance phone calls, most of them made from my dressing room at the Tropicana. I sent her seven roses, one for every day before the wedding, and I included a poem that read, "For everyday there is a rose, for every rose there's time. And when they've all been counted for, I'll come and make you mine!"

I was on cloud nine, and the night before our wedding I danced across the stage announcing our marriage singing, *I'm getting married in the morning!* It was great and I couldn't have been happier.

The morning after the show, July 16, 1974, I boarded a King Air chartered flight with Wayne as co-pilot. Father and Mother went with me along with our publicist, Frank Lieberman. Merrill and Mary flew with us to Provo.

Suzanne and her parents met us at the Provo airport, and we went directly from there to the LDS Provo Temple next to the Brigham Young University campus. It had been eleven days since we purchased our marriage license, and eleven days since I had seen her. I was ecstatic, and it was a happy day for both of us. We ran to each other. I picked her up and twirled her around.

When we arrived at the temple, we were met by family and friends, about fifty people in all, and Elder Paul H. Dunn, a General Authority of our Church. Elder Dunn was a close family friend and would officiate at our marriage and sealing ceremony.

Even though everything was rushed, our wedding was a beautiful and emotional day for Suzanne and me. I couldn't have been happier to make Suzanne my bride, and she was radiant in her wedding gown. We were married for time and all eternity in the temple, and it would remain in our memories as one of the most important days in either of our lives.

As Mr. and Mrs. Osmond, we didn't have the leisure of spending the day and evening meeting friends at a traditional reception or having a wedding breakfast for Suzanne's family. We had a few wedding photos taken, and then we were off to the airport to catch our flight to Las Vegas with my parents, and Merrill and Mary. We were doing an early and a late show with our brothers at the Tropicana.

The management of the Tropicana rolled out the red carpet for us. They booked us into their hotel owners luxurious penthouse suite. We gave a press conference, posed for pictures, and attended a small reception hosted by our family's business managers, Raymond Katz and Jim Morey. Our family was there as well as many celebrity guests, including singer Pat Boone and some others who were performing in Las Vegas at the time.

Then, it was time for me to get ready for the early show.

For Suzanne,

When I found you,
Twas the day that,
Dreams came true.
All I hoped for,
Or could be imagined,
Soon was mine.
I couldn't believe my eyes,
It made me realize,
I was blessed.
Seventy times seven,
My heart was overcome,
Much more than even ten;
More like eleven!

Love, Alan

Suzanne's Version of Our Courtship

Alan and I first saw each other at a basketball game in the Marriott Center on the campus of Brigham Young University.

Alan was in the stands and one of my fellow cheerleaders pointed him out to me.

I thought he was cute, but every time I looked at him, he would look away. So, when he looked at me, I looked away, too. Silly game!

The guy I was dating at the time had gone home for Christmas vacation, so I planned to ride home from that game with my parents.

BYU was playing Utah State University that night. I had met one of their cheerleaders at Girls State when we were in High School. She came to me immediately after the game because she watched my yell partner and me doing a stunt called, "The Torch." I put one foot in his hand, and he would lift me up. She wanted me to teach her how to do the stunt.

At the same time, my mother was walking toward me and so was Alan. I helped my friend with the stunt but kept glancing at Alan who was talking with my mother. When my friend left, Alan approached me.

My mother didn't say anything when Alan introduced himself. I didn't know much about him, but I did know that he was a celebrity, so I had already decided that he must be self-absorbed and conceited.

So, I played it a little cool, but we had a pleasant visit. Because my dad had already left, I drove my mother home.

I was shocked when my mother asked, "What if you married him?"

I couldn't believe she said that. "I just met the guy."

Between Christmas and New Year's, I traveled with some of the other cheerleaders to a basketball tournament in Portland, Oregon.

I was acquainted with Mary Carlson Osmond, who had recently married Alan's brother Merrill. She had been a varsity cheerleader when I was a freshman cheerleader at BYU.

While I was gone, Alan asked Mary to call me and set up a date. My mother told her I was out of town.

After I got home Mary called again on December 31, New Year's Eve, asking if I could go out with Alan that night.

Seriously? I already had a date, and frankly, I was a little offended that he hadn't called me himself, for the second time, and that it was rude of him to ask me *on* New Year's Eve, to go out *for* New Year's Eve!

Did he honestly think I would be available *just for him* on such short notice, and on a big night like that? He further confirmed my assumption of his arrogance that he didn't even arrange his own dates.

In late afternoon on January 9, 1974, while at cheerleading practice, Val Blackham told me Mary had asked her if she would go out with Jay Osmond that night, and to ask me if I would go out with Alan. It would be a big group dinner date in the Tree Room at Sundance Ski Resort.

This was now the *third time* I had been asked to go out with Alan by someone else. There was no doubt in my mind that he was a self-centered egotist.

I let Val know that I was annoyed.

She said, "Hey, it's a free meal, come on, we'll have fun."

So, I agreed to go, and a couple of hours later, Alan showed up at the apartment to pick me up. He seemed to be a gentleman; he opened my car door. Val and Jay were already in the back seat.

I didn't really know cars, but this one was different than any car I had ever seen. So, I asked, "What kind of car is this?"

Alan said it was a Mercedes Benz.

It still didn't register as anything special, but I did remember a song and I said, "So this is what Janis Joplin is singing about."

Alan confirmed that it was.

We drove to Sundance and met Merrill and Mary, Wayne and his date, and Mike Curb, their record producer who had been set up with another girl I knew. They had been recording all day and were ready for a break.

The conversation was very pleasant and fun. I was a little confused because Alan seemed quite nice. I typically dated students with limited funds so I would try to be careful and considerate when ordering food. But I was still a little miffed, so I ordered Fillet Mignon. I surprised myself because I had never done anything like that before.

As the evening progressed, I was getting to know a very sweet guy who was not only a gentleman but knew how to have a good time.

After dinner, we went back to the recording studio where we listened to the music they had been working on. I couldn't help but be impressed with his talents. I began to reassess who I thought Alan was.

When he took me back to my apartment, I was taken off guard when he gave me a very quick kiss on the cheek and then ran away. I stood there for a minute, *what just happened?*

When I got inside I told some of my roommates how I had misjudged Alan and what a wonderful evening we had just spent together.

From then on, Alan called me himself and arranged every date. We did a variety of things and got to know each other better each time.

I didn't really know very much about the Osmonds because my only exposure was hearing them occasionally on the radio. I never did see *The Andy Williams Show*, so I missed that part of his career.

I was in high school the first time I heard the name Osmond or heard them on the radio. I knew there were some brothers and was most familiar with Donny who had some solo recordings. I was at BYU when they moved to Provo. I learned they were members of my church and that they owned and lived in the Riviera Apartments just off campus. That was really the extent of my knowledge of him and his family.

I didn't have any of his records, so he gave me *The Plan* album. I was so surprised when I heard "One Way Ticket" and learned that he and his brothers had written it.

Bruce Bastian, conductor of BYU Cougar Band, had arranged that song and a few other Osmond songs for the band to play. That was one of my most favorite routines we did as cheerleaders but had no idea it was an Osmond song.

My walls were coming down.

Alan was always very kind but also confident and in charge.

One day he took me for a ride on the back of his motorcycle. He took me all the way up the switchback to the big "Y" on the mountain. It was one thing going up, but I refused to get on for the ride down. He didn't say so, but I think he was actually grateful for that.

We walked down.

We dated a lot, but never steady or exclusive, and we never talked about being serious.

May 11, 1974, was my twenty-first birthday. Alan took me to Merrill and Mary's home to celebrate with cake and ice cream. Sometime during the evening, Merrill took some trash out and saw some questionable people hiding in the bushes.

The next thing I knew, Alan and I were in the back of a police car. The policemen drove us to my parents' house in Spanish Fork as I had moved home for the summer. The policeman waited for Alan to walk me to the door and a quick kiss good night. I later found out about the death threat on Alan's family by the Symbionese Liberation Army (SLA). They had kidnapped Patty Hearst, and she had in her possession a copy of an Osmond tape. The SLA said they were against everything the Osmonds stood for and that they would annihilate the entire family.

I had a crazy experience with one of Alan's fans. She had been obsessed with him and some of the brothers. I started getting phone calls from her, and she told me terrible lies about him. I didn't believe any of it, but I told Alan about her calls. Apparently she was trouble; Alan's family had some bad experiences with this girl.

Merrill and Alan wrote the songs for the movie, *Where the Red Fern Grows* and he took me to the premier. That particular fan was also there and made me feel very uncomfortable. She always managed to sit behind me whenever she was around.

After we were engaged, she threatened to kill me, and I was told not to go anywhere alone. Even after we were married, she started coming to our church services and would sit right behind me in some of my classes. It was very unsettling.

Shortly after my birthday, Alan went to Los Angeles for five weeks to work on their new Las Vegas show. He called and even wrote a few letters during that time, and I looked forward to each one. Still, we were very good friends, but we had not discussed anything serious.

At some point I had started missing him and began looking forward to his return. He said he would be back for his twenty-fifth birthday on June 22, 1974, and we could celebrate together.

I had gone to school non-stop since I started in the fall of 1971 and worked in the BYU bookstore. I was ready for a little break, so I took the summer off from school, and a friend and I got jobs in a clothing store in Provo.

While Alan was gone, I started dating a guy who had just returned from his church mission. I had dated him a lot during our freshman year at BYU, and I was dating others, too, but no one steadily. A couple of years earlier I had been quite serious with another guy who was about to return from his church mission.

I did have a plan. I was going back to BYU, cheerleading, and begin my senior year. I would start back up with the guy on his mission when he came home.

I was a little stressed about what to give Alan for his birthday. I mean, the guy had to already have everything. What could I possibly offer that would have any meaning.

I decided to make a quilt he could wrap up in late at night while writing his music. My mother and Grandma Richardson helped me. We used red, white, and blue patchwork fabric on one side, and on the other we sewed BIG AL in large red fabric letters, on a navy-blue background. It was such a fun quilt, and we still have it today.

While we worked on it, we had it set up on quilting frames in my parents' living room. When another guy stopped in unannounced, I was glad the BIG AL was on the underside at that moment. He asked if I would go with him out of state that weekend to help paint his mother's house.

When I talked to my parents about it, my dad's response really took me back.

"If I were Alan and heard that you had done that, I would never ask you out again."

Alan? Why did he even mention Alan?

However, I respected my dad and always trusted in his wisdom, so I didn't go.

Alan's quilt was completed, and I was very pleased with the result and hoped it would be special to him, too.

On Friday June 21, 1974, I was getting ready for a date when I got a phone call from Alan. He said he had come home a day early and wanted to go out. I told him I was sorry, but I already had a date and couldn't go that night.

"Can you break the date and go with me?"

I was a little startled. "No. That wouldn't be right."

We hung up, both a little frustrated.

Alan called right back. He apologized but added, "Go on your date—but don't have any fun!"

It made me laugh, and we set a time for the next night, his birthday, which is when I had expected him to come home in the first place.

He came to pick me up on time and I was ready with his gift. Because my mom was so helpful in making Alan's quilt, I had him open the gift in front of everyone before we left on our date. He really liked it. I was relieved, and my mom was happy, too.

We went to dinner and then back to his recording studio. It was there, as we talked, that he said, *'I love you,'* for the first time.

At that moment I had a very personal spiritual experience that is sacred to me. I have only shared it with my closest family. It was overwhelming and brought tears to my eyes. It was *so* sacred that

I didn't even dare share it with Alan at that time. He had no idea of the meaning behind the tears and made his own assumptions, but that experience proved to be extremely helpful in making my decision to marry him.

When he took me home that night, he asked if I would go the next day with him and his family to their ranch near Logan. It was Sunday and we would be spending the night. At that time, I taught six little kids at church and told him I better not.

He decided to stay behind and go with me to Sunday School. He even sat on the little chairs with the kids. Afterward, we had Sunday dinner with my family, and I packed a few things to spend the night as his ranch.

I found it very interesting that my dad didn't say I shouldn't go; it was very uncharacteristic of him. I absolutely trusted my dad and it was obvious he trusted Alan. We attended Alan's afternoon church services in Provo on the way to Logan.

All during the service he held my hand and would occasionally squeeze it three times. He eventually told me it meant *I love you.*

Alan had a little convertible Mercedes sports car that only seated two. After church we started our drive to the ranch. It was a hot, late afternoon in June and the heat and wind whipping my hair became unbearable. I'm sure it didn't occur to him. Guys don't usually think about that stuff.

So, for some relief I climbed down onto the floor. He got the message, pulled over, put up the top, and we continued on—with air conditioning. Now we could actually hear each other, not to mention arriving without a sunburn.

Alan's family was already there when we got to the ranch; Merrill and Mary who were married, and Wayne with his date Kathy White, who he later married. We sat around a campfire, roasted hot dogs and marshmallows, and had a great time.

When it came time for bed, Alan's family went into the little farmhouse to sleep, and we three couples were assigned to a large travel trailer. Alan, Wayne, and Merrill slept in the front of the trailer and Mary, Kathy, and I slept in the back on bunk beds.

The next morning, we had breakfast with everyone, went tubing down the river, and rode horses. We had a marvelous time, and my walls were quickly coming down.

It had only been forty-eight hours since our date on his birthday and we were talking, and acting, serious with each other. We went home and the next day, Tuesday, I went to work during the day and out with Alan again that night.

We were both feeling even more comfortable, and more attached to each other. On Wednesday, another guy had asked me to go water-skiing with him on Deer Creek Reservoir. I had made the date before Alan came home so I kept it. But I was feeling a little uncomfortable that I would be alone on the lake with him so I asked if I could bring along my fourteen-year-old brother, Brian.

He picked up *both* of us and we headed toward Provo Canyon. He said he needed to make a quick stop for something and pulled into the Riviera Apartments parking lot. My heart was pounding worrying that Alan might see us. How awkward would that be?

Thankfully, we were finally on our way and the *three* of us had a fun time on the lake.

I had a date with Alan that night and thought I would have plenty of time to get ready after water-skiing. But when the guy took me home, he didn't leave. He just kept talking and talking and didn't take any of my hints that it was time to say goodbye.

My mother kept looking in and making remarks that he didn't pick up on either. Finally, my mother called from the other room, "Suzanne, he's going to be here!"

I was embarrassed and he was shocked. He immediately left and I quickly got cleaned up just in time for Alan to arrive.

He took me to dinner at the place of our first date, the Sundance Tree Room. It was sweet and sentimental. He gave me a gold necklace; the little pendant had my initials, SP, on one side, and his initials, ARO, on the other. I felt like things were getting very serious.

When he took me home, we sat on the hood of his car. We leaned against the windshield and watched the stars. We talked about life, each other, and the future. Even though my feelings about him were getting stronger and stronger, I was surprised how fast it was all happening.

Thursday, I went to work in the clothing store. When the guy who had taken me water-skiing the day before came into the store, I was nervous to say the least. We had only dated a few times, but it was still uncomfortable when he confronted me.

"I want to know where I stand with you!"

What?

I told him the truth; I had been writing to a missionary for nearly two years who would be home in about six weeks. I said I wasn't going to get serious with anyone until he got home and see how we felt about each other.

He was not particularly happy, but he left.

That night, June 27, was my Grandma Pinegar's birthday, and we had a big party at our family cabin/ranch in Hobble Creek Canyon in Springville. I gave Alan directions so he could pick me up there for our date that night. He was a little late, but was able to meet *all* the aunts, uncles, cousins, etc. and they loved him.

We went to his home and watched *The Tonight Show* with his family because Donny and Marie were on that night. Afterward, we all decided to go swimming in the apartment swimming pool.

Alan was acting differently.

He said a few times, "I need to talk to you."

By his tone and demeanor, I thought that he probably wanted to slow things down. Even though we had known each other and dated for six months, our relationship had advanced to a serious level in only the past five days.

We played a game where everyone lined up with legs apart and one person had to swim through the tunnel of legs with only one breath. On my turn, I went a little too deep and hit my chin on the bottom of the pool. It hurt, and it left a scrape.

After the swim, we dressed, and he took me to his parents' living room. His mother had decorated it all in white. Couches, carpet, draperies; everything was white. They called it their "Celestial Room."

I was casually dressed, wet hair, and no make-up; hardly dressed for this beautiful room.

He sat me down and pulled out a sheet of paper; I could see that it was in his handwriting. I later learned he was late picking me up that night because he had been fasting and praying about us. He had gone to the Provo Temple to have time to think, pray, and get answers to his questions about our path forward together. He got his answer that we were meant for each other and should get married. He had recorded his answer on the paper, and then he read it to me.

I was stunned! Was this my marriage proposal?

I had pictured that moment all my life, but this was not what I had visualized. I was not looking my best, not even close to my best, and I had a scraped chin. Yet he still wanted to marry me?

Now that's love!

I told him I would like to say yes, but I needed to do my own homework. I wanted to fast, pray, and get my own confirmation.

He agreed and took me home. I was still living with my parents, and they always left the front door open when we were out in case we came in late. But this night, everything was locked up tight. We had to walk around to the back patio and knock on the sliding glass door to my parents' bedroom.

My mother got up and opened the door in her nightgown. It was dark and I was just going to say good night and step inside. But Alan came right into their bedroom behind me.

He blurted, "I'm sorry we're so late. But we've been talking about making our relationship more permanent."

I couldn't believe he said that to my parents in their dark bedroom. Mom in her nightgown and my dad lying in bed!

All I heard my dad say in the darkness was, "U-Huh, U-Huh."

I took Alan by the arm and walked him quickly through the house to the front door. Everyone was asleep so we didn't say much. We would be together the next night, and we could talk more then.

The next morning, Friday, I was back at work at the clothing store. I was fasting, praying, and feeling quite overwhelmed with the decision that was suddenly before me.

Alan called the store, and I answered.

He asked, "Have you decided?"

"No."

A little while later he called again. "Have you decided?"

"No."

A third call from him pushed me to the edge and started my stomach churning. I needed to leave work, so I could spend some time alone and really spend some time on my knees talking to my Heavenly Father. I needed direction at this critical time. I told my boss I didn't feel well and went home.

I spent the afternoon in prayer and shedding many tears. My dad happened to be home that afternoon and I was able to counsel with both of my parents.

There were two experiences Heavenly Father brought to my mind that confirmed for me that I should marry Alan. One was the experience that I had the night he first said, "I love you." The other was an experience I had a year before I met Alan. I didn't understand it at the time, but it made perfect sense now as I was making this critical choice in my life to marry. Both experiences are sacred to me, and I have leaned on and recalled them many times through the years.

I made my decision that marrying Alan was the right thing to do. I was crying as I told my parents, and just then my older brother walked in and wondered if someone had died. I told him, too. He approved and was excited for me.

Now three people knew, and I hadn't even told Alan. I dried my eyes and got ready for our date.

Just before Alan arrived, the guy I had gone out with the previous Friday called to say he was sorry, but he was going to be late for our date.

What? Oh no!

In the whirlwind of events the past week, I had totally forgotten that I had accepted a date with him. Well, I couldn't tell him that I was getting married because I hadn't even told Alan, so I told him the truth, that I was sorry, but I had forgotten about it and would not be able to go.

Alan was taking me to my friend's wedding reception and came dressed in his Sunday best. When we came to a stop sign, he turned to me, and for the fourth time asked, "Have you decided?"

I looked at him, nodded and said, "Yes."

He slammed the car into park, honked the horn, and began shouting "Yes!" Then he jumped out and ran around the car, while I laughed.

We arrived at the reception on cloud nine. They had dancing at the reception and did we dance! My friend later told me that I had signed in her guest book "Mr. and Mrs. Alan Osmond." I don't remember doing that, but she has proof.

Alan wanted to talk to my dad and get his blessing; sweet and old fashioned. They sat alone in the living room to talk and of course Daddy gave his approval.

The next day was Saturday. Alan and I, with Merrill and Mary, drove to Los Angeles. Dick Clark arranged a press conference for us to announce our engagement. Alan took me shopping for a suitable dress and shoes and I later wore that same dress after our wedding ceremony to travel to Las Vegas. I still have that dress and shoes.

We had to find a ring and were referred to a Jeweler in downtown LA named Mr. Glass. When the setting was ready, we picked it up, but Alan wouldn't let me just put it on. He walked me outside and into a dark alley. It felt unsafe to me, standing there in downtown LA with a diamond ring. He asked me to marry him again and put the ring on my finger, I was happy, but relieved to get out of there.

The press conference was held on July 3, 1974, at the Beverly Hills Hotel. Reporters had a lot of questions, and I let Alan do most of the talking. I was really out of my element, but he was experienced with the press. We went to the Los Angeles Temple grounds and took some pictures for the press and then off to the airport to fly back to Utah. We arrived back home, exhausted but happy.

The next day was the Fourth of July. My family tradition was to go to the parade in Provo, followed by a family BBQ. To be married in the temple of The Church of Jesus Christ of Latter-day Saints, I needed to obtain a recommend. My dad was a councilor in the Bishopric, leading clergy in my ward, and was able to give me my first interview. It was so special to me to have his name personally signed on my first recommend.

From there we went to Cougar Stadium, sat on the grass, and watched the fireworks. It's crazy to think that only seven years later, Alan produced his first *Stadium of Fire* in this same Cougar Stadium.

Who knew?

The next morning, July 5, 1974, we were up early, and I went to the Provo Temple for the first time. Alan, my parents, grandparents, brother, and his wife were there with me. We went from the temple to the courthouse to get our marriage license.

After that we took Alan to the airport in Salt Lake City so he could fly to Las Vegas to open his new show with his brothers. I drove on with my family to Star Valley, Wyoming, for a Richardson family reunion.

Alan and I didn't see each other again until our wedding day eleven days later.

At the reunion I announced that I was getting married and learned from Grandma that Alan and I were step second cousins—really?

She told me my great uncle married Alan's Grandma Osmond after they had both lost their spouses. Alan's dad and my mom are step first cousins—*Crazy!* I learned that our grandmothers had been good friends growing up in Star Valley.

To find fabric for my bridesmaid dresses, I went shopping with my mom, sisters, aunts, and cousins at the only department store in Afton, Wyoming. Time was of the essence. We bought two bolts of fabric to take back home with us. My mother was an amazing seamstress and made all nine dresses.

A few days later we drove home and were met by police who

said a fan, the same girl I talked about earlier, had threated to kill me for marrying Alan and I was advised not to go anywhere alone.

My head was spinning so fast; things were both exciting and frightening. I went to the ZCMI Department Store in Orem with my mom, and bought a wedding dress. We took it home and Mom glammed it up a bit by sewing little pearls on it.

The missionary that was due home in a few weeks learned of the engagement and called me from his mission asking me what was going on. I can't deny—it was a little awkward, but I knew I had made the right choice, and I felt it had been spiritually confirmed to me.

What more was there to say?

One week before the wedding Alan sent me seven red roses with a note that read,

For every day there is a rose, For every rose there's time. And when they've all been counted for, I'll come and make you mine.

He is such a romantic—and I love it.

The night before our wedding, during his show in Las Vegas, he did an impromptu rendition of, "I'm Getting Married in the Morning."

Early the next morning and with very little sleep, I went with my parents to meet Alan. His parents, Merrill and Mary, and Wayne as co-pilot, all flew in a small private plane from Las Vegas to the Provo Airport. They had already landed when we arrived.

We hadn't seen each other since we parted eleven days earlier and were so ready to be reunited. We ran to each other and he picked me up and twirled me around.

I was *home* again.

We all drove to the Provo Temple where we met family members and friends. A good family friend of the Osmonds, Elder Paul H. Dunn, performed the marriage and sealing ceremony. It was beautiful. We took pictures afterward, talked to some press and then drove straight back to the Provo Airport.

There was no time for a wedding luncheon, or any kind of celebration because Alan had to get back to Las Vegas for two shows that night. We said goodbye to everyone and boarded the plane. Shortly after takeoff, they passed around a box of donuts, and everyone took one.

Then everyone fell asleep, except me and—*thank heavens*—the pilot.

Holding my *lone little donut* in my open hands, I looked around at my new in-laws and the sleeping man who was now my *husband.*

What just happened? I'm married!

Our reception party — over a month after our wedding day

Overwhelmed, I tried to catch my breath. I was a mixed bag of crazy emotions, but I was so happy.

The press met our plane and took pictures. Then we were quickly taken to the Tropicana Hotel where the Osmonds were the headline entertainers.

That night, my *wedding* night, was the first time I saw Alan on stage. I was taken to the showroom and sat in a booth with Alan's parents, and Mary. I had no idea how talented Alan, and his brothers were. I also didn't comprehend the massive following of fans they had.

Wow! I was beyond surprised by what I saw and heard. The incredible singing, harmonies, flawless dancing, and multiple musical instruments.

I had seen Alan play piano and guitar, but he was also playing trumpet and saxophone. I remember thinking,

You would expect a wife to already know these things about her husband, and I'm just seeing and learning this for the first time?

After the show, I went backstage and found him dripping wet with perspiration from performing. It was hard to find adequate words to describe what I had just experienced.

"Wow! You guys are *really* good!" Alan just smiled.

It sounds silly now that I didn't know the extent of the Osmond's accomplishments, but I was speaking my newly found truth. They were REALLY GOOD!

Between shows, his manager held a reception at the hotel for some of our family and some people in Las Vegas, then we went back for the second show to do it all over again. I was equally impressed.

I noticed a group of about fifty screaming girls down front and asked him, "What's with that?"

This was all new to me, but I soon learned that this was nothing compared to the thousands of screaming fans I would see in London a few weeks later.

My family came to Las Vegas a week after the wedding to see the show for the first time. They were equally as impressed and learned new things about Alan like I had.

Only two days after our wedding, Jimmy had to do a TV show in LA and Alan was assigned to take him. No one else, just Alan and Jimmy. I wasn't allowed to go because his father said I would be a *distraction* to Alan, and he wouldn't be able to help Jimmy like he needed to.

He had always done this willingly, but having been married just two days, he was reluctant to leave me. Even though he felt the request was unreasonable and he resented having to go, he did as he was asked.

For me, having Alan run off so soon after we were married was an immediate indicator of what my life would most likely be, being married to Alan Osmond.

So, Wayne was given the chore of taking me shopping at the Mall. That is so *not* Wayne, and only married for two days, I didn't dare spend a penny. We just walked around for a while and then drove back to the hotel. I was so happy when Alan returned that night.

After a couple of weeks in Las Vegas, we stopped in LA where the brothers did *The Tonight Show*. Then on to London for three weeks. This was my first time overseas and the first time I had flown on a 747.

Because the fans had caused so much destruction to some hotels where the family had previously stayed, the Osmonds were banned from the hotels, so we stayed on a beautiful estate in the country near Ascot. Rod Stewart lived in the estate next door.

During the three weeks we were there, the family did six nights of thirty-minute live TV performances and interviews. These were free to the entire country. If the press said something false or misleading, the brothers could explain the actual facts on the next evening show.

I was amazed to see thousands of screaming fans and had no idea of the following they had. They took pictures of us, and I was taking pictures of them. Sometimes to get safely out of the studio, we climbed quietly into the back of a bread delivery truck. We drove one direction and as a decoy the limousines drove in another.

Sometimes we had to carefully drive through crowds of screaming girls that would hit our windows so hard I thought they would break. They even ripped off the windshield wipers. At times it was very frightening.

A magazine asked to do a story on Mary and me. They came to the estate with several gowns for us to wear for the interview. They offered each of us a gown to keep for trying them on and modeling them. The lady in charge stayed in the room that Mary and I were changing in and made recommendations on the accessories. They took all of the gowns and left saying that they would later return the gowns we'd chosen to keep. It seemed legitimate. Instead, they sold the photos to *The National Enquirer* and other *RAG* magazines, and we *didn't* get to keep the gowns.

During our five weeks away after the wedding, my mother and sisters were back home in Utah planning and preparing for our delayed wedding reception. Invitations were mailed and the caterer booked.

With just a few days left before our departure home, the brothers received a call from celebrity Ann Margaret. She was filming a special in London and one of her guests fell out. She needed the brothers to fill in, but it would mean moving our wedding reception at the last minute. They all asked me to call my mother to see if she could move the reception just one day.

Are you kidding me?

I made the call, but I already knew the answer. They didn't know my mom like I did, and she confirmed that loud and clear. "NO!"

There was no way she was going to change the date of our wedding reception two days before the event. She was a strong woman who wasn't shy about saying what she felt.

As it turned out, Ann Margaret rearranged her shooting schedule to accommodate our departure from England. We arrived home in Utah the day before the reception; we were also dealing with jet lag.

On Aug. 21, 1974, we had our wedding reception in my church's Stake Center Building in Spanish Fork, Utah. Many invitations were sent but many more came beyond the expected guests. Spanish Fork was a small town where everyone knew each other, and I think some just wanted to see Alan's family.

We arrived at 5:00 pm for pictures and we didn't leave until 11:00 pm. We ran out of food and had to cut our large wedding cake for refreshments. According to our guest book, we estimated over four thousand people attended. The next day we left for a concert tour of State Fairs and other commitments. During this time, we were away much more than we were home. My new life as an Osmond had begun.

❧ **11** ❧

I THOUGHT WE WERE RICH

SUZANNE AND I rented a half-duplex in Provo, Utah, that my family owned. Merrill and Mary rented the other side. We were all such close family, so we had a door cut into the adjoining wall under the stairs so we could more easily go back and forth.

But we weren't home much. My brothers and my career were at its height, and we were just one year out from launching *Donny & Marie.* We were making regular appearances in Las Vegas, making recordings, doing TV specials, and performing to sold out audiences all across the world; Mexico, Europe, Asia, Australia, Taiwan, and the Philippines.

Money was pouring in from all of our endeavors so, you would think money would be of no concern to us. But we began our married life pretty much like any other young married couple, on a tight budget.

You would never have known we were wealthy by the way we lived. Our family accountant's name, if you can believe it, was "Mr. Costly." His attitude was, "They're newlyweds. All they need is some toothpaste and a little hamburger." He had Father and Mother's approval to see that we had little more than that. We were expected to live on a very modest monthly allowance—just as Merrill and Mary had been doing. We had to pay our rent and other monthly expenses out of that allowance. We even went to a store in Spanish Fork and bought a television on time. We could have bought the entire store, but we paid for it in monthly installments.

Father and Mother had always been frugal, and they carried that into our lives as performers and even after we were married. They had lived through the Depression and had seen some lean times. They managed the family's money, and they were very conservative. I think our success was a little unreal to them, and even though they saw a lot of dollars coming in, their attitude was that it may not last. They saw to it that most of our family's income was put into savings accounts, invested in real estate, farms, orchards, ranches, etc. That was the way they had always done things. Little did we know how grateful we would all be for those reserves later in our careers.

I really didn't mind it; we didn't need luxury items. It never was about the money for us, it had always been about family and promoting family values. Suzanne and I had sufficient to live on, but sometimes it was a little annoying not to have access to some of the money. I had a wife to care for, and it was frustrating to have to wheedle to get at the revenues my hard work was helping to generate.

12

"THE GIRL I MARRIED"
(from Suzanne)

I WAS BORN in Payson, Utah, to Kenneth J. and Ruth Lavina Richarson Pinegar. I was their third child and oldest daughter in a family of seven children, three boys and four girls who grew up in Spanish Fork, Utah.

My dad, Kenneth Pinegar was a building contractor and also held public office for many years. He first served as a city councilman in Spanish Fork and later as Utah County Commissioner. He held a variety of positions in The Church of Jesus Christ of Latter-day Saints. As a presiding officer in the church, he often sat on the stand behind the pulpit in meetings while Mom managed us children in the pews.

Mom grew up in Brigham City, Utah, but her family roots were in Star Valley, Wyoming. My mother was a homemaker and stay-at-home mom whose focus was on her family in a traditional home. My siblings and I all attended the same schools in Spanish Fork, and all later attended Brigham Young University.

Being the oldest daughter, I was given a lot of responsibility and learned to cook, do laundry, take care of children, and clean the house. The Pinegar's were a large family with kin scattered all over Utah Valley. Much of my social life consisted of reunions and family gatherings.

Many of my fondest memories were centered around my grandmothers. I was fortunate to be close to both of them. For a while, Grandma Richardson even lived with us, and she and I shared a room.

One night my two older brothers, Richard and Gary, came home from a church youth activity wearing hideous Halloween costumes. Grandma stayed with us as she recovered from surgery. They thought they would be clever and sneak into our room to scare us. I opened my eyes to see them lurking over me. I wanted to scream but I was afraid what that would do to sleeping Grandma. I whispered to them to get out and they snickered as they backed out of the room. As soon as the door closed, Grandma burst out laughing. She had been awake the entire time.

Grandma Pinegar lived in Provo, and for many years our family would go to her house after church for a family gathering and Sunday dinner. Those were wonderful times where we created special memories with cousins.

Grandma Pinegar was a wonderful example to me, and the kind of grandma I wanted to be. She had slumber parties just for us granddaughters. Sometimes we would go to a movie and out to dinner and then back to her house to sleep. When we did that, Grandma and Grandpa would sleep downstairs and let us have their bigger bed. One night we got a little rowdy and ripped the sheet. In a feeble attempt to fix it, we got out the sewing machine and tried to mend it.

The next morning Grandma would set a beautiful table with a little gift for each of us. She did the same thing for her grandsons, only the boys got to sleep out in the backyard.

Grandma Pinegar attended all the important moments in our lives, such as baptisms, school plays, games, and other such events. She did the same for mine and Alan's children.

I was blessed. I grew up with great examples of what it takes to be a good parent and grandparent. Family always came first.

I was taught solid values by not only my parents, but my extended family as well. I felt secure and I knew I was valued, cherished, and loved. My parents had certain expectations of us, but sometimes I would go against the rules, which usually resulted in disasters. One Sunday when I was ten, my eight-year-old sister Laurie and I were assigned to do the dinner dishes. But instead, we decided to sneak away on our bikes. We rode them to a house that had a Tarzan swing rigged up in a tree. We knew better. We were breaking two rules—not doing our dishes, and playing on Sunday. But we were feeling adventurous and gave into the lure of the swing.

The end of the rope was looped through a crotch high up in the branch of the tree; so, I leaned my bike on the kickstand and stood on the seat to reach the end of the rope. But when I threw the rope, I slipped and fell off the seat. I crashed landed on my back with my arm under me.

My arm looked deformed, and I started to scream. The lady who owned that house took me home. We couldn't find our regular doctor, good old Dr. Moody, so another doctor saw me and could see that it was broken. He set it and put it in a cast. I went home in pain and feeling weak, but Mom said it was time to get ready for afternoon church services. So, I put on my dress and went. I had been fine that morning with my friends in Sunday School. Now I had to explain to them why I was now wearing a cast. I guess I looked pale, because halfway through Mom took mercy on me and drove me home.

Another time, when Laurie and I were again assigned to the dishes, Laurie kept teasing and hitting me. I turned my back to ignore her, but she wouldn't stop. I thought, *If she does that one more time, I'm going to turn around and let her have it.* I turned away and tried to ignore her.

Laurie didn't stop, so I turned around and took a swing at her. Unfortunately, she was drying a sharp knife and when I swung at her, the knife sliced my hand severing an artery between my thumb and forefinger.

At the time, Mom was in the living room talking to Mr. Murphy, an insurance salesman. I started screaming, and they came running in to see blood pumping out of my hand. Mom wrapped my bleeding hand in a towel and called Dr. Moody, but he wasn't available.

Daddy was in a meeting at the church, so Mom called him to come home. He brought Grant Jensen with him who was a veterinarian. Dr. Jensen looked at my hand, wrapped it to stop the bleeding, and advised that I needed stitches.

By then Dr. Moody had been located and Daddy drove me to his office. Daddy was watching, but as soon as the towel was removed, blood started spurting and he had to put his head between his knees to keep from passing out. Though Daddy had seen all kinds of gruesome things in his life, he wasn't able to tolerate seeing any of his kids get hurt.

After I graduated from high school, I enrolled at BYU and was the first one to ask permission to live on campus. My two older brothers had attended BYU but lived at home and commuted to school.

Daddy was not in favor of my decision, but with Mom's help we convinced him that it would be a great experience for me. Dad said if I wanted to live on my own, I would have to pay for my own expenses. I knew that would be no easy task, but I was determined to make it work. The only job I ever had was babysitting, so I applied at the BYU bookstore where I was hired as a clerk at $1.65 an hour to sell over-the-counter drugs and candy. I would receive a ten cents raise every year. I set the precedence in our family though, because later on when my sisters asked to live on campus, Daddy didn't object.

Being Married to Alan, In the beginning

We moved into a duplex the family owned. Merrill and Mary lived in the other side. We shared a wall, and even had a secret door put in under the stairs so we could go back and forth without going outside. We were very close to them and had several of our babies close together, too.

There had been speculation that I agreed to marry Alan because of his fame and wealth—that I was simply star struck. But honestly, nothing could have been further from the truth. To Alan's credit, he didn't even let on about his fame. He was just Alan the man I fell in love with. If anything, he downplayed his celebrity status.

I had lived a normal childhood and grown up with traditional ideas of finishing my education and earning my teaching certificate from BYU. I had accumulated china and silverware and kept them stored in my cedar chest in preparation for the day I would be married. My plan after I was married was to settle into having a family and taking care of our home. Most of my friends were doing just that, living in Utah Valley, and raising families.

But that was not to be my life.

When we were home, I was happy and relieved to be there. I was uncomfortable in the spotlight, and the crowds were not only overwhelming, but they were scary sometimes. Along with other members of the troupe, I often felt like a prisoner in some of the places we stayed, and it was stifling to me to be the center of attention. I just wanted to go home to Utah and get back to a life where Alan and I would be treated like average people. I had suddenly been thrown into the public eye and this was going to take some getting used to.

But there were, and still are, so many great and wonderful advantages being married to Alan. We love each other so much, so the inconveniences that came along with the craziness of a public, crazy life, have been more than offset by the amount of sheer happiness we have had.

Yes, life with Alan Osmond was, and is, different than I ever imagined married life to be, and has been filled with more than a few surprises. But I wouldn't trade my life, or him, for anything.

✳

Journal Entries 1975 — Alan

March 28, 1975

We're in Hawaii now after having finished a month of touring. We started the tour off in Manilla after a short stop in Guam, then to Hong Kong which all went well. Father and Mother bought me a Nikon F2 camera with a zoom lens plus souvenirs for Suzanne's family and a Mumu and shirt for Suzy and me. Japan is next—Tokyo and Osaka with two shows each. Masanobu Ono, our Japanese intern was of great help, plus he cued the lights with our assistant manager, Jim Morey. Hawaii was very successful, but we hardly had any time to enjoy the sun or the beaches. We went to New Zealand with a stop in Pago Pago. We had to cancel a few things because a lot of expenses crept up. We finally made it to the New Zealand temple. The concert was wild! Suzanne has been having morning sickness since Hong Kong. We did one show only in Auckland, then went to Australia and played in Sydney, Brisbane, and then Melbourne. The shows were wild and we really 'stirred them up'! Ha.

We also did some press conferences and three firesides in Tokyo, Sydney and in Brisbane, Australia where we bought sheep and kangaroo skins, a kangaroo purses for Suzy and boomerangs for Suzanne's brothers. It was a really good tour, but though we didn't make much money, we "opened up those markets for future tours."

We're staying in Hawaii for a few days to relax and enjoy our condominium. We'll probably leave Wednesday. I sure love my Suzy. It's amazing how our love grows with each day. We've had no fights and always work our problems out together. It's amazing how much alike we are! We rented a car and are going to get away and enjoy ourselves. We'll probably have a family next time we're here so, while there's only two of us, we'll enjoy our second honeymoon and "see the world."

March 29, 1975 — Saturday

Merrill, Jay, Donny, Jimmy, and I went golfing today on an eighteen-hole course. Tied Merrill on the last 9, while the girls all got sun at the condominium. We went back and Suzy, Jay, Don, Jimmy, Father, and I went to Mockapu Beach and went body surfing. Wow, that was a lot of fun. I took pictures. We stopped and got groceries on the way back. We had hot dogs with all the trimmings. Suzy and I went shopping after and bought two more Moo Moos because they're great for pregnant women. Ha. Got some sandals and a huge root beer float for both of us. Had a great time watched TV.

April 28, 1975

We took off for L.A. to rehearse the band for some TV appearances. We're carrying seven musicians with us most of the time. Organ, Guitar, Bass, Drums, Trumpet, Sax, and Trombone (plus our own instruments). Donny and Marie did the Hollywood Squares TV Shows and Merv Griffin Talk Show and did two songs and promoted the book: "Osmond Story." We also had some fittings of some wild costumes that Bill Belew (Elvis's wardrobe designer) and we helped design. They looked great and we decided to have a photo session with the clothes for pictures and promotion before we get them dirty.

May 2, 1975

We went to Guadalajara, Mexico and got ready for our concert there. The promoter didn't even have any tickets for sale to the public until a day or so before the concert and No promotion at all! Finally, the record company put some posters around and we did a few interviews and took pictures with some fan members. We did a fireside that wasn't set up by Elder Paul Dunn but decided that we'd do it anyway. We got there and had more people than at Stake

Conference and all went well for a while. With an interpreter, Father spoke, we did a song, then Jimmy spoke. He just got started, when the power went off! There was a moment of pandemonium. Finally, some candles and flashlights were brought out, but the P.A. system was out, and half of the people never heard Jimmy's, Donny's, and Marie's talks. I told Jay to go out halfway into the audience to give his talk while standing on a chair. He did this with the interpreter and Wayne, Merrill and I followed suit. We sang a couple more songs. I was really touched by all the challenges that the saints have had there and in my comments warned them against depression and discouragement; to pull together and hold on to truths, because the Church and prayer and family were the important things in life.

We sure felt Satan's influence strongly. First, for not wanting to do it, because of the way it was set up. Second, for the sick way we felt. Third, the power failure and interruption of the Spirit that happened. Fourth, Mother fell down and really hurt her knee going out, and Fifth, because our car

George and Alan

almost wrecked! We screeched to a halt as a truck with no lights pulled out in from of us! But we did feel good about trying and giving it our best.

May 6, 1975

We went to Laia to see the Polynesian Cultural Center where they gave us a personal tour, feather lei's, and took us to dinner, the show, and ice cream after. The weather was great, so we went through the Laia temple after. We flew home and Mom and Dad Pinegar met us at the airport. We gave them 'leis' and we all went to a relative's wedding and then home.

During the next couple of weeks, we put some new songs together for our Mexican and European Tour. Tom Nolan (a reporter for Rolling Stone Magazine) came up and lived at our place for five days and later Annie Liebervitz (one of the best photographers today) followed him up with pictures for the *Rolling Stone* Magazine.

We sold our fourteen-foot Ford truck and bought a Diesel truck with a Cummings engine and a twenty-seven-foot trailer for our summer tour. "Dad," Kenneth Pinegar, and Suzanne's brother Gary helped us since they really know a lot about trucks. I bought some Cutco knives for Suzy without telling her. I wanted to surprise her for her birthday since she really liked them. Since we share everything, it's hard to do something without her support because we have become much like it says in the scriptures" "As One." One day Father and I had a disagreement, and we both felt badly about being a bit snappy towards each other. We sat down together alone, and Father opened up his heart. He told me that he knows that he's not always right and is trying to do the best he can to hold us all together as a family and watch out for our futures; that sometimes he gets up tight and throws his weight a bit too much maybe, and that he feels sometimes that he's not needed, that the only place he can do some good is up on the Avon ranch. He expressed how he has nothing to do when he goes on tour, that he has always held the reigns of our careers as we were growing up and though he's glad we have "pro's" helping us, and were taking over more of the responsibilities, he doesn't feel as needed. We both really broke down and told each other how much we loved each other. Father sold all of his companies just to give us a chance to make it in entertaining. I think that of all the brothers, I understand Father the best. What a giant of a man he is! Oh, if I can only be like him!

Suzy bought some maternity clothes for the tour. I contacted Elton John, and after a few conversations, he's agreed to produce our album for Donny. I called him in Australia and then L.A. His manager said that he might even come to Utah to record! It all depends upon our meeting in Paris. I called him, because you don't get anything done unless you do it yourself! Elton is very popular now and I think it would be a "plus" for Donny's career right now. At least we're all excited about it.

May 11, 1975

We did another fireside in Mexico City which turned out great on May 11th, Suzanne's Birthday and Mother's Day. I gave her a Louie Vuitton purse from Paris that she really wanted.

May 12, 1975 - Monday

We went to Madrid, Spain and then to Paris on Aero Mexico Airlines which was not very good, and Suzanne is still feeling the same way experiencing morning sickness.

May 13, 1975

I tried to contact Elton John for our meeting with him in Paris. He evidently had to be in the USA and so we'll have to get together at a later date.

May 22, 1975 - Gothenburg, Sweden

We had our chartered Caravelle jet waiting for us, and we soon took off. Our bus met the jet on the runway and after a few pictures for the press we went to the hotel through the kitchens and back doors on loading docks because of the fans swarming all over the place.

We finally tried out Donny's new cape which has a battery pack with lights and mirrors all over it that Bill Belew had made for him so Donny can be seen as he swings out over the audience as a way for him to get closer to the audience.. It works great! Show time came and we still weren't feeling very well. We put extra songs in the show trying to gear up the pacing of our show for London which were filming for the movie and recording for a 'Live' album.

13

THE PLAN

My desire or goal musically for writing The Plan *album was to help others remember Who we Are, Why we are Here, and Where we are Going; God's "'Plan of Happiness.'" Music is the medium of sharing thoughts and feelings. I learned as a songwriter that with the right words expressing what I feel in my heart, the right music will carry those feelings to the hearts of others.*

IN THE 1970's we hit international stardom with songs such as the hard rock hit "Crazy Horses" and the pop song "One Bad Apple."

After our *Crazy Horses* album made its mark, we started thinking more like the Beatles and that we ought to write our *White Album.* I said to my brothers, "We need to say something—something important!" I told the brothers that since we had a number one album, the fans would buy the next album the moment it came out. And that this was the time to talk and sing about God's Plan of Life. It was something we always loved sharing spiritually, but, now to do it musically. It was sometime in 1972 when I felt impressed that we say more with our lyrics in the songs we would write and to give everyone "a reason for the hope that is within us." Our patriarchal blessings had some personal indications that we were to use our musical talents to bless the lives of others.

Like the Bible said, "to give every man that asketh you a reason of the hope that is in you" (1 Peter 3:15), we were determined to approach this project very seriously and spiritually knowing that much of it would not come from us but through us, from the Spirit of the Holy Ghost. We prayed, fasted, pondered, read scripture, shut out worldly noises and interruptions, and would spend hours isolated together in our basement in Westwood, California, addressing a work that would not only change our lives but many lives of those who followed our music and lifestyle. It had to be what the Lord would want and of the Spirit. Of course, it would also have to be musically appealing and played with feeling in order to grab the ear and attention of the listeners.

After so many years of writing and singing songs, I wanted to share the truths of our Christian faith, by explaining to our audience why we believe the way we do. My brothers and I felt we could create an innovative concept similar to the Beatles *White Album* and speak of spiritual things in a contemporary fashion and not the typical gospel music style. I knew it could be risky but also vital to the core of our beliefs. I kept notes, ideas, and inspirations in a notebook that I carried everywhere I went, so I could write down any ideas and any musical melodies on music paper that we felt were worthy of this sacred project. This went on for several months leading into a tour we had to make across the country. Of course, I took that notebook with me everywhere. I used whatever free time I could find to pray, ponder, and write, or re-write songs for *The Plan*. I felt like the Holy Ghost was with me whom I called my "ghost writer." My brothers and I jammed and leaned heavily on the revelation we received through the spirit. We created ideas and themes for songs that we thought might fit the messages we wanted to share. We tried to express where we all started in the pre-mortal life, and down to real-life concepts with lots of variety. We used various chord structures including diminishes and augmented with different time signatures and key changes. We used numerous musical instruments as well as an orchestra, with rock, and special sound effects.

We added a little humor, some tap dancing, all recorded by me and my brothers. We used other great musicians in both MGM's studio and our own Kolob Studios which was adjacent to it. We did *everything from heaven to heck in order to achieve the objective.* (an Osmond truism).

Some songs came harder than others. Some came together quickly with inspiration flowing from above, but either way, we took as much time as we needed to create a variety of songs filled with meaning of those concepts we were trying to share. With much prayer, dedication, and in searching the scriptures diligently to only share truth in order to better understand how I might share Heavenly Father's great *Plan of Life*, also known as the *Plan of Happiness*. I had always prepared for and planned to serve a mission for The Church of Jesus Christ of Latter-Day Saints, and when the military changed those plans, I knew there had to be other ways that we could share and remind others of the *Plan of Happiness—* through our music, service, internet, and social, as well as at live concerts.I started *The Plan* with the premise that nearly everyone seeks to know where we came from, why we're here, and where we're going after we die. Like birth, I look at death and leaving this world as a *graduation*. I began taking notes, creating melodies, along with my brothers Merrill and Wayne, and identifying pertinent topics that I wanted to include in the songs. I kept my notes and lyrics in a dedicated notebook that I carried with me.

While at the piano playing chords and lyric ideas, Merrill would add additional melodies while playing his bass, and Wayne on guitar would add rock riffs and discuss lyric options. Jay was most influential when jamming with us for the right feel and when we put the songs on their feet for recording, and when Donny joined in, he was incredibly talented on the keyboards and special effects. But I felt the personal drive and responsibility to make this project happen, and we were all blessed by receiving many promptings from the spirit with much help and inspiration.

My brothers and I had discussed the idea of *The Plan* before. They all supported the idea and were more than willing to join me that we might *be instruments in the Lord's hands* in doing

179

good where we could in the world. Ideas started coming, and yes, old Satan also often knocked on our door with discouragement, contention, interruptions, and anything he could do to stop the process of this work. We prayed often and would cast Satan and bad spirits out as we recognized the negative discouraging influence and often talked with each other about the importance of this effort. We realized there are no hymns in the 'Top 40' music charts. Our songs would have to be contemporary and catchy musically but carry a message.

We have been so blessed to have "goodly parents" (George Osmond = GO OD= Olive Davis) who were good examples and taught us well. After having had many conversations, living examples, and discussions to lean upon, especially our mother's with her extensive knowledge of the gospel and our father's never giving up determination and to remember, their training gave us wisdom in how we might share the gospel with our music.

Whenever we had free time, we would jam to create musical ideas and themes for songs that might fit the messages we felt were the most important to share. This was a process, and it took us quite a while to finally get to the end result of a tangible pressed record to sell to those who would listen. We had a good idea of what we wanted to say, and a few songs picked out that we would use after our tour started, knowing that the best songs are not written, but re-written.

We did not seek permission from our church leaders to record this concept album, but we told them what we were doing and sought their blessings. The Plan album contains songs to help us remember that we all lived before we came to earth, and that we are all children of God.

Our tour at that time was very tasking and went really well, and we had a lot of success. I remember the day when we were in Memphis, Tennessee, and went to check into our hotel. The hotel was swarming with fans without much security. The hotel manager rushed us up to the top of the seventh floor and to our rooms, then shooed away those fans who followed us. The fans were all over the hotel and so they locked the fire doors on our floor to keep them out.

Wayne and I shared a room, and inside it there was a huge pile of gifts all wrapped up from the fans that were stacked up unopened on the floor by the door. We were due for a sound check soon, and Father had ordered some room service with a huge platter of fresh shrimp for the entire family to eat together in his room. We were enjoying the food together when one of my brothers said, "I smell smoke!" I remember walking out of the room and into the hallway, and sure enough, smoke was filling the halls, and it was coming out of Wayne's and my room.

I yelled, "FIRE!!!!" Soon others came running out of their rooms, and the fire alarms started blaring loud like crazy. We tried to make sure all of us got out and didn't use the elevators, but the fire doors were locked to keep the fans out, and now we couldn't get out either.

Before we could do anything, our lead trumpet player, John Rosenberg, who was an expert in karate Tang Soo Do Korean style, did a flying side kick into the fire doors and broke them open. We all quickly ran down the seven flights of stairs to the lobby where many people were nervously evacuating the building. We ran out past them and jumped onto our chartered bus and then remembered that our costumes were still in our room that was on fire. Fortunately, we remembered that we had another set of black jumpsuits that were dirty and in the cleaning bags under the bus. We'd just have to wear them again.

We arrived at the venue just in time to get dressed and do the show. "The show must go on."

After the show, we were in a hurry to get back to the hotel to see what was going on. I remember walking into the lobby filled with people and fans only to see all our personal belongings heaped in a pile and hotel guests were picking through and choosing souvenirs from among our stuff. Some fans had taken things yet returned them to us later like my retainer/braces for my teeth, my scriptures, etc. It was then that I panicked. I was looking for my notebook of *The Plan* album and I couldn't find it. After another thorough search through the debris, I knew it had to have been burned up in the fire, along with our white jumpsuits and all kinds of personal belongings.

From a hotel fire, our costumes were all gone, burned up, and the gifts were destroyed. As well as my *only copy* of our notes, inspiration, and music, pertaining to our next album that we had worked so hard on for many months now! I couldn't find it. I was just sick. We all were.

On the bus to our next concert, we tried to remember as many and as much of the things we had written. It was almost impossible as it had been a month or so being on the road and focusing on the Crazy Horses tour. *The Plan* was gone!

Humbly, we all gathered together. We were grateful that we were protected, but then we started asking ourselves what we were going to do. We couldn't remember all of those new lyrics and song ideas we had written. It was then that I said to my brothers, "Someone is trying to stop us." With somewhat of a sigh, I said, "We must re-dedicate ourselves and start over again. This project must really be important for it to be stopped. We now have to work even harder than before and make it happen."

We rededicated ourselves to *The Plan* project and to God. We thanked Him that none of us or any others were hurt in that fire; promising to complete what we had started and to not get "stuck in the mud" because we lost so much. I immediately tried to reconstruct what I could remember, *which honestly wasn't much,* and started a new notebook for *The Plan*. We reminded ourselves of how important this project must be, and that the adversary was not going to discourage us from getting this message and music out! We fasted and prayed for guidance as we readdressed the project and promised each other and the Lord that we would work even harder, as we started over on *The Plan*.

I remember one night, in a quiet, isolated, bedroom all by myself, petitioning the heavens that they would talk to my heart and mind and give what I needed to say with music.

I sat upright in my bed, and with pen in hand, waited for inspiration to come. I waited patiently until 2:00 a.m. when I felt a spiritual presence come over me with not only words, but chords and even notes of what the music should be to one of the main pieces of the album which ended up being the song, "Are You Up There."

Abruptly, I started writing down words, and as I looked at the piano, I could see in my mind's eye exactly what the notes and chords should be, all coming out of my head and through my pen to paper as fast as I could write them down. I started to cry and to thank my Heavenly Father for one of the most spiritual moments I have ever had. I knew that it came out of me, but it was not of me. It was proof of the Spirit working within me even as the scriptures promise, that "whatsoever thing ye shall ask the Father in My name, which is good, in faith believing that ye shall receive, behold, it shall be done unto you." The work was one of the songs that we Osmonds would close almost every show we would do together for years to come and segue into the song, "I Believe."

With much effort, after starting over, we finally *re-wrote The Plan* and recorded it!

I have always known there must be opposition in all things, and fully expected it when we embarked on this project. I honestly felt the adversary trying to stop or block the progress of this work through discouragement, contention, and interruptions.

I remember in post-production after recording all the tracts how we cut pieces together of songs that we didn't use in the album, singing about the two options given to us all in our pre-mortal life before we came to this earth. One was what Jesus might have said to His followers, as we sang, "Let me take care of you and keep an eye on you." . . . and what Satan might have said to his followers, which we also sang: "Gonna tame you, make you mind!"

We recorded the tracks and vocals at our Kolob Studios and the orchestra at MGM Studio which was adjacent to it. I was the Executive Producer; our Recording Engineer was Ed Greene. We took the album into the studio to record it, and Tommy Oliver orchestrated it with such power and inspired music that he himself told us that someone else was helping him orchestrate the music.

Great musicians like Reggie Powell, the piano player of the Beatles, who played on their *White Album,* plus great drummers Hal Blaine, a Los Angeles musician and Ronnie Tutt, who was Elvis Presley's drummer, and Glenn Campbell the entertainer, who is amazing on the guitar, and Joe Osborn on bass, who played in the orchestrations and sweetened our music tracks that my brothers and I played and recorded.

I remember when it came time to record with a full orchestra the song, "Are You Up There," Tommy Oliver handed me the baton and said, "Here Alan, you know this song better than anybody."

I had never led a full orchestra before, especially in a recording session, but I humbly stood on the platform and directed the orchestra and the beautiful and spiritual orchestration and recording. After it was over, I had to leave the room and break down with tears of joy for a moment, thanking Heavenly Father for the blessing and feelings I felt.

The rest of the songs from the album came one at a time. I remember the song, "Movie Man" which we recorded in our studio. I sang between two metal music stands to give it a metallic sound. Reggie Powell did a masterful job on the piano that we featured and added to that track. The lyrics sang of somebody who is always watching over us and knows even our every thought, so there is no fooling anybody when one tries to cheat, lie, or run away from one's deeds and actions. He is called, "The Movie Man," as if he is filming your life that would be a "movie show" that you could not deny, that everyone would see and know— your conscience.

The album opened with "War In Heaven," an orchestration representing the premortal battle between good and evil, that we were all involved in choosing who to follow, either Jesus or the devil.

One of the hardest songs to lyrically express, though the music came to us quickly, was, "It's Gotta Be the Last Days." We tried really hard to find words that rhymed together, and I had my rhyming dictionary, etc. as we worked on the lyrics for days. All of us, even our mother, was contributing words that expressed prophecies of what it would be like during the last days. And "If that's what we see . . . It's Gotta Be the Last Days!" Wayne sang lead on it with his deep bass voice.

"Darling" was a simple, pure, and true love song about one's special wife. It was as if she were dressed all in white, with ballet dancers on toe dancing around her as we sang this song expressing eternal love and marriage.

"One Way Ticket To Anywhere" is a song expressing that while seeking heaven after this life, there is no place we can't go, if we never give up. Whenever we got discouraged as young boys, we would picture in our minds our father saying "You Can Do It!"

This song expressed that we are on a "One Way Ticket To Anywhere," and that whatever you choose in this life, you can do it!

"Traffic In My Mind" started off with a guitar riff Wayne came up with, and melody by Merrill to my words, expressing the often-asked questions in life, "Who Am I? Why Am I Here? Where Am I Going?"

I likened the lyrics to traveling on a congested freeway with many highway signs and alternate directions one could travel in life, causing confusion, and not knowing which way to go.

When we released *The Plan* album, it was as if someone was trying to stop it. Mike Curbs MGM Records Distribution system was changed which made it difficult to distribute. The record label had no idea how to launch a marketing plan for it, and we were told that more of our albums went out the back door than the front. All we could do was pray for them.

Finally, Ben Scotti and his brother Toni, who were over Curb Records Marketing, visited with us and came up with an idea for me to walk into KHJ radio, the number one top radio station in Los Angeles as *Alan*, NOT Alan Osmond.

I did just that!

I entered their station and met the main program director for the KHJ radio station. I told him, my name was Alan and that my band and I just recorded a new album and wondered if he would take a moment and listen to it and see if he thought we had any chance of getting any airplay. He was nice, and as a friend of MGM Records, he took me into his office and started to play a song or two.

During the first song, "Traffic In My Mind," he smiled and said, "Boy, that sounds a lot like Led Zepplin."

He asked, "So you wrote and played this?"

I nodded, "Yes, we did."

He listened to another two cuts and started with interest to ask me more questions, and then he said, "I really like it. I think you have a great chance to get some good airplay."

"What is the name of your group?"

I grinned. "The Osmonds."

He was trying not to laugh. "Not the Osmonds on *The Andy Williams Show?*"

I said that we were.

Now, he just started laughing and couldn't believe we could record such music that he heard. He looked like he had an idea come to his mind.

"Hey, do me a favor. I want to go get two of my top DJ's (Disc Jockeys) who really know their stuff to come and meet you and to listen to a couple of the songs, okay? Do to them what you did to me, and let's see what they say and how they react."

The two DJ's came in. They were dressed kinda hippyish, acted nice, but a little cocky. They were probably wondering, *who is this kid?*

The program director said, "Hey you guys, I brought you out to meet someone who just recorded an album with his band and see if you think he has a chance to get it played on the radio."

After shaking my hand and saying hi, they sat down with me, just *Alan*. They went through the same songs that the program director heard and responded much like he did. They said it sounded really good, like some top rock bands of the day. Finally, after expressing how they liked it, the director introduced me as Alan Osmond of the Osmonds. They squinted, cocked their heads, and looked at me smiling and laughing.

One said, "Are you kidding me?"

I said, "No, I am Alan Osmond, and this is our new album."

He said, "Woah! Wouldn't it be fun if we did the same thing to our listening radio audience to see if they can guess who the artists are? We could have a contest and give prizes to the winners, tickets to a sought-after upcoming concert."

They asked me if I could hang around for the next hour as they played our music to see who could guess which group it was.

Of course I stayed.

We finally went on the air at KHJ, the number one top pop radio station in the country, and they played "Traffic In My Mind" asking, "See if you can guess who this is!"

After a minute or so of playing the song, they opened the phone lines, and the guesses started coming in as Led Zepplin, Steppenwolf, Deep Purple, the Doors, and other heavy metal bands with no guess or maybe even an idea that it was the Osmonds.

Finally, after a couple of songs and giving away gifts, they said, "Now we would like to tell you who it is and to have you meet the leader of the group, Alan Osmond of the Osmonds!"

The reaction by the listening audience all over California was amazing. The phone lines all lit up, and KHJ decided to add it to their rotation of songs played. With KHJ playing it, it launched the album, and the Scotti Brothers finally knew how to take this out to the world.

The Plan album was purchased by literally thousands and thousands of young and old people. After listening to the music and words, many felt that it "sounded familiar" like they had heard it from somewhere before and would seek out church missionaries to learn more about the meaning behind the songs on the album by Kolob Records.

Harold B. Lee, who was then our Prophet and President of the Church of Jesus Christ of Latter-day Saints, said of *The Plan* album, after reading the lyrics, "*This* was inspired."

———————————— ✖ ————————————

NOTE: Full lyrics and song descriptions for *The Plan* are in the back of the book.

14

DONNY & MARIE

IN 1974 our younger siblings, seventeen-year-old Donny and fifteen-year-old Marie were hired as co-hosts on the Mike Douglas Show. The following year, Fred Silverman, then a senior vice president for ABC television, liked their chemistry and proposed a weekly variety show centered on Donny and Marie.

We could have moved forward with our own careers, but Father called us together for a family meeting where we discussed this opportunity and voted on it: I would be one of the executive producers of the new show with Ray Katz and Jim Morey, and we would all get behind Donny and Marie to help make it successful.

We would make guest appearances on their show, but for the most part, we would only be involved behind the scenes. Our busy touring schedule had been full for several years, and I was now married with our first baby coming soon. The TV show could possibly give us not only an opportunity to expand our popularity globally, but to spend more time at home with our families.

My brothers' and my careers had put us on the concert circuit year-round, and the idea of expanding to larger audiences and especially having more family time not only intrigued us but was an answer to prayers. The family was unanimous in our decision, and we all agreed to support Donny and Marie which was one more example of the mantra, *It doesn't matter who's out front, as long as it's an Osmond.*

Marie and Donny

Our concerts were not dropped all together, but with the quick popularity of the show, more and more of our engagements were placed in the hands of our management team, and the decision of where these tours would occur became more select.

Our international tours became the focus, especially in the European arena. Merrill and I worked closely with the producers of the show, Sid and Marty Krofft, and that kept our creative juices flowing week after week.

Jimmy, along with Wayne, Merrill, Jay, and I, were sometimes incorporated into the format of *Donny & Marie*, and the success took our Osmond name into more homes—not only in the U.S., but also throughout England and elsewhere in the world. American audiences now watched us grow up on television.

The show was a top-notch production with perfectly written monologues, comedy skits, and lavish production numbers—and some even performed on ice with our "Ice Angels" ice skaters. We had an ice rink set up on a second stage where we taped our opening production numbers that opened each show. I even wrote the theme song "May Tomorrow Be a Perfect Day" for the highly successful hit TV series.

In 1972, I first realized the Osmond's existed. I was eight years old and saw my sister removing pictures of a young guy from a magazine. I asked her who he was, and she told me, 'It's Jay Osmond and he has four brothers.' She showed me pictures of the five Osmond Brothers, but it wasn't Jay who caught my eye. I thought Alan was the most good-looking guy I had ever seen. There was something about that dimpled smile that just had me hooked, and in the last fifty years that has not changed!
– Gaynor White

We were living in Westwood, CA, and driving back and forth to the studio at KTLA which took its toll on us, especially on Marie who had to get up really early to get her hair and makeup done. So, in our apartment building basement our father George had an area of our parking garage reduced, and we built a sixteen (16) track recording studio with access to our home at Manning Avenue Apartments. Our sound engineer, Ed Green, would pre-record the orchestrations recorded earlier, and then would bring the audio tapes to our home basement so Marie could pre-record her vocals and then Donny did the same. That way, Marie could have dinner and go to bed early followed by Donny. Then, Merrill,

Wayne, Jay, and I would often stay up late at night and record our background vocals on the songs, and then mix the audio for the videotaping at the studio the next day.

Art Fisher, our long-term director, and Rhett Turner, who created lavish costumes for the entire cast, required a substantial weekly budget by the network. But they believed in us and our ability to consistently bring the greatest of the great celebrity names each week. Most of the major television and some motion picture stars of the day appeared on the TV variety show *Donny & Marie*—which earned the number one position in the ratings on Friday nights—including Bob Hope, Lucille Ball, Sid Caesar, Paul Lynde, Danny Thomas, Buddy Hackett, Ann Margaret, Tim Conway, and many more.

I used my babysitting money to support my habit! LOL! I went to their concerts from 1971 through 1978. In total, including trips out of Toronto to Ottawa (1975 and 1978), Allentown (1976), Pittsburgh (1973), and Las Vegas (1977), I saw twenty-two shows throughout those years. I am so glad I found a great bunch of amazing people to become a fan of. I am proud to say I am still a fan fifty-three years later at sixty-six years of age. I will say, with honesty, those teenage years were some of the best times of my life. – Darlene Richards

Even with the success of the show and the wide audience it provided for all of us, it took a toll on the brothers' careers. It became evident to us that the more contemporary rock-styled image we had worked so hard to establish was being reduced to trivial performances as a back-up, slap-stick ensemble for the true stars of the variety show. While we were propelling Donny and Marie and their tremendous talents into a whole new direction with the Osmond name, the slap-stick nature of the variety show tainted the legitimacy and talents of the brothers and we feared that the music industry might not take us seriously as musicians and recording artists.

Marie loved to take our wives shopping, to spend our money!

My three brothers and I became more known as producers than artists. To keep the show costs more manageable, if singers or dancers were needed, the Osmond Brothers would fill the spots without needing much rehearsing. This change in focus kept us together as a family but did not suit every brother.

Wayne particularly lamented our lost rock 'n' roll gigs. He had been doing what he loved, and now he played a dancing lobster in one of the *Donny & Marie* show skits. It was hard to stomach—and though it was funny when we became a four headed dancing Santa on their Christmas show, Wayne thought our credibility as rock stars was over.

Even though we had agreed as a family to support one another, it did not sit well with Wayne and our newfound listeners who had started following us for that reason. We were serious about our music even though our fans knew we would never live the lifestyle of hard rockers. It just wasn't who we were.

In 1977, when Fred Silverman renewed our deal with ABC and agreed that the *Donny & Marie* variety show could be produced in our new one-hundred-thousand square foot studio in Orem, Utah, we all moved back to Utah and took the show back home with us to the mountains.

In 1979, we started building beautiful homes on Osmond Lane in Provo and settled in near the studio.

> The Osmonds are down to earth and the nicest people you could ever meet. Alan has a lot of deep faith and wisdom and has given me guidance several times.
> – Annette Eder-Blacknik, Grand Forks, ND

In our first year of production in Utah, to make sure we maintained continuity in the show, we hired one lead person in each key area of production from California—a television camera man who was one of the best; one lighting director; one audio engineer; Art Fisher, a top Director; and the Sid and Marty Krofft Producer team to make sure that our number-one rated Friday night *Donny & Marie* TV series maintained its look and feel. We had these amazing people backed up by an excellent Utah staff, that were just as creative and talented but just hadn't had the opportunity to prove themselves until we gave them one.

As an executive producer, I acquired skills from our television director, Art Fisher, and learned that it wasn't television, but "tele-*vision*"! People want to *see* something.

Alan working on The Donny and Marie Show

To keep our audiences engaged, I introduced some visual ideas like the Osmond Brothers flying onto the stage UPSIDE DOWN while singing "Hang On Sloopy!" or a balloon drop at the end of each show. We were among the first to use fireworks and explosion effects on television. Vocal arranger Earl Brown even helped come up with a funny idea—instead of hitting Donny with a pie, to throw Donny *into* a pie! These crazy ideas earned me the name: OSMONDO BIZARRO for coming up with unusual visual moments both for TV and live productions

"I've heard a lot of good about this group and read a lot about them and I must say everything I've heard and read is true." – Stan the limousine driver

America loved *Donny & Marie,* and we were pleased to provide it. The entertainment world of television became our own, and we were anchored in it for much longer than we ever anticipated.

When we performed in England, we wanted to get closer to our audiences. So, our studio team and I came up with the idea of flying Donny over the top of the live audiences wearing a purple cape with lights on it.

We hooked Donny up to a cable attached to the top of the ceiling in the center of the arena and pushed him from the stage, swinging him out and over the crowded audience, all who tried to jump up and touch him as he swung overhead, then back to the stage again. He got *rave* reviews, and it wasn't long after that performance that Mick Jagger did the very same thing.

I first seen four little Osmonds at the tender age of four on The Andy Williams Show, I am now sixty-four!! I was immediately impressed by these four little talented boys with the huge smiles that melted my heart. The more I watched them, the more I was smitten! In 1975 I got to go to London Earls Court to see them for the very first time! This would turn out to be, not only my first ever concert, but the BEST concert of my life! There they were, before my eyes! Little dots on a stage. I tried to focus in on them. That was hard to do with all the screaming and scarves waved in my face, and the tears streaming down my face. It was like a frenzy! You are all very much loved.   – Trudy Appleby

By producing the show, I learned even more about visualization and showmanship. For instance, "Crazy Horses" the song we wrote about automobile pollution, was made more visual by shooting out clouds of smoke from CO_2 tanks. (We were the first to use CO_2 tanks for that effect.) It was highly effective and the crowd loved it.

I also had raised platforms made for Wayne and me to stand on while being featured playing our guitars. I wired flood lights around the base of the platform so that they would flash bright lights as we tapped a foot switch so that they were synchronized with our guitar accents. We built those in our Orem studios, and then we hauled them around the world.

I personally learned a lot about the TV business at our studio and, as an Executive Producer, I had all the tools and opportunities to organize and create high-quality visual entertainment for our millions of television viewers around the world. This allowed my brothers and me, with Marie and our celebrity friends, to share our talents and fulfill our goal and mission of bringing happiness, laughter, and hope to others wherever they were.

Ironically, in spite of our fears that the *Donny & Marie* show hurt our legitimacy as serious musical artists, the popularity of the show created a surge in our music sales and increased demand for our live performances.

This fulfilled what my father had privately said to me that "After investing millions on this television studio, somebody had better come out with something from it all, and it better be you."

And I did. We all did. But most importantly, it kept us close and together as a family. Even though, show business was our living, it was never our life.

15

OSMOND STUDIOS

MOTHER ALWAYS WANTED US to move back to Utah. During the success of the *Donny & Marie* show, the only thing keeping us from doing so was that there wasn't a decent production studio in Utah. So Mother said, "Let's build our own."

As a family we came up with an idea that, at the time, seemed almost preposterous. What if we built our own specially designed, state-of-the-art television and audio recording studios in Utah.

In addition to our success as performers, our parents had been successful in real estate and investing so we had substantial capital to start such a venture. We had a lucrative touring schedule, and a popular variety show. We even had a successful line of *Donny & Marie* dolls by Mattel™.

In 1975, I met with Fred Silverman, the president of the ABC entertainment division, where he congratulated us for having the number one hit television series on Friday nights, *Donny & Marie*. He told me that the show had been renewed for another year.

I thanked him then said, "Now we'd like to do it from Utah."

Silverman didn't hide his distaste for the idea. "Utah?" he said sourly. "What's in Utah?"

"Well not much yet, but we're building a state-of-the-art television and recording studio there now."

Fred Silverman's response was, "Well, we'll have to get back to you on that."

As a family we got together and had a meeting of the minds and prayer over the matter.

Father and Mother believed in our futures, and our creative talents, but also knew that building a world class studio would be a huge financial risk. We discussed the work, dedication, and time it would require for the entire family, including our brothers, Virl and Tom. We went over the pros and cons, and then had a family vote. It was unanimous that we would move forward.

We knelt together in prayer and promised each other and the Lord that we were united as one and asked that the Lord accept our decision. We asked that His hand would be in our project and committed to being an instrument in His hands for doing good for mankind and our family.

We had a family hug, and ended with Father saying, "We can do this!"

Father had a real estate background, and we hired one of the top architectural designers to build a massive studio. Our plan was to fly in guest stars and treat them like royalty, Utah style.

I reached out to Jerry McPhie who was the physical plant manager of the NBC Burbank Studios. Jerry was the first person we met when we went to California to audition for Andy Williams and had taken a liking to us from the first time we auditioned. He agreed to offer help and advice.

Fred Silverman finally agreed to the move if we were willing to start the first half of the season in California, we agreed.

We called our principal architect, J. Shirl Cornwall, and gave him the go ahead to build the 'Osmond Entertainment Center.'

We purchased several acres of peach orchards in Orem, Utah, near the mouth of beautiful Provo Canyon with the majestic Wasatch Mountains as a backdrop.

We had to form our own union in order to build it fast enough, and we created the finest modern studio with state-of-the-art equipment.

Right after we purchased the land, we had a groundbreaking ceremony, and had it dedicated by then President and Prophet of the Church of Jesus Christ of Latter-day Saints, Spencer W. Kimball. We placed a copy of the dedication prayer in the cornerstone along with written thoughts, feelings, and pictures of our family.

Blaine Stewart, our audio/tech guy, made this observation in 2024, "I have visited or worked at Paramount, Fox, NBC, Universal and Motown. None of these legendary studios were even close to the Osmond's Orem facility in class, studio equipment, and especially cleanliness. Most the studios I mentioned were dumps. The Osmond employees took pride in keeping the facility up-to-date and nice looking. My experience there launched my career and opened many doors for me when I went to *Hollyweird*."

Osmond Studios

We didn't want to bring Hollywood to Utah, but take Utah to the world. We hired local talent to do the work, and also Utah-based technical artists, skaters, and dancers, and employees. We invested in people—many of whom learned their trade, began their careers, and started their own companies after working at Osmond Studios. We also brought one expert from California in each area of production to come to Utah and to teach our Utah based team what they needed to know.

We had put the very best into the building of our studio—the best cameras and recording equipment in lighting and sound equipment as well as wardrobe, set building, painting, printing and seamstress shop. We were as good or better quality than any studio in Hollywood.

We had a specially-designed large motorized soundproof door that enabled us to move a portable ice rink onto the main stage floor. Our production team came up with the idea of putting it on wheels, in order for the live audience to see our *Ice Angels* ice skaters perform on the main stage. We could silently lift up our motorized door and roll the ice rink on stage. This saved us from having to build another studio just for the ice rink.

Jerry McPhie had the idea of designing a light trough for our back lighting so you couldn't see the large lamps. The stage look would be seamless.

> Osmond Studios was state-of-the-art. If I were to look back in my career, if it wasn't for Alan Osmond and the opportunities he gave me, I wouldn't be doing what I'm doing today. – Johnny Whitaker

Because we had the best and latest equipment, Jerry McPhie told us that in our first year of broadcasting our delivery quality of production broadcast was voted number one, above all of the Networks; ABC, CBS, and NBC.

We didn't know if celebrities would come to Utah to guest on our shows, so we made it fun for them. We provided a chauffeur with a four-wheel vehicle or a private limousine, so they could explore the mountains and Robert Redford's nearby Sundance Resort.

They could stay in one of his cabins in the mountains or in one of our newly built "Star Quarters" which were high end private condos. They were built with elite design, comfort, and a view of the majestic Mount Timpanogos Mountains. We also provided a private cook and a security team.

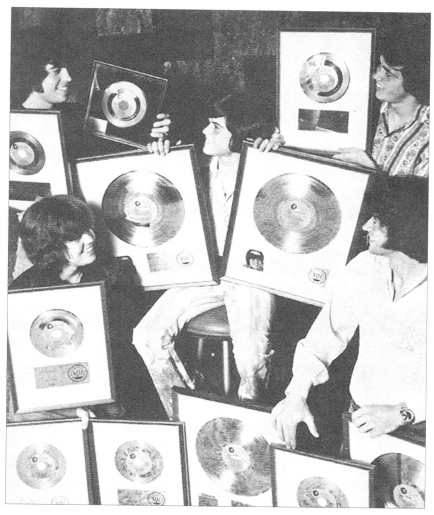

Some Osmond gold records

Back in the 70's they built a studio here and—man!, what an amazing facility that was. We learned so much from Alan, all of us that worked with him over the years, especially on Stadium of Fire shows. - Cliff Maag

All four of our Celebrity Dressing Rooms had fireplaces and were close to the main stage, each with a different design; modern, western, feminine for the ladies, and rustic for the men. (sometimes the celebrities fought over who would get a certain dressing room).

We had our own hair and makeup salon, large rehearsal halls and a top audio recording studio where we could prerecord or play live any orchestra, or vocals needed. We provided our audiences with the nicest bleachers that were moveable when needed.

The studio was an 81,000 square foot complex, including 17,800 square feet of office space and 21,300 square feet of production studios. The main production floor had sectional seating for 280.

We had 5,000 square feet of rehearsal hall that was connected to a state-of-the-art twenty-four track recording studio with the capacity to accommodate a full-size symphony orchestra.

We had nine dressing rooms, a makeup room, a wardrobe and fitting room, audio, and video control booths, still photo studio and lab, lighting department and set design shops, set construction and painting shop, scenery storage areas, electric shops, reception area, lounges, an exercise and weightlifting room, and a sports club. Later, we added tennis and racquetball courts near our homes and Star Quarters.

Being directly south of Mount Timpanogos near the mouth of Provo Canyon, our main entrance boasted photos of all our celebrities taken by "Merritt Smith" and mounted on the walls of the foyer. Since we had snow in the winter, I had an idea to create an outside lighted "Star Wall," we put the celebrity's hand and footprints in cement for the fans. Our wall included such notables as Lucille Ball, Milton Berle, Mel Tillis, Mickey Rooney, Roy Rogers and Dale Evans, Roy Clark, Ricardo Montalban, Danny Thomas, Buddy Hackett, Groucho Marx, Bob Hope, Ruth Buzzi, and many more. John Wayne wanted to put his cowboy boots in the cement.

In our first year of production, we hired one top television camera man, one audio engineer, and Art Fisher, a top Director. Sid and Marty Krofft, our Producer team, wanted to make sure that our number one rated *Donny & Marie* TV Series maintained its look and feel. We had these amazing people backed up by great Utah staff, and eventually we had a totally Utah based talent pool.

with The Bee Gees

I think all those kids would probably be dead by now if it were just Alan. I owe my career to the Osmond family and Alan took a huge gamble on me. – Sam Cardon

Gil Howe moved from Wisconsin to Utah to train and become a producer at Osmond Studios. He said he, "kept getting *fired* by studio head Bill Critchfield and Alan always reinstated me. I appreciated Alan's faith in me. Alan has always been so generous.

I don't know how he found out that my father had died because Alan and I had not seen each other for a while. But I was so surprised to see him, and Suzanne come to my door with a big bouquet of condolence flowers. The two of them are such a class act."

The "Starwall" featured lasting imprints of guest artists

My office was across the hall from Alan's and Merrill's offices. I considered our end of the building to be part of the most creative juices that flowed every working day. The dedication was unique and powerful, with many promises. The studio's potential was unlimited. We had so much to accomplish. At the time, the studio was unmatched as a state-of-the-art facility with no competition from the Mississippi River to Hollywood. I remember the number of programs we produced there, including the Donny & Marie show, The Specials, and other TV series. Even Paramount used our studio to film the original Footloose in 1984. The complex holds many fond and exciting memories for me. – Gil Howe

Getting Bob Hope's footprints for "The Wall"

Some of those professionals who got a start at Osmond Studios:

- **Cal McCorder,** our Scenic Construction Manager's assistant, started his own scenic set construction company.

- **Seven Nielsen,** a creative artistic designer. Gilbert Howe, production, and creative director started 'First Vision Entertainment.'

- **Devon Tu'ua,** head of security, started his own security business, Facilities Manager at Canyon Technology Park.

- **Denny Crockett and Ike Egan,** our music directors, started 'Broadcast International,' a major satellite and broadcasting company.

- **Kurt Bestor,** our music director, became a producer, artist/celebrity.

- **Sam Cardon,** our music director, is now a major composer and orchestrator.

- **Blaine Stewart,** who was our audio/technical, launched his own audio studio.

- And many more…

16

THEN THERE WERE BOYS...
AND MORE BOYS...

IN THE FALL OF 1975, I was in California taping the pilot of the *Donny & Marie* show, and Suzanne was in Utah awaiting the birth of our first child. I talked to her several times a day, but when she called me on November 4th, to tell me she was getting close to delivery, I immediately left the taping. I tried to get a commercial flight from LA, but the airport was fogged in. I was finally able to get a flight to Salt Lake, and a private plane was there to take me Spanish Fork.

My brother-in-law, Gary Pinegar left my car there and when I landed, I drove and picked up Suzanne and took her to the Payson hospital. I missed the first day of taping which is why, in the pilot, there were sometimes four Osmond brothers and sometimes only three.

Five hours later, Michael Alan Osmond was born. He was a loud baby, and almost immediately introduced to newspaper photographers who were anxious to document his arrival. But I couldn't stay. I made sure all was well with Suzanne and Michael and the next day flew back to LA to finish the pilot.

Our career was in full swing at this time, so our life and schedule was nonstop. When Michael was fifteen months old, Nathan was born on Valentine's Day.

Michael had been running a high fever with frequent bouts of vomiting causing him to become severely dehydrated. One night when Nathan was just a few days old, we heard Michael crying, and I went to his room to find him in convulsions.

I took him out of his crib and ran downstairs to the main floor while calling out to Suzanne for help. Michael suddenly relaxed but stopped breathing. All we could think of was to get him to the hospital. As soon as we stepped out into the cold air Michael gasped and started beathing again. Suzanne drove with Nathan on her lap, and I held Michael.

It took us five minutes to get to the hospital and when Suzanne stopped at the entrance I jumped out and ran inside with Michael. She was apparently running behind me with newborn Nathan, carrying my bathrobe, and yelling at me to put it on. One of the attendants took Michael from my arms and it was then I realized I was dressed only in my underwear. I put my robe on, and Suzanne stayed with us the entire time in emergency, but when they admitted Michael, they told her she had to take our new baby out so there was no chance of him catching anything, but I didn't leave Michael.

Michael was diagnosed with severe dehydration and for three days remained in the hospital where he was given intravenous injections fluids. It was awful. Michael's little veins had deteriorated so they had to stitch a temporary IV tube in his ankle to get the fluids into his body. It was painful waiting helplessly for Michael to get better. After three days, he was well enough to go home.

A month later we had another traumatic experience. Suzanne and I were moving from our apartment to a home in Provo. I was carrying a load of clothes still on hangers and when I reached in to lay them on the back seat, I lost my balance and one of the hangers sharp points caught my lip and ripped a horrible tear. Suzanne could see a nerve hanging from the gash and wouldn't let me look in a mirror. It took stitches but only three weeks later I was back playing the trumpet in Las Vegas.

When Suzanne was seven and a half months pregnant with our third child, she was going down the stairs carrying one-year-old Nathan. She tripped, tried to grab the railing and Nathan rolled out of her arms to the bottom of the stairs.

Nathan wasn't hurt but Suzanne tore her placenta and immediately started to hemorrhage. She ended up in the hospital and five days later we were told if she and the baby were to survive they would have to take the baby by c-section.

Her sister Laurie was getting married and instead of being her matron of honor, she gave birth to Douglas. He was five weeks early, but still weighed in at six pounds. However, his lungs weren't developed sufficiently, and he was struggling to breathe.

I was taping Douglas' delivery, and it was obvious to me he wasn't turning pink. Doctors put him on a respirator, and we were told our baby may not survive. If the oxygen in his blood got out of balance, and he survived, Douglas could end up brain damaged or blind.

We were terrified to say the least. We prayed and left him in the Lord's hands. I pleaded with God to spare his life. I covenanted with the Lord, promising that I would take special care of him, no matter how extensive that care might be. We just wanted to raise our son.

His blood had to be taken frequently, so they pricked his heels, but soon they couldn't find any more spots on his tiny feet, so they tried an arterial tap in his naval. That was unsuccessful, so they installed one in an artery in Douglas' temple.

A week later Suzanne was released from the hospital, but we couldn't bring our baby home. Her mother came to help with Michael and Nathan and take care of Suzanne. I stayed with Douglas, which one night proved to be a blessing as an intern who wasn't familiar with Douglas's case stopped to examine him. He jiggled the shunt and accidently broke it off causing a leak, and fluid accumulated under the skin. I noticed our Douglas' neck was swelling, and I quickly got the doctor. The shunt was removed and now they would have to put another shunt in his other temple.

But we had an absolute miracle. Coincidentally, that same day the hospital took delivery of a state-of-the-art medical device that allowed the doctors to monitor the blood levels of a patients oxygen by attaching sensors to the chest, rather than continually drawing blood. Douglas was the first patient at Utah Valley Hospital to use the machine. It helped him survive without any permanent physical or mental damage.

The night Suzanne was released from the hospital her Grandmother Richardson passed away. It had been an exhausting week; Laurie's wedding, Grandma's death, and Douglas was born. We brought him home the day of the funeral.

Suzanne would have her hands full. We now had two-year-old Michael, twelve-month-old Nathan, and a newborn. For the first few weeks we had to wear surgical masks and constantly wash our hands when caring for Douglas, but he was no worse for the wear. He grew into a robust baby and in fact became somewhat of the family comedian. When we reprimanded him, even as a toddler, he would laugh. I used to tease him that they must have given him laughing gas instead of oxygen. Still, he just laughs.

Now with three rambunctious toddlers, seventeen months later we welcomed David, another boy and our fourth baby, happily with zero complications. What had become typical of our young family's life, immediately after he was born, I left Provo for Logan, Utah, where the Osmonds were booked at a business convention.

While David was in the hospital nursery with other babies, someone cut a whack of his hair for a souvenir. So we moved him to Suzanne's room.

Just a little over two years later Scott joined our family, which was a year after we moved into our new ten-bedroom dream home on Osmond Lane in Provo.

During the seventh month of Suzanne's pregnancy with Scott, the baby was turned the wrong way in Suzanne's uterus, threatening to be born breach, and another c-section delivery.

About a month before Scott's due date, Paul H. Dunn, who had married us, was at the studio one afternoon when Suzanne called me. She drove to the studio and Elder Dunn, and I gave her a blessing. We didn't know the gender of our baby, but in the blessing, Elder Dunn referred to our unborn child as "this little boy." The blessing was comforting to both Suzanne and me and on the ten-minute drive home she felt the baby turn, and a month later Scott was born. Unlike our previous babies, Scott's delivery was quick which was a good thing, because according to the doctor, the cord was wrapped around his neck and had labor been longer he might have been strangled.

When Jonathan was born on August 8, 1983, we had a whole different experience. Suzanne had a new obstetrician, a much younger doctor who not only allowed me to be in the room with Suzanne but to actually help deliver the baby. I distinctly remember one sentence from my wife, "Don't drop him!" I couldn't wait to call my family and let them know that I 'delivered' our sixth baby. We now had six boys all under eight-years old, adding tremendously to Suzanne's workload at home.

Four years later, we had Alex, our seventh baby. His closest brother was four and a half years older, and the boys were all excited about the birth of a new baby. Suzanne's parents brought them to the hospital where they heard Alexander's first cries and watched him have his first bath.

Two years later Tyler was born. Ultrasound had been available since Doug was born, but we hadn't ever had the boys present until we went to learn Tyler's gender. This time our boys had the unique opportunity to go with us to Suzanne's first test. They were thrilled to learn they were about to have yet one more brother.

Our family was complete—eight boys and we couldn't be happier. Our household was full of activity—lots of it, and even though we had our challenges with a large family, we also had many happy times and memorable moments. Some funny—some not so much.

Suzanne said she knew that Tyler was our last child, "So I held and rocked him longer than I had my other sons."

17

PRESIDENTS AND FIREWORKS

IT WAS THE END of a long tour and I was performing at the Rodeo Grounds with Wayne, Merrill and Jay at Kewanee, Illinois, the *Hog Capitol* of the world. We were in the middle of a massive thunder and lightning storm. There was a full crowd in the bleachers who had been sitting and waiting for a show. Even though it was pouring rain on them, they wouldn't leave. Dressed in our fancy country outfits, we were told to run and get into a small trailer near the stage and wait until the rain stopped.

I joked that the trailer was so small that even the mice were hunch backed. Here we were looking out the windows and seeing the crowd getting drenched. We sat very tightly together with our guitars in the mini trailer when a lightning bolt hit right next to us. We suddenly got serious. We were risking our lives being on tour while missing our wives and our children back home.

I said to my brothers, "Is this where all our Gold Records got us?"

After we each expressed some tender feelings, we agreed that this was going to be our last show. We were going to quit and put our families first. We started smiling, then crying, and then laughing. Then I asked them, "What are you all going to do for a living?"

Merrill said, "I'll probably do Real Estate or something with Father's Real Estate company."

Merrill, Alan, Jay, and Wayne – Country Singing

Wayne said, "I'll do anything. I'll haul garbage, sweep floors, anything."

Jay said, "I'll go back to school and get my college degree."

Then it was my turn. "I'm not sure what I'll do but I'll figure out something. Anything is better than being away from our wives and children."

We did the show, and it turned out to be among the best performances we ever did. In fact, Wayne got so excited and carried away that he was going home he jumped off the stage, into the mud, and lost his cowboy boots. He didn't even care he was so happy.

—※—

When I got home, I worked with Merrill and Tommy Walker, the manager at Disneyland who the Dapper Dans had introduced us to, and had given us our first job at the theme park. Tommy got me interested in fireworks. It was later that he and Merrill formed a company called *Osmond Entertainment*. They were invited to produce Ronald Reagan's Inauguration including the Opening Ceremonies, various balls, and the main parade, all of which Merrill asked me to help.

We had the Opening Ceremonies set up in front of the Lincoln Memorial the day before the inauguration. We had erected two twenty-foot square firework set pieces mounted up high on scaffolding, one on either side of the stage where the Mormon Tabernacle Choir, as they were then called, would perform. Lt. Colonel Mike Bankhead, conductor of the U.S Airforce Band would also be on the stage directing the band. During their performance the fireworks would light up and display colored lances in the image of The Presidential Seal on one and a portrait of President Ronald Reagan on the other.

It was so cold that members of the choir were getting sick, and high-speed winds were very bad that day. While a member of the crew was finishing up working on one of those set pieces, the wind blew the scaffolding over with him on it, killing him. It was an accident, and we were feeling terrible when the Secret Service informed us that the show had been cancelled.

This would be a disaster, as we had at Nancy Reagan's request, personally raised two million dollars just to fly and house the Mormon Tabernacle Choir in Washington D.C. to perform. On top of that were the Pyro Spectacular's fireworks cost and labor for the show. Merrill and I went to our room and knelt in prayer saying to the Lord that the show was now in His hands. It was only a moment after when there was loud banging on our door and the secret service yelling, "Ronald Reagan just called, and he said the show is back on!"

We couldn't believe it. With tears in our eyes we gave thanks that we could complete the show we had worked so hard to produce. And it was fantastic. We were still a little worried because we couldn't light the fireworks if the wind was blowing too fast, but just as we started the show, there was a hush in the sky and the winds calmed down. They almost stopped completely.

The U.S. Airforce Band and the Mormon Tabernacle Choir gave a marvelous performance. The fireworks were amazing. One firework blew a pigeon out of the air that landed at the feet of Ronald Reagan causing the Secret Service to come running.

During the inaugural parade, the choir was also to sing while riding on the largest float ever constructed—one that we had built especially for the parade. President Ronald Reagan, First Lady Nancy Reagan, and their family watched from the viewing stands of the presidential review box.

We had cleared it in writing with the parade committee for the float to stop in front of the Presidential viewing stands while the Tabernacle Choir sang "Battle Hymn of the Republic." That's when a young military man came up and told us, *"This parade is NOT going to stop."*

Well, that wasn't going to work for us or Nancy Reagan.

Merrill told his assistant Bill Critchfield to approach the guy who was driving the float, explain the situation, and that we have permission to stop the float. Then he handed the driver five hundred dollars, and told him if he did, Bill would match that with another five hundred dollars after the parade. He gave him the cash and we all went to our seats in the viewing stands.

Mormon Tabernacle Choir singing "Battle Hymn of the Republic" for U.S. President and Nancy Reagan at the Inaugural Parade

*To Alan –
With Warm Regards – Ronald Reagan*

Nancy and Pres. Ronald Reagan with Alan and Suzanne

Soon, here came the Tabernacle Choir and 'doggone it' if that tractor pulling the float didn't have an engine problem. The driver got off the tractor, opened up the hood of the engine and tinkered with it while the Mormon Tabernacle Choir sang their spirited version of "Battle Hymn of the Republic."

During the song Ronald Reagan started to cry which was seen on national television. It brought tears to everyone's eyes both on TV around the world and to those at the parade. It was such a strong statement when the choir sang "Glory, glory, hallelujah . . . His truth is marching on!" There couldn't have been a more inspirational moment for all Americans—and that includes Ronald Reagan. And yes, we did pause and give thanks above for such an amazing outcome.

Journal Entries

9/30/85

As I sit here in Atlanta waiting for an early flight home to SLC, from Nashville where Wayne, Merrill and I finished recording five new songs for Capitol Records which we're sure excited about. I hope we have a hit sometime soon. The Brothers are all a bit emotional. We had all discussed how hard it is to be away from our wives and families. Elder Paul Dunn commented to Merrill that we seem to be reaching beyond for more; that we are giving personally to try to spread the good, and helping others and are not the only ones sacrificing, but our wives and kids too, by us being gone. We all shed a few tears. It really gets hard being away sometimes. I am heading home to work on Marie's next video. It needs a lot of advance preparation work to shoot it in one week. Sometimes as I am alone on the road, I worry. I have so much to live for, with six great sons and a beautiful wife! I was thinking about Suzanne last night and how I want to do more fun things with her. My boys are also waiting for me to help them fix up the spook alley in our basement with unfinished basement walls and to help them fix dummies with masks. They are sure excited about it. I'm trying to stay awake, so I don't miss my flight. I had two hours of sleep last night and spent it worrying about whether I would get my wakeup call or not! Scott and Jon will be meeting me at SLC Airport with Suzanne.

Letter to Donny, 14 December 1985

Dear Donny,

I love you brother and want only the best for you. I probably push too hard sometimes, especially when I believe in something as strongly as I do this. I respect your decision and will have Jill get all of your *Fab Club Kits* that might still be left over and get them put together awaiting instructions from 'Fin.'

I have enjoyed working with you these past few days and respect your talents a lot. I have always been a "background" person in our group and have had to find other things to do to "justify" my contribution and position among the brothers. I have thus tried to become more of a support to the group and career with behind-the-scenes efforts. By being aggressive with our fan club and by building an "army" out there, I have felt more needed and helpful. I do feel good about the things I heard last night regarding your direction. I know you'll make it BIG again. I need to do what I do and learn to stay in my own 'niche.' I do know for a fact, deep within my heart, that we all have a very important mission to the rest of the world and don't want anything to stop us or slow us down. If I think that there is something or someway to speed up our efforts, I start pushing—sometimes too hard! Ha.

Anyway, if there is anything that I can do for you, you know I'll do it. Give my love to your family and I look forward to seeing you in Pittsburg.

With brotherly love,

Alan

❧ **18** ❧

STADIUM OF FIRE IS BORN

CARL BACON, a great friend, was one of the leaders of Provo, Utah's *4th of July Panorama* celebration. Carl was used to watching spectacular events at the legendary Hollywood Bowl and was accustomed to more visual excitement. About 74,000 residents called Provo home in 1980, and *Provo's Panorama,* with minimal fireworks, only attracted a few thousand people The established holiday event had plenty of small-town charm, but executives of America's Freedom Festival knew the show needed to be more exciting.

Carl immediately thought of the Osmonds. He knew that our values represented those of the festival, God, family, freedom, and country, so he met with Merrill and me, and asked us if we could help liven it up.When we got involved with Provo's 4th of July fireworks celebrations, we not only produced it but also performed in it as a family for *free*, because we didn't want to charge our neighbors. We loved offering energetic, visual, and fast-paced entertainment filled with special effects and surprises.

Over the next few years, we changed the Panorama's name each year. Merrill and I wrote "The Hope of America," the original theme song. I also wrote "Red Hot and Blue" and "Circus in the Sky." We also pulled in other celebrity talent, thrill acts, and a lot more fireworks. This was all very time consuming, and eventually, Merrill said to me, "Alan, you are the 'Dick Clark' of the Osmonds. You need to take over this event."

Suzanne and I didn't know if we wanted to take on all of that financial risk ourselves, but after a considerable amount of prayer and consideration, Suzanne gave me her consent. I have a tremendous love for creating new ideas, so it seemed like the perfect fit. I took it over and produced it under *Alan Osmond Productions* from the basement of our new home on Osmond Lane, in Provo, Utah. I recruited a small staff and went to work. The Provo *Daily Herald*, offered a full page newspaper write up each year about the event.

I also had a good friend, Kirk Matson, who worked for M&M/MARS. He was able to get me fifty thousand PB Max candy bars for free to give away to our *Stadium of Fire* audience. When the truckload of candy arrived, Kirk came running to me and said, "BYU won't let me bring the truck into the stadium." I told him I would handle it. I made a phone call to BYU, and we got the truck inside where we distributed those fifty thousand free candy bars to everyone in the stadium. They responded with huge applause!

One of the first things I told my staff was that it was time we had a permanent name for our 4th of July Extravaganza. That's when I came up with *Stadium of Fire*, and I even wrote a theme song that sounded like what you would see at the event. This song, written to fit the production, is still being used today after over forty years.

"Putting our personal finances on the line, I have to admit it was a bit scary," said Suzanne. "I still remember cutting checks from our personal accounts and passing them out after the show. That's how committed we were to giving Provo families amazing entertainment."

I told Suzanne that I wanted it to be successful and my dear friend at AT&T, Jack Schiefer, said he believed in me and that he would be my first lead sponsor with a $65,0000 donation. In order to encourage ticket sales, we bought a new car and gave it away free to promote the event.

Stadium of Fire was a lot of work every year, but I had a blast. I always knew that audiences crave something exceptional, so I concentrated on designing extraordinary shows. I brought in dozens of celebrities and included tons of fireworks, and thrill acts with military flyovers which we broadcasted live around the world via *The Armed Forces Network*. We had an *International Fireworks Competition*, using fireworks that came from various countries. I even had my brother Donny flying in while singing, on the outside of a helicopter standing on the landing rung. He was leaning out, held only by a cable wire, as he flew over and around the audience at BYU Stadium!

Later I asked the *Foys*, who fly *Peter Pan* on a wire, to fly my brother Donny over the BYU Stadium as he did somersaults with attached fireworks shooting off his shoes as he sang. Another time I was going to shoot him out of a cannon. That's when Donny said, "I may be your brother, but I'm not stupid." We had a look-a-like, dressed like Donny, and we did a magician's "switch-a-roo" with him before and after he got in the cannon and was shot out. We hired *The Human Bomb* who climbed into what looked like a coffin and blew himself up. We had the U. S. High Diving team dive from a platform one hundred (100) feet above the stadium into a pool of water, plus, the 'Dancing Waters' fountains.

I wanted a way to get blasts of fire on demand, so I asked the local firemen if they could help me find a way to do it. One of them said, "We burn houses down fast with what we call a fire tree." He asked if I wanted to see it and of course, I did. After I saw what it did, I asked him if he could make it five times bigger. Those became my *Fire Trees*. I had the firemen make me a dozen and we placed them up high in the south end zone of the stadium with other fireworks that lit on cue. Flames of fire as tall as twenty feet all cued to the music of the *Stadium of Fire* theme song that made the stadium look like it was on fire.

The show always has an exciting opening song every year with hundreds of young *Stadium of Fire* singers, drill teams, drum corps, dancers, sky divers with smoke, and an unfolded and American flag that extends the length of the football field.

> *Alan loves a big production. His only desire in any production would be that people walk away and had the time of their life. His million firecrackers? Give a little boy a match look what he did to the Stadium of Fire...I really thought he was going to blow up Provo! I think people look at the Osmonds. Are they really as good as they say? Are they really as sweet and as kind, but they are that and a whole lot more.* – Tina Salmon, Family Friend

Another time, I had an idea to have dancers with flame throwers blast fire accents to music! At show time, one of them hesitated to do it so I said, "Give it to me." I knew the choreography and so I did it myself with them. We fired cannons, lit stages on fire, on purpose and once, accidentally, when Mary Hart performed.

Parachute jumpers sometimes brought in the American flag for the National Anthem. Thousands of young dancers and singers sang our theme song, "The Hope of America." High wire acrobatics with the Knocks Family on tall sway poles thrilled the audiences as I rotated a Ferris Wheel inside the Stadium mounted with lit fireworks flares shooting up from it as it rotated.

Mr. T., David Hasselhoff with Kit the Car, dog acts, Wayne Newton riding his white stallion horse and Willard Scott singing while riding on top of a run-away bouncy elephant in our *Circus in the Skies* Production. Anything visual for a family-based audience. Country, Rock, and Roll, you name it. Though we had top name celebrity artists perform, we did not want to be a concert, but a visual extravaganza that people want to see. Some of the first celebrity guests included Bob Hope, the Beach Boys, Lee Greenwood, the Oakridge Boys, Roy Clark, Toby Keith, Natalie Cole, Martina McBride, Crystal Gayle, and many others.

We had great *fun* and many of our celebrities ask to come back again.

The exciting part for me of course was the fireworks. I love creative "idea-ing" and lighting fireworks and we made it happen, thanks to some awesome talented friends at Pyro Spectaculars, and Austin Fireworks who both blew the sky away. I learned from the best in designing and painting the sky with fire, all electrically programmed and synchronized to the music. Eric Krugg was also there and continues getting us 'all fired up' and setting new standards on the 4th of July.

I had an extreme amount of respect for Paul and Brad, of Austin fireworks. They were literal geniuses and together we set a new standard for Fourth of July activities.

One day I came up with the crazy idea of lighting one Million Firecrackers *in six seconds!* It had *never* been done.

Paul Austin made it a reality and ordered a boatload of firecrackers. As it had never been done before, I had them fuse it from both ends. I invited a young boy who won a coloring contest by our sponsor *Fred Myer*, to come forward on stage and push the plunger as we counted down to zero. When he did, it literally blew him off stage. The fireball shot sky high in six seconds, and from the noise the crowd made, you would have thought we had just won the Superbowl. The crowd wouldn't quit screaming and yelling for several minutes afterwards. A large group from another of our sponsors, Nu Skin even made tee-shirts after that said, *I Survived The Stadium of Fire.* That explosion guaranteed us sold out shows for the next four years because of the excitement we created.

with Bob Hope and his wife Delores

- One time my buddy, Brad Bone, my fireworks guru, helped me think of a way to make the stage look like it was on fire. With help of our fellow fireworks comrade, Eric Krug, we put rain gutters around the edges of the stage and filled them with water. Our plan was to pour a flammable liquid on top of the water so it would burn tall flames, just before our celebrity Mary Hart came on stage. When the flammable liquid was added, one of the stagehands got some on their shoes and walked across the stage leaving footprints of the flammable liquid. When we announced Mary Hart, we lit the rain gutters—and the entire stage started on fire! Mary asked me, "Alan, what should I do?" I told her, "Just go out there and sing around the burning stage while we put the fire out." It was a great idea gone bad—but the audience loved it. So did Mary.

- On several occasions, Hill Air Force Base provided military jet flyovers. When they did, hundreds of young volunteers dressed in red, white, and blue, unfurled an American flag that nearly filled the entire football field followed by the singing of the National Anthem.

- I had Rocket Man fly around the stadium with his backpack of rocket engines.

- Mr. T hosted the *Human Bomb*, who went out into the stadium, got in a coffin, then blew himself up. Not really, but it appeared like he did, then Mr. T came out for his applause.

- For one of our shows, we had a huge Ferris Wheel at the south end of the stadium covered with fireworks; we lit them as the wheel turned giving a spectacular visual.

- We had a fully lighted hot air balloon filled with people launch from the center of the stadium.

- One year, Willard Scott, the famous weatherman on NBC, entered the stadium on the back of a running elephant. He was bouncing around and holding on for dear life. It was hysterical and the audience loved it, though I'm not sure if Willard did.

Donny practicing his wire flying stunt

- We had Donny hooked to the outside of the KSL-TV helicopter, who sang as he entered the stadium. When it landed he unlatched himself and, still singing, he ran out onto the main stage. (A short time later, Vic Morrow was killed doing a similar trick for a movie, so we never tried it again.

- Wayne Newton sang and rode his beautiful white stallion into the stadium.

- Another year, with the help of my good friend Paul Austin, we had an *International Fireworks Competition*. He ordered fireworks from various countries and with the help of John Whitaker, mounted colored firework lances or flares on the perimeters of large moveable scaffolding. They created amazing visuals, including moving ships, landing on the moon, the Statue of Liberty, the Liberty Bell, George Washington, the American Flag and flags of other nations, Abraham Lincoln, Chinese dancers, Japanese lions, and various other displays that represented the countries where the fireworks came from, all put to music. It was similar to the production Merrill and I did for Ronald Reagan's Opening Inaugural Ceremonies. It was another huge success.

- The thrilling Nytro Circus rode their motorcycles up a huge ramp twenty-forty feet in the air in the center of the stadium. They did flips and stunts while free falling then landed while waving to an appreciative audience.

- A team of skydivers jumped, trailing smoke behind them while they did twists and tricks landing in the middle of the stadium carrying both the Utah State and the American Flag. Then we all joined in singing the National Anthem.

One of my favorite ideas and visual effects was when I choreographed a routine for eight dancers that had flame flowers strapped to their backs, shooting coordinated synchronized huge flames in the air as they danced to the music. Just before it was time to go on, one of the dancers got cold feet and decided she couldn't do it. Since I knew the routine, I strapped the flame thrower on and performed with the dancers.

Here is a list of our amazing *Stadium of Fire* performers:

1981–1983 – The Osmonds

1984 – Lee Greenwood, Donny Osmond, Marie Osmond, and Jimmy Osmond.

1985 – Roy Clark, David Hasselhoff, Miss America Sharlene Wells, The Osmond Brothers

1986 – Crystal Gayle, Mr. T, Donny & Marie Osmond

1987 – Bob Hope, The Osmond Boys (2nd Generation), Miss America Kellye Cash, Thurl Bailey

1988 – Rich Little, Mary Hart, Emmanuel Lewis, Osmond Brothers

1989 – NBC weatherman Willard Scott, Keshia Knight Pulliam, The Osmond Boys, The Jets

1990 – Osmond Family, Wayne Newton, Highway 101

1991 – Andy Williams, Phylicia Rashad, Lorrie Morgan

1992 – The Beach Boys

1993 – Kenny Loggins, Jeffrey Osborn, Miss America Leanza Cornett

1994 – The Oakridge Boys, Mormon Tabernacle Choir, Mickey Mouse & His ToonTown Friends

1995 – Barbara Mandrell, Jay Leno, Utah Symphony

1996 – Donny Osmond, Kurt Bestor

1997 – Natalie Cole, The Jets

1998 – Huey Lewis and the News

1999 – Gladys Knight, All-4-One, Harry James Orchestra, Lex de Azevedo

2000 – Alabama, The Osmonds Second Generation

2001 – Sawyer Brown

2002 – Toby Keith

2003 – Martina McBride, Sean Hannity

2004 – Reba McEntire, Sean Hannity

2005 – Mandy Moore, Lone Star, Debbie Reynolds, Lucy Lawless, The Osmonds

2006 – Taylor Hicks, Lee Ann Womak

2007 – Brooks & Dunn, Corbin Bleu, Glenn Beck

2008 – Miley Cyrus, Blue Man Group, Glenn Beck

2009 – Jonas Brothers, SHeDAISY, Glenn Beck

2010 – Carrie Underwood, The 5 Browns, Jenny Oaks Baker, The Osmonds Second Generation, Eric Dodge

2011 – Brad Paisley, David Archuleta, The Whits, Eve Asplundh, Artie Hemphill, and the Iron Horse Band

2012 – The Beach Boys, Scotty McCreery, Ryan Innes

2013 – Kelly Clarkson, Carly Roe Jepsen, and Cirque du Soleil

2014 – Carrie Underwood, Studio C

2015 – Journey, Olivia Holt

2016 – Tim McGraw

2017 – Little Big Town, Brian Regan, and Hunter Hayes

2018 – One Republic and Lexi Walker

2019 – Keith Urban

2020 – Because of the covid epidemic, there was no show in 2020, although we still provided free synchronized fireworks from three different locations.

2021 – Lee Greenwood and Collin Raye

2022 – Tim McGraw and Marie Osmond

2023 – Journey

2024 – Jonas Brothers and Zion's Youth Symphony
and Chorus

I produced *Stadium of Fire* for twelve years. It was a lot of work, but equally rewarding, and I feel blessed to have had these opportunities and experiences. At the end of our reign, Suzanne and I moved our family to Branson, Missouri in 1992. Children's Miracle Network took it over, then gave it to KSL, who then handed it off to the Freedom Festival. At that time, I was put on the Board of Trustees.

Some wonderful Board of Trustees and Board members I worked with: Alan Ashton, Ralph Baruch, David McDougal, Carl Bacon, Taylor MacDonald, Paul Sabrowsky, Lothaire Bluth, Boyd Craig, Steven Hales, Douglas McKinley, Brad Pelo, Reid Robinson, Paul Warner, Sherry Petersen, Steve Shallenberger, Cameron Martin, Andrew Howlett, Frank Davis, Nancy Mann, Susie Bramble, Vicki Garbutt, Adam Robertson, Kristen Johnson, Jeff Rust, Jim Evans, Robyn Pulham, Bill Freeze, Chad Mustard, Alan Dewitt, and Bill Fillmore.

Stadium of Fire started in 1981 and is still going strong.

19

SOMETHING'S WRONG

DURING THE LATE 1980'S CONCERT TOUR I noticed the fingers on my right hand were not moving as quickly as they usually did. I scolded myself to get with it as I tried to keep pace with the music. It took every ounce of determination I had to finish the song.

But it was more than a one-time occurrence. I started to notice it was getting harder and harder to play my guitar. I also couldn't hold my saxophone steady, and there was a marked weakness when I played the piano.

What was happening to me?

The weakness I felt wasn't all in my hands. I was tripping a lot. Then, looking back to see what had caused my falls, I would find nothing. I decided that I was dragging my feet or shuffling. I was getting scared.

I knew I had to find out what was going on. One of my first stops was to Dr. Tom Myers, a neighbor from Osmond Lane in Provo, Utah. Dr. Myers recommended a more comprehensive diagnosis and referred me to the University of Utah Medical Center in Salt Lake City. Several physicians there offered multiple diagnostic alternatives, including one doctor who suggested I had a sort of foot drop.

Foot drop? It sounded ludicrous to Suzanne and me.

Another doctor speculated it was a slow disease, whatever that meant.

"We almost laughed it off," Suzanne said, "Until we realized these were indications that something was seriously wrong."

They told me to relax more and take it easy, which was hard for me, since it wasn't in my nature. One doctor even told me to take aspirin and come back in six months.

Suzanne and I visited doctors all over the country, and finally found the problem. After an MRI and a spinal tap, the doctor said it sounded like multiple sclerosis (MS).

Unfortunately, he was right.

At the time, the only thing I knew about the disease was that Suzanne's mother visited a woman bedridden with it. MS is a chronic disease of the central nervous system, that would follow me for the rest of my life.

Interestingly enough, Suzanne and I didn't panic. I don't think we even asked, 'why us?' We told ourselves we would learn everything we could about MS and look at all our options for fighting it.

We learned that MS was difficult to diagnose because its initial symptoms are similar to many other diseases. Early indicators can include depression, fatigue, tingling, numbness, forgetfulness, and problems with balance and walking. MS disrupts the flow of information in the brain and the signals sent from the brain to the body. Another challenge to diagnosis is that symptoms can vary substantially from person to person.

I was treated by more medical professionals than I care to remember but we wanted to try everything possible. We sought help from doctors in Utah, California, Arizona, England, and finally from Dr. John Rose, a neurologist at the University of Utah who specialized in MS.

Dr. Rose gave me a complete checkup and another MRI that confirmed the existence of white spots (lesions) in my brain that suggested primary progressive multiple sclerosis. MS causes the breakdown of the myelin sheath surrounding the nerves and because I had so many lesions on the left side of my brain, it especially affected the right side of my body. My version of MS is relatively rare affecting only about fifteen percent of the MS community. There are no flare-ups, but there are no periods of remission, either. With this complex disease, the body attacks its own central nervous system and exhibits symptoms that vary depending on which nerves are affected.

One of the first things that became immediately apparent was the encompassing nature of MS. It not only affects the person with MS but the entire family.

At first, I was embarrassed. I didn't want anyone outside of my immediate family to know. I don't know if embarrassment is the exact word to describe my feelings, but I definitely wanted to keep my MS private. I didn't want to let down my brothers or my parents, and I did not want people to see or treat me any differently. I wanted my life to continue without being defined by a disorder, so I decided to hide my diagnosis.

I am an optimist by nature, and I told myself that I could beat it. In the meantime, I worked hard to continue on as normal as possible. I was able to keep my disease hidden for several years.

A few years later, when I could no longer compose on a keyboard, I had to learn how to write music without a musical instrument.

Finally, after the dexterity was completely gone from the right side of my body, including my penmanship, I taught myself how to write and sign autographs with my left hand. I had to adapt and embrace each day as it came.

I developed a new perspective from Proverbs 23:7, *As a man thinketh in his heart, so is he.* I always told myself, 'You become what you think about. If you think you are sick, you are. If you think you can't, you won't. So, with faith in God, I keep moving forward.

Suzanne has been a constant witness in my life and rarely leaves me alone. She said, "Alan has faced this debilitating disease for more than three decades, but he doesn't ever use it as an excuse." I didn't want to be member of a club no one voluntarily joins, but I found kindred spirits who also struggle with MS. I visited several celebrity friends, including actor Teri Garr, Mitt Romney's wife Ann, TV host Montel Williams, and an original Disney Mouseketeer and childhood friend, Annette Funicello. She told me that the challenge was not the disease as much as the hopelessness.

It was inevitable that the public would eventually learn that I had MS, but I let them know—on my terms.

Then I was warned that a tabloid planned to write about my MS and claim I was dying. A *Globe Magazine* writer called and insisted I give an interview, or, in his words, "he would make up his own story." I had no intention of letting the magazine spread lies about me, but I wasn't sure what to do. So, I contacted Annette Funicello and told her about the article scheduled for publication. I can't lie, I was worried about it.

Annette told me, "Alan, the best thing to do is to be open about it and announce it to the world."

I did, and beat the tabloid to the punch. I called members of the mainstream media and got booked on *Good Morning America* with Joan Lunden and *Entertainment Tonight* later that evening. I let the world know my way, and the tabloid story never ran. A short time later, we invited a *People Magazine* writer to our cabin in Fairview, Utah. They ran a three-page feature highlighting my battle with MS.

Then I gave that tabloid writer a stern warning, *don't you ever threaten me or my family again.*

One day I was reading over a letter from Annette Funicello's son, Phillip. I paused for a minute and looked at her name— it ended in ETTE. This had been one of our family's slogans— 'Endure to the End.' It means to remain firm in a commitment and to be true to the commandments of God despite temptation, opposition, and adversity. We have always tried to live this and so did Annette. Doug came up with that idea when he was on his mission in South Africa. Our family often used that expression when hard challenges came—we even had rings made with ETTE to remind us.

One of my favorite scriptures says: *'Wherefore, ye must press forward with a steadfastness in Christ, having a perfect brightness of hope, and a love of God and of all men. Wherefore, if ye shall press forward, feasting upon the word of Christ, and endure to the end, behold, thus saith the Father: Ye shall have eternal life.'* (2nd Nephi 31:20)

I kept the disease a secret, even from Ron Clark, my former public relations director. He was a close friend, and I considered him, my eighth Osmond brother. Ron was broken-hearted, and I told him that I would probably need him when my MS diagnosis hit the public. Ron fielded many, many phone calls from concerned people.

After coming out with my disease, I felt a deep sense of freedom. My secret was out, and I could be as candid about my life as I always had been.

Once the public learned of my condition, I was inundated with treatment suggestions. One concerned fan even suggested submitting to bee stings.

To start, I decided to eat only healthy foods, exercise, and learn all I could on the subject. But I also tried many suggested treatments, including blood tests, bone adjustments, exercise programs, a bio-modulator, magnets, vibrators, acupuncture, hot and cold showers, goat serum, a hyperbaric chamber, a leg brace, more vitamins than I can remember, frankincense, and other essential oils.

But there were side effects. Some made me gain weight, some made my mind fuzzy, and others affected my memory recall.

In the early stages of my disease, I created an acronym to help me get through this difficult time. It helped me to focus when things got rough, and I shared it with my sons as well.

T.U.F.F

"Life is T.U.F.F."

T= Target. Identify your challenge.

U= Understand all you can about it.

F= Focus. Don't shotgun it, but rifle in on it with precision.

F= Fight! You have to fight hard for what you want in order to win at anything.

Suzanne and I talked it over and knew our family wasn't complete. So, going against the doctors' council, and with a lot of faith, we had two more babies. Now Suzanne was satisfied that everyone was here.

I wasn't going to let MS get the best of me. My new mantra was, *'I may have MS, but MS does not have me.'*

❧ **20** ❧

WHERE'S THE MONEY?

EVEN WITH all of our performing success and our collective family's assets, by 1983 we were financially broke. The devastation was overwhelming to all of us, and a prominent San Francisco law firm recommended that out family's partnership file bankruptcy.

But there was one person for whom that was not an option, our father, George Osmond. He insisted we would pay every bill we owed. Father would not consider bankruptcy because he knew by doing so it would hurt neighbors and friends. At a family meeting at the studio, we instructed our attorney to sell our assets and pay off all creditors in full. We had all worked too hard to have our good name and reputation damaged.

In the beginning, when I was just a young boy, our father George and mother Olive owned a real estate business, an insurance company, and a post office building in Ogden, Utah. They had a home residence, as well as a summer home. They also owned other properties and investments in Utah, which they tried to pay down without mortgages, until they sold most of them and in 1962 moved our family to California. Our parents were frugal with the income we made from performing, and they kept it working and invested it as we all were young and working together while living at home. Our parents' philosophy was 'of one heart' and 'of one mind.' They paid all the bills, and provided for our needs, until we started getting married and moved into our own homes. But even then, we only took a modest monthly salary to cover our living expenses. They kept our income working with various investments, all guided by our parents with the advice and assistance of an accountant and lawyers.

The decision to build our own television and recording studios in Orem, Utah, was a major investment, so we hired a management team to take over the fiscal responsibilities to handle all our assets, including the new studios. That same management team also took control of the income we brothers and Marie made. This included performing and concert tours, endorsements, commercials, and earnings from our writing and publishing of original music.

When we each needed cars or homes, we would purchase them as a family. We never took much, keeping our money in various investments, allowing us to focus on our creative endeavor. Meanwhile, the management team focused on controlling and managing those. With our hit records, performance royalties, records sales, studio profits, investments, and by remaining frugal in our spending, collectively, we were worth millions of dollars.

Our financial and spiritual advisors met on a monthly basis to lend advice, but even with that, our Public Relations manager, Ron Clark explained, "Every time we came in from an extended concert tour, I carried the money belt containing hundreds of thousands and many times millions of dollars directly to the financial manager's office as I was instructed. I would say, "Here's our pound of flesh..." to which he coldly responded, "Just shut up, get back out there and bring me more.""

Our studios struggled after the cancellation of *Donny & Marie*, but over time, bad decisions, gross mismanagement, and eventually betrayal by those we trusted, we were left financially destitute.

To add insult to injury, we had purchased one of only three existing Rank Cintel film transfer machines—equipment that transferred film to video tape—and we returned from one tour to find that some of our employees were using our equipment for transferring X-rated films to video. Everyone involved was immediately fired, and we shut down that profitable division of our business.

We had to clean house, and we began by letting go our financial management team. We were flattened financially by unscrupulous business advisers who kept two sets of books as they absconded with a fortune between eighty and one hundred million dollars— leaving us with a debt of about $30 million.

We learned that much of the money from our concerts had gone directly into the pockets of some of these disreputable men. Some served prison sentences for what they'd done, but the Osmond family fortune was gone all the same.

Even with the betrayal and devastation we felt, we were also blessed as we experienced a miracle of epic proportion. We were able to liquidate or sell properties for cash, and the studios were leveraged with substantial debt to continue operations until we sold them.

We also sold the Riviera apartments in Provo, Grand Central stores, almond orchards, and several other major investment properties, including ranches, land, high rises, office spaces, racquetball courts, student housing, homes, and more.

That still wasn't enough, so our family 'tightened our belts.' As performing Osmonds, we hadn't vanished. In fact, we continued to maintain active touring, recording, and performance schedules. We even had a surge in our worldwide appearances plus more recording success to our impressive crowds and fan base.

We went back on the road doing what we did best. Traveling in busses instead of planes, we all worked extremely hard. In the end, the partnership avoided bankruptcy, paid off all creditors in full, and the remaining assets and cash were divided equally among our family members. Nobody got hurt.

These experiences solidified in my mind the fleeting of worldly possessions, and the opportunity for me to remind our eight sons, thirty grandkids and now four great grandkids, that besides our experience, intelligence, and many priceless memories, all that we get to take with us when we leave this earth, is family.

21

HERE WE GO AGAIN

On May 5, 1986, *People Magazine* did an article on our boys. It was titled, "Oh Brother! Here Comes Another Generation of Osmond Boys Making Beautiful Music Together!" They included a black and white picture of our six boys standing in a line from tallest to shortest. They were dressed identically and standing in a performance pose each holding a black derby hat. I'm in the photo as well with a big grin. (I couldn't help it.)

Another photo they ran in that same article was taken a few years earlier. Suzanne and I were sitting with our boys on a rock in our backyard on Osmond Lane. We used to gather our boys together whenever we had something we wanted to discuss with them or just spend time together. There my boys could tell me anything. We called it our *talk rock*.

In 1990 I hired a close friend, Mike Reese, to be road manager for my sons, the Osmonds Second Generation. Mike had worked for us in some of our other enterprises. That summer Mike and I took Michael, Nathan, Douglas, and David, on a seventy-city tour. The boys appeared at malls, gave concerts, did store signings, and performed at fairground shows up and down the eastern seaboard of the United States, from Boston to Florida and back again.

Hershey's Chocolate Company sponsored the tour, and we traveled in a motorhome packed with their equipment. It was a grueling four and a half months.

It was exhausting, setting up to perform, packing up the equipment, then driving to the next gig.

Mike and I drove the vehicle and shared all other production tasks. The boys became very familiar with what it was like being a professional entertainer. They took to it easily and seemed to enjoy it, but they also discovered being on the road and performing was not all fun and games.

It was not always an easy ride. When we arrived at a few mall sites, the advanced publicity hadn't been done and there was no crowd to greet us. But it didn't take the boys long to attract attention. As soon as they started to perform, crowds of mostly teenage girls quickly gathered.

At one of the malls, we nearly caused a riot. The center of the shopping mall where we were performing had been decorated with beds of freshly planted blooming flowers. Well-meaning girls tore them out to throw at the boys on stage. It was so much like what my brothers and I had experienced, and even though the boys were young, ages ranging from eleven to fifteen, their star appeal caught the attention of these young girls.

The Osmonds Second Generation

Even in the 1990's, the Osmond name was still marketable.

Mike traveled with us long enough to get to know the boys well and see them at their best and worst. He made this observation, when the boys had spats, he would hear me remind them, 'The enemy is outside the bus, not on the bus.' He said our boys were quick to get over their disagreements, that they were talented, fun loving, and it had been a joy to travel with them.

251

The Osmonds Second Generation

The boys also did some work promoting *The Children's Miracle Network* by visiting hospitals. They were given the privilege of seeing how their singing could bring joy to other people, and they developed a feel for humanitarian work.

Once the boys showed an interest in performing, it was natural to me, just like my father had, to push the boys to be the best they could be. I told them if they wanted to perform, they needed to be serious and that meant putting in hard work. I wanted them to achieve the same level of excellence that my brothers and I had.

Our boys not only performed but became positive role models to their fans. We were happy that parents felt comfortable with their kids listening to our boys' music and following their careers.

Mike also commented that the Osmonds Second Generation reflected the values they had been taught at home, and that our boys referred to us as Father and Mother, a symbol of respect for us as parents.

Our boys have been photographed for teen magazines, and were often asked to take off their shirts, but without any coaching from us, they refused. They made a conscious decision not to compromise their values. They had no problem taking the ribbing they would often get from DJ's about being too goody goody or too Mormon. But after talking with them for a few minutes those people would change their opinion and discover the boys' terrific sense of humor and engaging personalities.

They were the same with their music. They met and did some recording with British record producer Nigel Wright. Occasionally questionable lyrics would surface, and on their own our boys would insist the lyrics be modified so there was no suggestion of vulgarity or immorality.

Travel schedules had an effect on the schooling and social life of our sons. Attending school regularly was difficult, just as it had been for my brothers and me. The start of my sons' singing career was surprisingly organic. Michael, my oldest son, said,

"We used to watch videos of Father and his brothers performing, and, on our own, my three brothers and I just started singing. We started out small, performing at a hearing aid center.

"I was sixteen when we moved to Branson, we moved from a great big house in Provo, Utah, to two tiny apartments in Missouri. Still, life was good. We traveled all over the world, we recorded with Epic and Capital Records, and the shows were always fun. We did a lot of TV and radio, sometimes doing as much as twelve interviews a day. We even had girls camping in front of our hotel.

"We did a few gigs with the wildly popular New Kids on the Block. On one occasion, we performed at the Tokyo Dome in front of eighty thousand people, then flew straight to Branson to perform in front of just two thousand. We wondered, *what the heck?*"

The Osmonds Second Generation performed with me, Wayne, Merrill, Jay, and Jimmy. The show ran for almost seven years.

Mother of the Band

Suzanne and I always wanted to have a big family. I was the third of nine and Suzanne the third of seven. Parenthood would prove to be nothing like we expected, but honestly, our life together wouldn't be *anything* like we expected. Being married to an Osmond and our crazy lifestyle, Suzanne's life has been anything but typical.

Always impeccable in her appearance, Suzanne graciously met dignitaries and celebrities, traveled from one end of the world to the other, by plane, bus, car, and any other form of transportation known to man at the time, maintained our beautiful home, and managed to consistently prepare a healthy meal for our family every evening at 6:00 PM. We were like the Brady Bunch, minus the girls but replaced by five boys, and maybe one or two Alice's over time. But at the core of it all, she was, and is, *our rock.*

Suzanne made it a practice to rise early and get ready to face whatever the day would throw at her. She was ready for a stage appearance or whatever was expected of her at any minute of the day.

She kept our young family on a schedule, including naptimes, dinner, practices, and bedtimes. Childhood rituals were important to both of us. We wanted our boys to have friends, parties, participate in scouting, and enjoy boyhood experiences that I didn't have. She kept our family in order and was stressed when it wasn't. One of our favorite family stories is when Suzanne was grocery shopping with our four young sons. She had our eight-month-old sitting in the child seat of the cart, our two-year-old inside the cart, and our three and four-year-old's hanging onto either side.

A woman passed her in the isle and shook her head. She said, "I'm sure glad it's you and not me."

Suzanne smiled, "So am I."

That is my Suzanne—bold, confident, and a wonderful mother. Even with all the amazing experiences of our lives, she will tell you that her favorite and most prized role is being mother to our eight boys.

Suzanne says, "As a child, I remember coming home on a cold day and being greeted with smells of bread and other baked goods permeating the kitchen. I felt enveloped by warmth and love, and I wanted that for my own home."

with Marjorie and Gordon B. Hinckley, then President of
The Church of Jesus Christ of Latter-day Saints

We went through twenty gallons of milk a week, and Suzanne made a cake every day. She bought twelve dozen eggs at a time since it seemed our boys were always hungry. We had two refrigerators, one in the pantry, and one in kitchen, and she went to the store every other day. Whenever the weather was cold, they knew they would be coming home to homemade treats their mother made especially for them.

Besides gathering for evening meals, Sunday was a day for friends, family, a meal, and conversation. It wasn't unusual for friends, VIPs, studio executives, and extended family to crowd around the table and enjoy Suzanne's hospitality.

It was around those meals that we learned things about our family we may not have otherwise known. The boys would share stories and thoughts about their day. Suzanne said, "We also used that time to teach them manners—at least the best we could. We used to laugh, because with our huge all-boy family, dinner was often *survival of the fastest.*

The other time we spent together was in the morning when we did our scripture reading and prayers.

Alan and Suzanne with their eight sons —
all of whom earned their Eagle in the Boy Scouts of America

Parades and Branson

In 1987, the Heinz company called and asked if the Osmonds Second Generation could participate in the Macy's Thanksgiving Day Parade, however in order to qualify, the boys had to have a song recorded by a record label. So, I created my own recording label, ARO Productions and I pressed some 45 RPM vinyl's so they could qualify.

For the first parade, the Heinz float was a stagecoach, and the boys sang Kay Thompson's rendition of "Jingle Bells."

In 1988 we were contacted again, this time by Comfort Inn Hotel. I did the same thing with their vinyl records and this time the boys sang "Mr Sandman."

After the parade in 1987, we were joining Marie on a tour through Christmas. Because Suzanne wasn't allowed to ride on the float with the boys, they gave her a place under a little awning in front of Macy's store. Alex was a baby, and that allowed Suzanne to go in the store whenever she needed to.

The night before we were all in the huge FAO Schwarz Toy Store and it was about thirty minutes to closing. I took the boys outside while Suzanne got Alex bundled up in his snowsuit. Suzanne explained that all of a sudden, the stroller tipped over and when she was trying to pick things up, she discovered her purse had been stolen.

Beside the fact that it had her driver's license and everything else she carried in her purse, it was of sentimental value because it was a Louis Vuitton that I had given her. She was quite upset about losing those valuable things when, out of nowhere, one of the boys said, "Aren't we grateful they didn't take Alex." In that moment, everything fell into perspective.

We're Going *Where?*

One year, Andy Williams was a guest star at my *Stadium of Fire* event. He told us about Branson, Missouri, which was becoming a center for wholesome entertainment, and that he had built a theater there. Some of the stars that also had theaters and performed there were Wayne Newton, Roy Clark, Mel Tillis, Shoji Tabuchi, Jim Stafford, Tony Orlando, and the Lawrence Welk Show, to name a few.

In 1960, Branson, Missouri was a sleepy little town in the picturesque Ozark hill country, but by the 1990's it had grown into a major tourist destination. It is now a sprawling city filled with lights, marquees, restaurants, hotels, motels, craft boutiques, T-shirt shops, factory outlets, souvenir shops, a wax museum, water slide, strip malls, and every other tourist attraction imaginable.

The main thoroughfare is a winding two-lane road with more than thirty theaters. The bumper-to-bumper traffic is impacted as well by a myriad of tour buses.

Typical audiences in Branson are retirees who want to partake in one of the nostalgic experiences offered in the town. Many of the audiences are of the age who would remember the Osmonds from our recording and performing years. Branson is popular for family and patriotic entertainment where you can bring your kids and your grandparents, without the fear of off-colored jokes or other embarrassing entertainment. The usual way of addressing a Branson audience is *'folks.'*

My brother Jimmy has always had a good business head, and since live entertainment is the draw there, in 1992 Jimmy purchased an existing theater in Branson. He then approached us older brothers, and invited his entire family—parents, siblings, children, and grandchildren—to join him. The five of us put our heads together and came up with a five-year plan which included renaming the theater, *The Osmond Family Theater*, and we would become the featured performers there.

Suzanne and I were not so keen on going at first, but we knew this was a great business decision for our family and would be the means for all of our families to reunite, work together, and use our talents for good. For the past ten years my brothers and I had not traveled together on the road much because we wanted to be home with our families. Also, we each had started our own business ventures to manage. We were on the verge of getting out of showbusiness after forty years of wonderful success, but there was something intriguing about being together as brothers and also having our families in one spot where the audiences were coming to where we were, instead of us traveling the world to get to them.

Setting up in Branson looked like a good move for Suzanne and our boys, and after much consideration, Wayne, Merrill, Jay, as well made the decision to make the move.

For Suzanne and me, it wasn't an easy decision. I was forty-three years old, had started *Alan Osmond Productions* and created *Stadium of Fire*. Plus, with my MS becoming more and more debilitating, I had pretty much planned on retiring from performing. Moving to Branson would mean pulling up stakes in Utah where we were comfortably settled with our eight sons ranging in age from two years to sixteen.

But along with performing together as brothers, a huge positive for our family would be performing with our eight sons— the Osmonds Second Generation. It would be a great way to stay close as a family and to work together as father and sons. They could attend school and participate in church and other activities and would be a part of our shows doing two performances a day, six days a week, after school and in the evening.

Suzanne had some very real concerns about the move. She said, "I wondered about the idea of leaving Provo, where we had been really happy. It would mean selling our dream home on Osmond Lane, closing down, or selling some of Alan's companies and various productions. It would also mean uprooting our family and making a big change in our lifestyle. Our sons were all involved in school and their social activities, and I wasn't sure I wanted to ask the boys to give all that up."

We finally decided to make the move, and in August of 1992, I had already gone to Branson ahead of my family and started performing with my brothers. Suzanne was still struggling with the idea when in October, she had to take our sons alone, on a scheduled performance tour of Japan. Suzanne's parents, Ken, and Ruth Pinegar, stayed with the four younger boys in Provo.

We had discussed with our sons about going to Branson and everyone agreed we would give it a try. None of us were very excited about leaving Utah. While in Japan, Suzanne had a dream that convinced her that the move to Branson was the right thing to do for our family.

She and the four older boys flew from Japan to Salt Lake City, where Suzanne's parents delivered the four younger boys to her so they could all fly to Branson. After two months separation from me, we were once again reunited as a family.

Suzanne said, "We had traveled non-stop from Tokyo, Japan to Salt Lake City, to Denver, and then on to Springfield, Missouri. Alan met us and drove us all to Branson. We arrived at 11:00 pm and we had our first exposure to the Branson Strip.

Alan drove us to where we would be staying for the next couple of months. Two condos side by side was the best he could do with such short notice. Alan and I and the four youngest boys stayed in one, and the oldest boys stayed in the other. I didn't like the fact that we were not all behind the same door at night."

Suzanne had shared her dream with me, and we were both in agreement that the move was necessary. But we knew we could not make that decision without the boys consent and input. We met together as a family and Suzanne shared her dream with the boys.

After the boys discussed their concerns and feelings with us, we asked them to take a vote, and we all agreed to make the move. We enrolled the boys in public schools, and they began performing with me and my brothers, doing two shows a day, six days a week for two months. The Branson entertainment season runs from February through December. We then went back to our home in Provo for Christmas. We were exhausted but happy to be home.

After the holidays, we went back to Branson but moved into different condos that were closer to the theater, but again, we were separated. That was hard. Our family was literally in two different condos, one on top of the other. Imagine that with eight kids. And

Suzanne got plenty of exercise just maintaining the double decker residence.

Later, we purchased two more adjacent condominium units which were located just a block from the Osmond Family Theater. Our new housing was great because we were finally in the same house again—almost. The condos required a little remodeling to make that happen. We cut some doors through the walls to create one single house with six bedrooms and six bathrooms. Now it was spacious enough for our growing family. We weren't adding any more kids, but the ones we had were growing and taking up more space! After living in a seventeen thousand square foot home, we felt cramped at first, but we adjusted. The boys were used to doubling up in bedrooms. The kitchens were small and located in separate areas, requiring Suzanne to utilize both spaces—two separate refrigerators and two separate stoves. Our boys joked with Suzanne that she had two *Coleman* kitchens.

It was a relief to be together as a family and only one block from the theater. Our sons could actually walk there and easily get home between shows for dinner and homework.

The theater was closed for the month of July, so we all went back home to Utah. We started packing up everything so the movers could store all of our belongings, until we could sell the house on Osmond Lane. Getting ready to sell our home and organize a move for ten people was not an easy thing.

I remember Nathan sitting on the porch of our Provo home and weeping while holding his school yearbook. He was fifteen and looking forward to dating when he turned sixteen. He had circled the pictures of all the girls he wanted to ask out and realized he wouldn't be going out with any of them.

My brothers and I, the original Osmonds, consistently filled the theater with enthusiastic audiences. Eventually, because of MS, which affected the right side of my body, I couldn't raise my right arm up high on our closing song, *Are You Up There/ I Believe*. So, my brothers and I adjusted our choreography to accommodate my mobility issues by changing most hand movements to be on the left side. However, as my MS progressed, I eventually had to stop dancing altogether.

It was also becoming more difficult to stand, climb stairs, or play my instruments. I just couldn't do it anymore. I told my brothers that I wasn't sure I could continue, to which they all said "we're not going on without you." So, I positioned myself back by the keyboards where I could sit, play the piano, and still sing and interact in the show.

I told my boys, to be in the show you'll have to put in the work. They became fabulous performers and were a real hit with their singing, dancing, and engaging the audience. In fact, they were recognized and awarded *Best Young Group of the Year* for three consecutive years, and one of their biggest achievements was being inducted into *Branson's Hall of Fame.*

The Church of Jesus Christ of Latter-day Saints organizes its members into *wards.* However, if there are not enough members in a particular area, the organization will begin as a *branch.* With so many of our Osmond family moving into Branson, the branch grew into a ward; it was divided into two wards of which I was called to serve twice, as a counselor in two of the Bishoprics.

Our family was greeted warmly at church, but the same couldn't be said for the town's residents.

In the nineteenth century, members of our church were informally nicknamed Mormons, and, at that time, experienced severe persecution from the local residents of Missouri. We soon learned that the deep anti-Mormon sentiment in Missouri was still alive; it surprised Suzanne and me, but especially our boys. For the first time in our lives, we were outsiders. Our boys were discriminated against solely based on our religious faith. They were mocked, kids spit on and threw things at them. One of our sons even had a knife pulled on him. Once some of our boys were invited to a slumber party and one of the parents told their kids to watch closely at midnight because their "Mormon horns would grow." Needless to say, our kids didn't go. We were shocked that a myth like that could still exist. Still, I cherish our time in Branson. I was able to reinforce the lifelong love and admiration I felt for my brothers. It was not only a rewarding time for us all but an extremely busy one for our family.

With so many performances, our sons honed their performing skills and gained valuable experience, but even with that demanding schedule, they still participated in church and scouting activities, school, family, dated and even had a social life. We grew as a family with newfound friends, and our kids grew as individuals. If handled right, challenges can make us better, and they certainly had plenty of those.

Suzanne and I returned to Branson to rehearse for the 1996 season which was starting on March first. We decided to drive our red Pontiac across country so I would have a car in Branson, then she would fly back home to our boys in Utah.

But that was not the only reason she went with me. She didn't like the way I was walking and had no intention of me driving that distance by myself. Our boys were attending four different schools in Utah, and Nathan was now serving a church mission in Chile, so it was less than convenient for her. However, she was undaunted, Her most important responsibility, in her mind, was to me. Such is the love and devotion of my amazing wife.

After we arrived back in Branson, we learned that three teenage girls had broken into our condo. Apparently one mother discovered her daughter holding some Osmond photographs and precious family videos, claiming she had found them in a dumpster. Her mom wasn't buying it and marched her daughter over to return the items and apologize to us.

I was having major problems walking, and after a few rehearsals, my brothers and I decided it would be best for me to sit at the piano while we performed.

There is no way to adequately describe my frustration. I couldn't dance like I always had, I could only play chords on the keyboard with my left hand, and even handling the microphone was difficult. I had to walk with a cane. I couldn't even get to the theater on my own.

My life, as I knew it, was rapidly slipping away from me.

One morning after struggling through yet another agonizing shower, I was trying to get to the kitchen using the walls as support when, my legs suddenly buckled, my left side suddenly weakened, and I crashed to the floor in a heap. I have never felt more helpless or in such excruciating pain. I yelled for Suzanne, but she was in the shower, and I knew she couldn't hear me over the running water.

My knees were killing me, so I crept along the floor until I reached a chair to pull myself up, but I couldn't even do that. I was in agony, and I collapsed back to the floor sobbing unashamedly. To say I was terrified at that moment was to say the least. All I wanted was Suzanne.

Suzanne remembers, "I heard his cries, and when I saw Alan on the floor, I hurried to his side and helped him to bed. To see my husband so helpless caused my insides to coil in agony, but there was no time for that. Alan needed me, and *we* needed help."

In an instant the trajectory of our life changed; we had to go back home. Suzanne called my brothers, the news wasn't entirely unexpected to them, but they were still shocked.

Merrill explained, "My brothers and I had suspected Alan's MS would eventually rob him of his onstage career. His right side was clearly getting weaker. Over the previous two years, we had feared this day would come sooner or later. We had rarely performed as a threesome, but we adjusted the show, knowing that Jimmy could join us to complete our foursome."

For me, the cold hard reality was that my performing days had come to an end.

Our drive home was depressing. Even stopping for gas and a restroom break posed problems. I couldn't even navigate a one-step curb to get into the restroom without help.

After forty years of performing, I was still determined to do whatever the Lord had planned for me. I relied on my Heavenly Father and Jesus which are stronger than any cane, walker, or wheelchair I may ever need to use.

I had been dealing with MS for nearly a decade. I was acquainted with the gradual decline of my body, but I now had to lean heavily on Suzanne for not only emotional, but physical support as well.

In Branson when I was struggling with MS a rumor circulated that I had a wooden leg and that the Church stored sacred documents in it.

While we traveled, Suzanne and I discussed our years in Branson. It had been a difficult start—Missouri had been less than welcome in the beginning— but it gave us the opportunity to be with our family, our sons performed, and I could direct them from the performing center. Our boys were booked as the Osmonds Second Generation, and audiences packed the showroom.

It took us a little while to win over the Branson community, but we eventually did, and the Osmond name continued to draw crowds. We learned to love those people, made life-long friends, and established a life that, while we were there, brought us many joyful experiences.

I felt nostalgic whenever I watched my siblings onstage. My performing days were over—at least as they always had been. I had been the leader of the Osmonds since I was eight years old. After forty years of performing, it was time to step down. But my brothers were amazing, and I knew the show would continue. While they continued to wow audiences, I had to concentrate on getting well.

Back home in Utah, I visited with my neurologist Dr. Morgenlander, at Duke University and explained all that had happened in Branson. He recommended that I either fly in to see him or get insurance clearance for an MRI from a local neurologist in Utah.

I chose the local option and was given both good and bad news. It appeared that the scarring had affected my neck, but it was fading. That was the good news. But then came the bad news—there seemed to be some new areas further down my spine affecting both my legs. We were devastated.

Both Dr. Watkins in Utah, and Dr. Morgenlander in North Carolina, agreed that I should be given a heavy dose of cortisone called a *'cortisone blast.'* They explained that they had seen improvement in some patients, so we were grateful I had the option. They explained a normal heavy dose of cortisone is five milligrams. My dose would be *one thousand* milligrams a day for four days. It would be like shooting a gopher with a howitzer.

"We were willing," said Suzanne. "Anything was better than nothing, and if it calmed Alan's nerves even a little, it would be worth it."

I went to the hospital, and for four consecutive days, received an IV infusion intended to stop the flareup taking place inside my body. Doctors cautioned us to watch for possible drug side effects. We were advised that I might experience personality changes and say things foreign to me, such as swearing–but nothing alarming happened during those four days.

The cortisone treatment was followed by a wind-down regimen of prednisone to wean me off the cortisone IV's.

Suzanne said, "By the time we got to the end of the weaning off period, those side effects began manifesting themselves, and they hit hard. Alan was not himself. When the phone rang, or if he heard a noise, he would start to cry. He became paranoid, frightened, and insisted I be near him."

It was horrible. At the smallest sound I would start sobbing. Unwelcome thoughts battered my mind until I felt I was going to stop breathing. I developed tunnel vision. I became critical of everything. I could not bear for Suzanne to be out of my sight.

I was sure I was dying, and my physician was out of town and unavailable. How could this be happening? Only a year ago I had been onstage singing Osmond hits and entertaining enthusiastic audiences. Honestly, my heart was breaking, and I think Suzanne's was too.

Our sons also noticed that I had radically changed. They seemed helpless. A part of me knew I was frightening them and unsuccessfully, I tried to hide it from them, but they still heard me crying.

I was encouraged and seemed to improve when our oldest son Michael, proposed to Rebekah (Beka), his high school sweetheart. She had waited for him two years while he served a church mission to Denmark. We had decided to go to Las Vegas for spring break. Suzanne said, "Alan was having a reprieve from the medication and treatment, and his body was beginning to react normally once again. We thought we could finesse the activities in Las Vegas. But I soon discovered I could not leave Alan's side, and the improvement didn't last."

I was driving Suzanne and me to Las Vegas when suddenly I freaked out. I couldn't drive and I pulled over.

The drive was excruciating for me; oncoming headlights looked like pillars of light, and my peripheral vision was failing, it seemed like we were going through tunnels of blinding light.

I must be dying.

I wasn't particularly afraid of dying, but that thought remained with me for quite a while.

Our weekend included partying for spring break. I felt like I was ruining this adventure for everyone, so I suggested a trip to the Tower Ride atop one of the Vegas resorts. I knew it was something the boys wanted to do. Suzanne and I attended the temple, but the entire hour and a half was agony for me. Afterward, we went to one of the famous Las Vegas buffets with some family who lived in the area. But I was having a full-blown meltdown and I couldn't bear for Suzanne to leave my side. The effects of the heavy doses of cortisone were back, and my public behavior was hard for my family to witness.

I believed that everyone was there for my funeral, and no one could convince me otherwise. Every new sound caused me more anxiety. I was sure the security guards were questioning my sanity. I was doing the same. I started mumbling, repeating myself, until my tongue went dry. I was clearly losing it.

I asked my son, Doug, to take me outside and make me walk. I clung to him, and Doug was kind, but we both knew that a security guard was scrutinizing us, maybe wondering if I'd had too much to drink.

Suzanne had suffered a long, dismal night and she hadn't slept well for days. Her brother, Brian, and my sister-in-law, JaNece, had survived a near fatal head-on collision and they understood the pain we were going through. JaNece spoke comfortingly to me about her own grief and the experiences she had suffered.

I was starting to get a grip on reality again, so I attended the temple with Michael and Beka, and was able to spend a treasured forty-five minutes with Michael, who later said of this experience, "What I remember most about this time was not my father's melt-downs but the waves of love coming from him."

In the temple that day, I met a gentleman who was somewhere in his seventies or eighties and used a black cane just like mine. I learned he also had multiple sclerosis. We hit if off immediately, joked about our MS, and playfully challenged each other to a race to our cars. He had contended with MS much longer than I had. I honestly believe he was an angel sent to encourage me.

Michael and Beka's wedding was scheduled a week later. I felt much better, but the experience still proved challenging. My ever-stable Suzanne stayed by my side the entire evening. When my erratic behavior frightened our sons, Suzanne would tell them I was having a reaction to the medication and reassured them that I would be fine.

Suzanne is, and has always been, my rock—our family's solid foundation. From my marriage proposal to the present, she learned to expect the unexpected and to steel herself against anything that might be thrown in her path in the topsy-turvey cycles of our life.

I spent the next few months trying the best I could to heal. My doctor declared me disabled and advised me to get my financial affairs in order. I filed for disability.

That May I silently mourned when I was not able rejoin my brothers to perform in Branson.

Life is tough but so am I.

After forty-two years of performing, I remained determined to do whatever the Lord had planned for me, always, with Suzanne by my side. I put my trust in and relied on my Heavenly Father, and our Savior Jesus Christ, which is stronger than any cane, walker, or wheelchair that I may ever need. Our family would rapidly expand, and Suzanne and I were ready for the next chapter.

OTHER VENTURES (As if I didn't have enough to do.)

In the late 1990's, I started writing children's books. I had written two and started my third '*Twice Upon a Time Tales.*' The first two books are about *The Three Bears* and *The Three Little Pigs'* families. The third is a tale about *Cinderella's* boy.

Suzanne and I had a fun thing going when we were in Branson. We ran across these delicious jams, and I decided it would be a great idea to private label them.

We called our newest enterprise *Lazy River Farms*. It was going great, and we even got them in the local Walmarts in Missouri and Arkansas. But then the craziest thing happened. Someone went into Walmart, opened jars of our jam and stuck their finger in them. That ended our short-lived jam venture.

22

MY SON ALSO HAS MS?
(From a Father's Point of View)

IN 2005, David, my fourth son was twenty-six years old and his career as a lead vocalist of the Osmonds Second Generation, was in full swing. They had played to sold-out crowds of up to sixty-five thousand in the United States and multiple countries, and England loved them, almost as much as they had the original Osmonds.

My sons had relocated to Branson, Missouri, to perform with the *Osmond Brothers* in a town with more entertainment sites per capita than Las Vegas. With three top 40 hits in the UK, David signed major record deals.

December 2005, we were doing a Christmas Eve Show at the Missionary Training Center in Provo, Utah. When we got home, David was experiencing excruciating pain on the bottom of his feet. Then the pain moved to his legs, back, chest, and hands. Over the next few months, he would wake up gasping from paralyzing pain that shot upward to his diaphragm.

He had no idea what was happening to him.

It had been twenty years since my diagnosis of MS. *Could it possibly be the same?* The thought tore at my heart.

In 1998, David followed his three older brothers' examples

and entered the Missionary Training Center for The Church of Jesus Christ of Latter-day Saints and began his two-year mission in Spain. When he returned home in 2000, he re-entered the entertainment world as though he had never left. For the next five years, my sons enjoyed a successful ride to Osmond fame.

David had been dating Valerie McClain for eight months and was convinced she was the love of his life. She felt the same about him, and their relationship become serious. Still with everything in his life growing in a positive trajectory, he had been suffering intense physical anguish. We were all shocked and saddened to learn that David's problem was a form of multiple sclerosis. It was one place I didn't want my son to follow my example.

I was horrified assuming I had passed the disease onto my son, but we soon learned that only about two or three percent of people with MS have family members who also develop multiple sclerosis. It was most likely not genetic, and some physicians even believed that David's disease may have been the consequence of a mosquito bite that led to catching the West Nile virus, and then triggering MS.

David says, "I was angry and in denial at first. It had been hard to watch my father contend with declining mobility, but this was different. His symptoms were nothing like mine, and I struggled with more agony in the following weeks and months than he had in years. In my naïve arrogance I told the doctors the diagnosis absolutely could not be true."

David was positive he needed more sleep and that he just was suffering from a pinched nerve. He was willing to do about any-thing, but accept the multiple sclerosis diagnosis. Believe me, nothing would have made me happier for him at that time.

Of course, I was all about the *you can do this, and we'll get through it,* in public, but in reality, I was terrified. What is going on? How can this be? What will happen to my son? Will this happen to my other boys? The questions tumbled over and over in my mind, clouding my ability to reason logically. All I could do was pray, and that's what Suzanne and I did.

David said, "I know the optimistic part of father's personality comes out especially strong when he talks to others, and he works hard to hide his worries and concerns, but that cheerful mask failed him during an interview with Ryan Seacrest of *American Idol*. When the host asked Father about his son, he broke down, which was strangely heart-warming. I realized how much my father cares about and loves me."

Once we had David's initial diagnosis, it didn't take long for his body to deteriorate. Within months he was in a wheelchair, and his eyesight was fading.

He wondered whether he would have children, and if he did, how could he roughhouse with them?

Valerie supported her boyfriend and willingly took care of essential needs and pushed his chair. She stood by his side, helped him move or to get up when he fell. But I could tell that even with her devotion, MS frequently had sidelined him from center stage.

On top of everything else he was dealing with, David's spirit would be crushed whenever a stranger approached Valerie and say something like, 'Really dear, you don't have to do this. You don't want to marry a *cripple*.'

David would think, *I'm right here and can hear everything you are saying. What? Am I invisible?* The doctors who reviewed David's MRI found extensive damage to his brain, spinal cord, and optic nerves. His body was full of lesions. They said David's MRI resembled those of an exceedingly sick senior citizen and many of his symptoms were the same as the labored movements of someone much older than he was. I knew David was asking *'why me?'* because I had been in his shoes. It was all too familiar.

In true Osmond spirit, David did his best. He continued to

perform, and when he couldn't stand, concert personnel helped him onstage in the dark and carried him to a chair. With legs that didn't move properly, he headlined a corporate show for USANA at the Salt Lake City Delta Center.

After the performance, the president of USANA told David he wanted to give him a gift by sending him to a detox center in Mexico for a month to receive hyperbaric and other treatments as well as steroid infusions.

I had been given the same treatments but without effect.

David had gained some weight, a common side effect of some medicines, but while in Mexico, he lost the weight, felt his toes once again, and could shuffle using a cane. But it was short-lived and his MS symptoms returned. David continued to dismiss the doctor's assessment that he had the disease, but it was getting increasingly difficult to deny the inevitable. A spinal tap recon-firmed the findings, and he was hospitalized.

The doctors told David that his MS was very hot and extremely active. People with MS often wear cooling vests to manage their body temperature. If they get too warm, the heat short circuits their nerves and their bodies become more disconnected than they already were. He would start to drag if he was on his feet too long or if he didn't wear a cooling vest when he was hot.

For the second time, David contemplated asking Valerie to marry him. The first time had fallen apart when her mother died from cancer after a five-year battle. He wanted to give his sweet-heart an unforgettable proposal. He did, but it was not quite what he had planned. He booked a charming bed and breakfast nestled in the heart of the Wasatch Mountains near Provo Canyon. A gazebo was located next to David's room and as promised, the inn's personnel agreed to create a romantic atmosphere. However, getting to the gazebo would require he descend a stairway made with railroad ties.

David told us, "I held onto Valerie and managed two steps before I fell and both of us tumbled into the weeds. I couldn't believe it. Her mother had just died, her boyfriend was a mess, and she was in a heap in the weeds on what was supposed to be a romantic event.

Valerie started sobbing.

David told us, "I begged her not to cry, because I was about to."

Well, at least the gazebo was beautifully decorated. He then fell on his knees and asked her to be his forever wife. She said yes. On their wedding day, David desperately wanted to be walking, so he asked for a huge dose of steroids.

Suzanne and I were concerned, but he was determined. He said, "Steroids are like bandages on a swollen brain. The effects typically wear off after a few months and I just need them to last long enough to get married." He got his wish and experienced an incredible miracle that is still a blessing his life after fifteen years. He walked into his marriage ceremony on April 21, 2007, and miraculously hasn't stopped walking since.

He is grateful for every step he takes.

To his doctors, David is a miracle. At his routine visits to his doctor, the physician just stares at his scans and shakes his head. "According to your tests, you shouldn't be upright, but when I see you walk into the room I realize there is a greater power than me who is keeping you active."

David and Valerie are now parents of two daughters and a son, and yes, he can play with them. Recently, he went on a skiing trip with their daughter, Saffron. Though he had some challenges, including a wild run down the mountain when he couldn't navigate his right side, he says they had a wonderful time together on the slopes.

In addition to his ski buddy Saffron, David is the proud parent to Azalea and Everest.

"These are three of the most amazingly remarkable children on the planet," he said proudly. "Everest, as in Mt. Everest, is my only son, and I like to serenade him with the familiar melody *You Are My Sunshine*. I just made a few wording changes. My version goes, 'You are my son. My only son. You make me happy when skies are gray.'"

David walking on his wedding day with Valerie

David's version of MS, unlike my strain of the disease, leaves him in pain twenty-four hours a day–hours that turn into months and then years. His struggle ranges from discomfort to anguish. Despite his innate optimism, pinpricks of pain punctuate his life.

However, most people don't notice it. Typical of his performances was a spring 2022 concert at an Orem, Utah, arts center called the SCERA. He headlined an evening that had been sold out for months. Thousands had flocked to see our gifted entertainer.

Even though he lives with chronic pain, it hasn't stopped him from remaining warm and genuinely welcoming to others. David says, "Where much is given, much is required. And I've been given a lot."

David touches others with MS as a public speaker, fund raiser, advocate, and singer. In 2010, David received the National MS Society *Spirit of Life* award. David says, "I continue my MS activities with my wife now and will do the same in the future. I hope to inspire others to do whatever they can for their specific circumstances."

He has teamed with Novartis Pharmaceuticals International for a campaign called *Our Voice in Song* and has written the song *I Can Do This,* which is based on his own experiences. His speeches, heard worldwide, offer hope to the most unlikely audiences. He remembers how humbled he was to speak to an audience with MS who were all bed-bound and could do little more than push buttons indicating basic needs, such as *hungry,* and *bathroom.*

He adds, "I have learned to follow my father's mantra, '*I may have MS, but MS does not have me.*'"

When people ask David how he's doing, he typically says, 'great,' and that's true. He is standing, even though the doctors don't know how. And he is dancing, which is supposed to be impossible.

He had to put his career on hold for a while, but he continues to improve. "Besides," he says, "Whenever I hear the sweet little voices of my children as they pray for me and my struggles with MS, I know I will do everything possible for myself and others."

This is my son David's assessment of his MS:

"I choose not to be bitter, but to be better. My father may have MS, but his spirit doesn't, and it's soaring.

"Pain is inevitable, I suppose. But suffering is optional."

I am so proud of him.

23

ONE WAY TICKET TO ANYWHERE

In late 2021, I maneuvered my electric wheelchair into the elegant convention center in downtown Provo, Utah, to accept, with Suzanne, the community's 10th annual *Pillar of the Valley* award.

We knew the evening would honor us for contributions to Utah County and that five of our sons planned to be there and entertain the crowd. Our three sons living out of state were not expected to attend but surprised us by joining the group one at a time. First Michael, followed by Douglas. By the time Tyler joined the group, both Suzanne and I were in tears. All eight sons had united to honor their parents. It was the perfect moment for a perfect photo on a perfect night.

Nathan and David were emceeing the evening, and our eight boys gave a concert that blew the roof off the convention center.

My sister Marie flew in from Las Vegas to surprise her big brother and to perform with her nephews.

"You sing better than my brothers," she exclaimed.

Before she left, Marie also honored Suzanne by stating that, while she loved all her sisters-in-law, Suzanne reminded her most of her mother. Suzanne could not have received a better compliment.

The event drew community leaders from throughout Utah, and Suzanne and I were delighted by our boys' concert. Like I usually do, I quietly mouthed the words along with them. I can't help myself.

In July 2024, Suzanne and I celebrated our Fiftieth Wedding Anniversary. We wanted to go back to where it all began, so we reserved the Sky Room, on top of the Wilkinson Student Center on the Brigham Young University campus. It is near the Marriott Center where we first met and has a beautiful view of the mountains, campus, and the Provo Temple, where we were married together for eternity. It brought back so many wonderful memories. We were delighted to have ALL of our sons, daughters-in-law, grandchildren, and great-grandchildren in attendance. Suzanne's wedding dress and veil, and the dress she wore that day were on display, along with gold helium balloons. In Taiwan in 1980, we had a large Family Guest Book made, and it was there for everyone to include their thoughts. We have had this huge book at many events throughout the years and it has become quite a journal of the amazing life we've been blessed with.

50th Wedding Anniversary portrait

bedroom and the rug in front of the fireplace was crawling with thousands of them!

But after that year, I just took it in stride and positioned a boy at each fireplace with a vacuum to capture them as the ants came in."

Keeping the boys alive wasn't easy!

- Musician Sam Cardon, a friend who worked at *Stadium of Fire* joked, "I think all those kids would probably be dead by now if it were just Alan."

  He was probably right. Keeping eight boys alive wasn't easy. All eight boys had stitches, most of them had broken bones and, with traveling so much, many of them wandered off and got lost.

- Jon broke his arm twice.

- David once fell from a roof retrieving a Frisbee. He barely missed the concrete and fortunately landed on snow and grass.

- Doug cut open his chin and broke his leg.

Suzanne remembers...

- One morning, shortly after breakfast, Doug ran into the kitchen yelling, "David broke his arm!"

  I had heard this before, so I didn't get too excited and followed him to the boys' room. David was laying on the floor and Alan was giving him a blessing. This *was* serious.

  David had fallen off a Little Tykes slide. He hit his left arm on the edge of the window and had what looked like a compound fracture. We were afraid to move him because the bones might tear through the skin. Our neighbor was an Orthopedic surgeon and his wife was an X-Ray Tech, so I called her.

"I know his arm is broken but come and tell me it is!"

She came, called her husband at the hospital and we called an ambulance. EMT's arrived and Alan rode with David to the hospital. David had to have surgery, two temporary pins and a cast. He spent the night in the hospital.

Three weeks later the boys had to do a show at Disneyland, so the doctor adjusted his cast to free his fingers enough to play his saxophone for the show.

Alan remembers…

- One day Suzanne got a call from Sundance Ski Patrol telling her that Doug had an accident on the mountain. They had to bring him down on a sled and he would be transported to the hospital by ambulance.

  When Suzanne asked what his injuries were, they said it was bad and there was blood. Expecting the worst, I headed up the canyon and Suzanne went to the hospital to meet the ambulance.

  When the doors of the ambulance opened, Suzanne saw a smiling Doug who said, "Hi Mommy!" He had broken his leg, but there was definitely no blood. They put a cast on him, and we took him home. Someone had given us some very bad information.

- The boys created a magic trick where they would throw a stuffed animal out of a box to scare others. But one day, someone put a Matchbox car in the box instead of the stuffed animal. When the box was opened, the car went flying and hit Nathan in the mouth, breaking one of his teeth in half. Another trip to the dentist.

- We were at the theater in Branson doing the evening show when David walked between two curtains on the stage and, at the same time, another performer came through from the other direction. The guy's finger went into David's eye and actually took a small piece out of it. Later that night,

Alan remembers…

- When we visited St. George, the boys caught some tadpoles and brought them home. We had a large fish tank, but the boys put the tadpoles in a big fishbowl on a shelf under the tank. They watched them grow and develop into little frogs.

  Several times, nine-year-old Michael caught two-year-old Jon taking the frogs out of the bowl and putting them in his mouth. Michael stopped him each time telling him, "No, no."

  One day the frogs were all gone, and Michael was convinced that the only explanation was that Jon must have eaten them.

Suzanne remembers…

- One Sunday afternoon after dinner at our cabin in Fairview, Alan and Michael were sitting on the back lawn playing with Michael's two baby girls when a microburst of wind hit from the west. It was sudden and very strong. Michael grabbed a baby under each arm, so he was not able to help Alan.

  As Michael ran back with his girls, the wind blew Alan over. Michael ran all the way to the cabin yelling "Sorry Father! Sorry Father!"

  We still laugh about it!

Alan remembers…

- When we lived in Fairview we had two ATV's that we all rode. I remember on a Saturday evening, Alex caught a mouse and we let him keep it for the night. He put the mouse in an empty glass fish tank and promised to get rid of him the next day.

  The next day after church, I told him to get on the ATV and drive that mouse far away from our cabin so he wouldn't come back. Alex decided to drive him to the other side of the San Pitch River that ran along the back side of our property, that way he could never come back.

Alex was still in his Sunday suit as he started to drive across the river. But the water got too deep and the ATV, instead of going across the river, began floating down the river with Alex still on it. He had to get it to the side and then walk back home.

Suzanne saw him coming across the field with his Sunday suit pants rolled up and couldn't imagine what had happened. We still laugh about it.

- One cold morning after church in Utah, we were visiting with some members, our former bishop, stake president and two other church leaders.

  We hadn't noticed that Alex had climbed behind one of the curtains until it suddenly fell down. There was four-year-old Alex writing on the steamed-up window with his finger. He had displayed his writing talents by clearly printing POO.

  Suzanne was especially embarrassed and quickly explained, "Oh, he can't even write."

  Alex said, "Yes I can."

  He told us he had been writing *Winnie the Pooh*.

Suzanne remembers...

- In our Osmond Lane home, we had a massive shower in the master bedroom. I had just put the five oldest boys in that shower because it was easier to have them all in at once. I was in the nursery with three-week-old Jonathan when I heard a loud explosion, and the house shook violently. It scared all of us.

  The lights went out, the alarm came on and kept ringing, and, in the bathroom, the jet tub pump came on and would not stop running.

  I could smell wires burning, and I grabbed towels and told the boys to help dry each other while I grabbed the baby and tried to shut things off.

We learned that lightning had struck the TV antenna just above the master bedroom, and sent electricity all through the house, frying everything electronic as well as the wiring.

One of the firemen told me how lucky I was that the lightning hadn't come through the water and electrocuted the boys.

Alan was on the road, and our phones had been destroyed, so I went next door to tell my sister-in-law, Wayne's wife, what had happened and to pass the message on to her husband so he could let Alan know that I'd taken the boys to my mother's. It took about a month to fix the damage, and we had to purchase all new electronics.

As if that wasn't enough excitement, while we were on our way to my mom's home on a busy road, Michael had found a fire extinguisher in the van and pulled the tab, filling the vehicle with the smoke-like extinguisher dust. I had to pull over and roll down the windows to let it out so I could drive. I couldn't believe that day. I thought, I can laugh, or I can cry. I laughed.

- That wasn't my only experience with lightning. When I was in high school, I attended a slumber party with several friends. We spent the night at one of the friends who lived in Salem, Utah on a dairy farm. Their property had several barns, buildings, and cows.

Girls don't really sleep at slumber parties, so in the middle of the night we decided to play Hide and Seek in the barnyard. We divided into teams and went out.

I was walking with a couple of girls when lightning struck right next to us, knocking us to the ground. It felt like an explosion, and we all laid there trying to figure out what had just happened. I heard some of the other girls screaming in the distance and a girl with me said, "We have to get out of here!"

We came to our senses, jumped up and ran for the house.

I find it quite telling and interesting what we did next. When we got back to the house, we read our scriptures for comfort, and discussed how we had just been protected from what could have been a great tragedy.

Michael remembers…

- We did a Disney pilot when I was in 3rd or 4th grade. This kid at school named Eddie was a bully and was always picking a fight with everybody including me. He sucker punched me and cut my eye open, so I beat him up.

  I never saw Eddie again, but my mother wasn't very happy because we had the Disney people coming the next day and I had a huge black eye.

  Some of my brothers had trouble with kids in Branson who didn't like them. I didn't, but I did have trouble with my math teacher. He was the head of the local KKK.

Doug remembers…

- One year Brad Paisley was featured at the *Stadium of Fire*. I took my father back to visit with Brad and one of the festival workers stopped us before we got to the *meet and greet*. This person said, "Where do you think you're going?"

  I was infuriated. I wanted to tell that person, "Not only did my father start this, but he also sold more records than Brad Paisley could even dream of." But before I did, someone else came a long and took us back. When Brad Paisley saw my father, he said, "Oh my gosh, it's Alan Osmond!"

The Osmond Animals

Michael remembers…

- We had a lot of dogs, but a particular one was Buddy. I think Father found him and brought him home. Buddy caused a lot of trouble. Once he disappeared but returned home with parts of a deer. He also killed our neighbor's ducks. One of the worst things he did was when he got in the mud, then somehow got into a neighbor's house and climbed up on the bed in their master bedroom. I don't think my mother liked him very much.

Doug remembers…

• Buddy tore my brand-new down sleeping bag to pieces, and it looked like it snowed on the lawn.

More dog tales from Suzanne:

• Many times, Alan got dogs in pairs thinking it would be better for the dogs to have a buddy. We had Bud & Burt, Tom & Jerry, Bill & Ted, and Fuji & Max. There are stories about each pair, but I think Bill and Ted were the most trouble. Just before Christmas, Ted chased eight of the neighbor's baby sheep into the river and they drowned. We had to pay for each of those sheep.

   Then, a few days later on New Year's Day, I ran out of space in the refrigerator and put my big Honey Baked Ham in a big pot on the back porch to keep it cold. I opened the door just in time to see Ted grab the entire ham and run away. He never came home. I think he knew I was furious. (Either that or he overdosed on that ham!)

• Marie had a Rottweiler named Mr. T. She asked us if we would keep him for a week while she went out of town. She came back home but never came for Mr. T. We ended up having him for quite a while until we gave him to Merrill.

   Mr. T was nice to us but wouldn't let anyone else get close to our house, not the mailman, the paper boy, friends or family.

• While filming a Japanese commercial on Osmond Lane, the Japanese filming crew knocked over our cockatiel bird cage, and we had to put it upstairs in a room until we were finished. While they were filming, the cockatiel flew through the guest room into the kitchen then out the window. We never saw him again.

- We had an iguana and a turtle, and one time, Jimmy brought us a large parrot in a very big cage. That bird was always screeching—we could only handle it for one week.

THE OSMONDS NEXT GENERATION
Where Are They Now...?

From Michael

I grew up on the road. I'm the oldest, so that made me the oldest of my four brothers who were the original performers. We traveled with our father and the Osmonds, and then later when we started to sing.

It was hard being the oldest, I was expected to be the leader, just like my father was and that included when we were on stage. But I never feel pressured to perform, I enjoyed it. I always wanted to be like my father and make him proud.

I was sixteen when we moved to Branson, and I remember

wondering why Father was in Missouri looking at theaters.

Then I found out—we not only went from performing at the Tokyo Dome in Japan to a crowd of eighty thousand, to a little theater in Branson for two thousand people, but we also left our huge house on Osmond Lane and moved into apartments. It was a crazy transition for all of us—culture shock.

After high school, I served in the Denmark, Copenhagen mission. The day after I came home, I went straight back to work with my brothers in Branson, followed by the North American tour of *Joseph and the Amazing Technicolor Dreamcoat*. I was married right after my mission, so I didn't spend a ton of time at our cabin home in Fairview, Utah.

My greatest accomplishments to date are my six great kids, five girls and one boy, and three grandkids so far, two boys and one girl. All of them are my buddies. Suzannah, my oldest daughter and my parents first grandchild, is named after my mom. She was born at 1:00 pm on opening night of the Joseph tour while we were in Dallas. After she was born, I went back to the theater for final rehearsal.

During this time, my family was able to tour with me. It was fun—we did our shows in the evening so during the day we could go to the zoo and do other fun things.

My kids are Suzannah, Sarah, Sasha, Sean, Sophie, and Sadie, who is sixteen. Once my son and I decided to shave our heads— problem was that I forgot we were having a big family picture in three days; my mother was not happy.

Currently, we live in St George, Utah, and work in investing.

From Nathan

What an honor it is to get to say a few words about my incredible father in a book all about his remarkable life. Not only is he a rock star who has sold over 100 million records, but he was also trained in Karate by no less than the legendary Chuck Norris! He won three out of the four trophies in the Army and now he's a

published author. There really isn't anything that my father can't do. He is hands down my biggest hero.

I recall having dinner with my father at a little Chinese restaurant a few years ago. I asked him a very personal question…I said, 'Father, if you could go back in time and talk to your younger self, what advice would you give to yourself?" He made a smart aleck remark, then he got very serious. He looked me right in the eyes and said, "Son, here's what I would tell my younger self…It's not who you are, but who you become that ultimately matters." I hear those words echo over and over again in my ears daily. My father is full of wisdom beyond his years, and I find myself quoting him everywhere I go. He could literally write an entire book just on the "*Alanisms*" that he shares with his family daily.

I used to sneak into my parents' bathroom as a child so that I could read the poem they had hanging on their wall. It was titled, "The Man Who Thinks He Can," by Walter D. Wintle. I learned that this was the secret to my father's many successes. He had to believe that he could do anything he set his mind to. Heck, he became a regular on *The Andy Williams Show* at the age of 12! I remember him telling me, "Son, we wrote #1 hit songs in the '70's, simply because nobody told us that we couldn't." It reminds me of the words of John Andrew Holmes who said, "Never tell a young person that something cannot be done. God may have been waiting centuries for somebody ignorant enough of the impossible to do that thing."

He's become my ultimate life coach. When we were on *Good Morning America* back in 1986, Joan Lunden singled me out and said, "So Nathan, do you enjoy this entertainment business?" I was only 9 years old at the time and completely froze on National television. Only two words escaped my lips, "Uh, yes ma'am." My father saw that I wasn't going to say another word, so he jumped in and saved the interview. On the way out of that New York City television studio that morning, my father said something to me that would forever change my life. He put his arm around me and said, "Son, it's a talk show…TALK!" He followed up by saying these words, "People want to hear what you have to say!" On one hand, I was humiliated. I felt like I had let my family down on national television. On the other hand, I was liberated. He told me that people wanted to hear what I had to say, and I believed him. He looked at me with the eyes of Goete who said, "If you treat a man as he is, he will remain as he is. But if you treat him as if he were what he ought to be and could be, he will become what he ought to be and could be." He has helped me become who I am today.

Since that day on Good Morning America, my father became my brothers and my manager. As a boy band, we did a 100-city mall tour in the early 90s. I remember my father helping to set-up a stage in front of a Wal-Mart, where we performed. His MS was not helping him at all in that extreme heat as he was overturning shopping carts to create a place where the audience could stand to watch us perform. He told everyone, "Come listen to my boys. I swear, they're really good!" Now, that's a father. He helped us get three songs in the top 40 in the UK and inspired me to go after my own Country music career as a solo artist. I now have 4 consecutive #1 hit singles on the Country charts, thanks to the example and belief that my parents instilled in me. I have also spoken to over 1 million audience members as a keynote speaker, simply because he told me, "People WANT to hear what you have to say." I won the John C. Maxwell Leadership Award two years in a row in the category of Arts & Entertainment and even received the Ten Outstanding Young American Award from the JAYCEES for my musical achievements and humanitarian efforts. (This was Elvis Presley's favorite award as well.) All this was possible because two parents committed to never give up on their children. I've come to learn that if you doubt yourself, sometimes all you have to do is believe in somebody else's belief in you until your own belief kicks-in.

The greatest name I've ever been called is "Mini-Alan." What a compliment! I've tried so hard to be just like my father in every way. I usually fall short, but he's always been there pushing me to be my very best.

When I was just 19 years of age, I was called to serve a Spanish-speaking mission for the Church of Jesus Christ of Latter-Day Saints in the Chile, Santiago North Mission. My biggest fear before I left was my father's ailing health. I worried that his MS would take him from me and that I would never see him again in this life. I never told him about my fears, but parents have their intuitions. One evening, in our living room in Branson, Missouri, he said, "Son, if I die while you are on your mission…don't you dare come home. Because that way I can come and be with you and we can knock doors together." He's always known exactly what I needed to hear in the very moment that I needed to hear it.

When I returned home, I saw my family all standing there, waiting to give me a big welcome home hug. I gave my beautiful mother, Suzanne a kiss…and then I saw him…standing with a big poster board sign in hand that read, "Speak English!" I ran to him and gave him the biggest hug ever. He hugged me so tightly and whispered in my ear, "You didn't think I was going to be here, did ya?"

As you've read this book, there has been a common underlying theme to my father's story: "With God all things are possible." (See Matthew 19:26) He's taken his mother's dying words to heart.

When my grandmother, Olive Osmond, was dying, she suddenly came out of a coma and grabbed my father's hand. She couldn't speak as she had suffered a stroke and was intubated, so she signaled for my father to hand her a pencil and paper then wrote the following message.

Alan, there is no limit to the good you can do
if you don't care who gets the credit.

This is how my father has lived his life. He's the one who stood back and let his brothers and sister shine on stage. He taught soldiers how to pray who were about to be shipped off to war in Vietnam. He's in the Guinness Book of World Records for the most firecrackers lit off at one time: One Million fifty thousand in six seconds. He even produced both Ronald Reagan's and George HW Bush's inauguration celebrations and firework shows. But above all of his countless trophies and accolades, the title that he's most proud of is that of husband, father, grandfather and now great grandfather.

To Alan Osmond, family is EVERYTHING. I am SO blessed to have him as my father. I love you "Par Par!"

"I thank my God upon every remembrance of you." – Phil. 1:3

From Doug

There was never a dull moment growing up in the Osmond family. Although many of my childhood memories involve tour busses, sound checks and photo shoots, I admire my parents' ability to create magical moments that made it feel normal in all the best ways. Some of my favorite memories were traveling with my parents—seeing the world and performing with my brothers as a member of the Osmonds Second Generation.

My father was diagnosed with MS when I was young. He sat us all down and told us that he was sick and that if he were to die, to make sure that we took care of Mother. We were scared that he wouldn't be around much longer, but he still had such a positive

attitude. I believe this is the reason he is still able to walk today. To this day, I have never once heard him complain or ask, "why me?" He would always say, "I might have MS, but MS does not have me."

There are a few things I never had to doubt: my father's love for my mother, his family and his love for the Lord. Especially in his later years, he has been an amazing example to me on how to treat your spouse. He always puts my mother first in everything he does. She is the love of his life. My mother is also my hero. She has sacrificed so much for my father and quite frankly, all of us. I know that this book is about my father's life but without my mother, there would be no book to write. She is the backbone and the strength of our family.

After high school I served a 2-year mission for the Church of Jesus Christ of Latter-Day Saints in Johannesburg, South Africa. I learned so much about faith, life and resilience on my mission. I also learned to love the Lord and through Him, I found it easy to love the people I served.

After my mission, instead of flying home to Utah, I flew to Minneapolis and joined my family on their Broadway tour of *Joseph and the Amazing Technicolor Dreamcoat.* It was a good experience.

While on the tour, I spent my evenings reconnecting with an old friend I had met during my family's days in Branson, Missouri. Before I knew it, I had spent two thousand dollars on phone cards and had fallen in love. But let me back up. I met Tiffany when she was 11 years old. She comes from a very adventurous family. Her dad wanted a central location in the country for his new business, so he literally opened a map and moved the family where his finger landed. They ended up in Nixa, Missouri. I met Tiffany's brother at a youth conference, and we became instant best friends. It wasn't until later that we found out our moms had worked together in college at the BYU bookstore and even ran against each other for Homecoming Queen.

Tiffany is the love of my life. She makes me want to be better every day and strive to reach my full potential. She is the epitome of selfless love and lives her life the way the Savior wants all of us to live. I don't know what I did to deserve her, but I thank the Lord every day that we're together. Tiffany and I married in the Manti Temple and have five children. Our eldest son, Maximus, was a wrestler in high school, and was later called to serve a mission for The Church of Jesus Christ of Latter-Day Saints in Trinidad, Port of Spain. Due to covid, however, he served in Wichita, Kansas. He is now a devoted firefighter and emergency response specialist in the Arctic Circle. Our second child Ivy, and her wonderful husband Tyler, are loving life and expecting their first baby. Ivy is a talented singer, musician, writer, and entrepreneur. Tyler loves the outdoors, playing guitar, and the little things. Miles is currently in school and preparing for a mission. He loves basketball, playing guitar, and has become quite the song writer. Penny is also in school and enjoys volleyball, reading, singing, playing guitar, ukelele and piano. Our youngest, Jeslon, is full of energy and loves anything active or sports related. At three years-old he was smashing golf balls 60 yards straight down the fairway and he hasn't slowed down.

We have raised our children mostly in Utah and Missouri. A few years back, however, we decided to do something adventurous. We bought a rustic cabin, sight unseen, in Alaska. No power. No water. No internet. It was rough in the beginning, but we now have running water when we turn the generator on. Although we have grown to enjoy the simplicity of our new life, we began our adventure not knowing how long it would last, or should I say, how long *we* would last. For now, at least, we can't imagine being anywhere else.

I feel fortunate to be able to work from home and travel as needed. I have worked mostly in the sales and the nonprofit industry as an adult. I remember my father being heavily involved in charitable work when I was younger, and I attribute my career choice to his influence.

From David

Growing up the fourth son of the Alan Osmond family, from an early age, I didn't know music and performing were an uncommon way of life. I thought it was totally normal and every kid's dad did this thing called "showbiz." So, that's what I was going to do. Sing. And I did. From two years of age until my early tweens, I was performing constantly with my family. It was then that I realized doing two shows a day, six days a week, and traveling all over the world was not normal. A strange realization, but it brought a feeling of gratitude and immense appreciation for the cool things I was able to do and accomplish in my childhood—an opportunity I knew many other kids weren't afforded.

I was the lead singer for my brother's group, the Osmond Boys and, later, the Osmonds Second Generation. In my late teens, I started to become an individual music artist when Andrew Lloyd Weber and Tim Rice's team asked if I would be the understudy for my Uncle Donny in the lead role of their musical, *Joseph and the Amazing Technicolor Dreamcoat*, and ultimately take over that lead role as full-time *Joseph*.

I remember once overhearing a dedicated fan of Donny who had expressed major disappointment that I, not Donny, would be Joseph one particular night. After all, it was *he* who she came to see. I absolutely understood her plight. But, after the show, I was delighted to hear that same woman say how she had completely forgotten that I wasn't my famous uncle from the moment I started to sing, and how good the performance and musical were. Believe me, at that young age, I recognized what big shoes I had to fill, night after night, and I had the time of my life playing the title role for many years after.

In touring as *Joseph*, I successfully pitched my brothers for some of the parts of Joseph's brothers. Just as our grandparents Osmond had done, my parents traveled with us and attended every performance. Life growing up as an Osmond was always a family affair. I paused my musical career to serve a two-year mission in Spain for my church.

I met my wife, Valerie, at the last place I ever thought I would meet my soulmate, the love of my life, and my best friend—Las Vegas at the Hard Rock Hotel and Casino on New Year's Day. I was living in LA working on music projects, so we dated long-distance for a few months.

On Christmas Eve of that year, after a performance in Provo Utah, I vividly remember taking my shoes off and experiencing agonizing massive pain in my feet which came out of nowhere. I didn't sleep much—the pain soon advanced to my legs, waist, and chest. Doctors thought pinched nerves were causing the symptoms and I sought out physical therapy. However, my hands continued to slow down in movement and agility, and my eyesight diminished. I thought my music was finished. This continued through February, and by March I was falling a lot. By May, I was using a cane and then ultimately a wheelchair.

I was terrified. I had watched my dad gradually slow down physically when we were kids, but I didn't suspect I could also have MS. My decline was much faster and accelerated than I had seen with him. *It couldn't be,* I thought.

I had shows booked with my brothers, but I couldn't walk, and we didn't have any answers. They carried me onstage into a chair where I held a guitar and sang to get through the show.

I wanted to ask Valerie to marry me. The day before I planned to ask her, her sister called from Las Vegas to tell Valerie her mom had unexpectedly passed away. We went back to Vegas for funeral arrangements. I sat in a wheelchair to sing at my future mother-in-law's funeral feeling hopeless.

Valerie and I were weighted down with grief and the progressive decline of my health. Right after the funeral, I had an MRI in hopes we would find answers. The doctor simply said, "This looks like you do have MS. And son... from what I see in there, you've been through the war."

Even with this devastating diagnosis, I still needed to work and had a contracted performance at the Delta Center in Salt Lake City.

Since my original proposal plans were pushed aside with the passing of Valerie's mom, the night before my performance I arranged a private dinner in a romantic gazebo near my hotel room with flowers, lights, and candles. However, I hadn't expected to navigate down railroad tie steps to get to the gazebo. Valerie and I were walking down hand in hand, and my legs gave out and I fell hard; we both tumbled to the bottom, and both started crying.

I told her, "Please don't cry." I got down on my knees, well, I fell to my knees and asked her if she would be mine forever. She said yes! It was a wonderful moment, though not exactly how I saw it unfolding in my head.

With a wedding soon, getting my health in check was my number one priority. I stayed at a health facility in Mexico for three weeks. I received alternative treatments to calm the inflammation in my body. Back home in Utah, I visited a neurologist, and they confirmed my MS was very aggressive—that there were lesions all over my brain and spine. They treated me with a drug called Solu-Medrol giving me the max dosage of 1,000 mg every day for five days.

With an anti-inflammatory diet, I lost twenty pounds, and for the first time since it all started, I could move my toes. I was using a cane to walk and then back to the wheelchair to get around. I knew the steroids were a temporary fix, but I wanted to walk without assistance for our wedding. On April 21, 2007, Valerie and I were married, and I was miraculously able to stand and dance with her. It's been almost twenty years and I'm still on my feet.

Every time I see my doctor, he is shocked that I am still walking. MS is a progressive disease and though I still have MS, MS does not have me! No one knows what tomorrow holds, but today is a good day. Yes, I feel constant pain all over my body, fatigue like no other, broken systems and inabilities. Knowing what I can't do right now, it also helps me to see more clearly what I still can do. And those simple things mean more than they ever have before.

My father is a rockstar of life, not just music. Sharing the same love of music with him, and also the same diagnosis, has given me a much deeper connection and appreciation for the incredible man he is. I feel him in every step I am able to take. He's such an example to me. He always tries to live his best life. I have never heard him complain one time about challenges or misfortunes. Life can be frustrating and hard sometimes, but we have to keep perspective. I admire my dad's determination and pay it forward example to try to reach new levels of resilience. I stand on the shoulders of parental giants.

I've been blessed with so many great years, performing with my brothers, working with Uncle Donny on *Joseph*, appearing on *American Idol*, touring my own music all over the world, and performing alongside my Aunt Marie for over fifteen years. Being a versatile entertainer, music artist, Emmy-nominated TV show host, keynote speaker, and business leader, I've learned and experienced wonderful things over the years. Yes... pain is inevitable, but suffering is optional. I eat raw organic as much as I can, try not to push myself too hard, and have a genetic predisposition to smiling. But the greatest thing I've accomplished in my life is being a husband and father.

Valerie, the love of my life, and I have a beautiful, blessed life. We have three kids, Saffron Gloria who is fifteen, Azalea Mae who is thirteen, and Everest David Levi who is nine. They are my favorite people.

From Scott

My father instilled in me a strong work ethic and a love for music at a very young age. Many people don't realize it, but there is a lot of work that goes on behind the scenes in the music industry. We consistently practiced music and for many years I was able to sing together with him on stage. That lead to two national tour productions of *Joseph and the Amazing Technicolor Dreamcoat*. We were performing in eight to twelve shows each week and I had to take additional independent study classes and meet with tutors frequently to stay on top of school and fit music and singing into my schedule. It was physically demanding and many times, I would

> When my boys performed, Scott was the cute little kid, just like Jay used to be.

lay down on the ground backstage and take a five-minute nap right before the show to quickly recharge. When you are singing as much as we did, there are days that you don't feel the energy to get up on stage and smile, but I learned that I could do hard things and, in the end, really enjoy it.

Traveling and performing together as a family were some of my favorite memories and helped me develop a strong bond with my parents and brothers, as well as a love for the many different people and cities that we visited.

When I was nineteen, I served a two-year mission for the Church of Jesus Christ of Latter-day Saints in the Paraguay Asuncion North Mission, which forever changed my perspective on life and priorities. I loved the people, culture, and languages that I learned in Paraguay. I was able to use the Spanish and Guarani languages that I learned to translate to live events after returning home.

Later, I graduated with a degree in finance from Brigham Young University and received an MBA from Utah State University. Over my career, I've enjoyed the relationships I've made with others as

I've worked in financial planning and analysis, mergers and acquisitions, helping businesses grow and become more efficient, and leading while mentoring others.

My father and I both met our spouses at BYU (He met my mother at a BYU basketball game, and I met my wife, Annie, at a BYU football game). It wasn't a great season for BYU when I met Annie, but it was the best thing that ever happened to me. Watching BYU athletics brings back great memories for all of us. My wife Annie loves running and consistently competes in marathons. I love to snow ski, mountain bike and golf. We love to try out new restaurants. Most of all, we love our four children (Caleb, Jaynie, Jake, and Isaac) and two dogs (Leo and Lou).

Last summer, I returned to Paraguay with my son Caleb for a humanitarian project. Connecting with old and new friends was a highlight for me. Caleb is now serving a two-year mission for our church in Nicaragua. Seeing each of my kids share their love with others and develop their own relationship with God is one of the greatest joys in my life and I'm proud of each of them. I continue to sing and play my guitar often and love attending live music concerts together as a family. My parents' passion for life and commitment to each other continues to be a foundation for my approach to life.

From Jonathan

I grew up performing with my family. After high school, I moved out and started attending Utah Valley University a little before my seventeenth birthday. I earned my Associate degree in accounting and then transferred to Brigham Young University to enter their accounting program, (one of the top ranked accounting programs in the nation), where I received my Master of Accountancy degree. For eight years, I worked for PwC (Pricewaterhouse-Coopers, LLP) in their tax practice in Salt Lake City, Utah and in the national tax practice in Washington, D.C. I currently lead the tax function for Sunrun.

I married my wife, Laura, in August 2004 and started BYU's accounting program a day after our honeymoon. I met Laura at church when I was sixteen, just two weeks after she had seen me perform in Stadium of Fire. We became quick friends and eventually started dating a few years later. Laura served as a missionary in Quito, Ecuador at the same time I served my mission in Brasilia, Brazil. We wrote each other the entire time and shared the experiences we were having on our missions. I arrived home from my mission on my parent's anniversary which was the same date Laura, and I met four years earlier. We were married five weeks later.

Laura is the youngest of 10 siblings. Her parents converted to the Church of Jesus Christ of Latter-day Saints and moved from Ohio to Lehi, Utah when she was young. We had similar upbringings, both growing up in a large family. She is a great pianist and taught piano lessons for 11 years. She put her career on hold to help raise our children full time. Once our youngest was in school, she went back to school and got her Bachelor of Science degree in

Nursing. She currently works as a Registered Nurse at Intermountain Health. She has fond memories of listening to *The Osmond Christmas Album* as a child.

Laura and I have three children: Luke, Asher, and Kate. We have put our roots down in Utah and have been married twenty years. Our children are the center of our lives; we do everything together. We love to spend time together, including camping in our trailer, traveling, skiing, golfing, and nightly dinners around the table.

My father is a producer—he literally can't stop creating, it's in his DNA. He's always motivated and is the epitome of Stadium of Fire. He is a "go big or go home" type of guy. Music runs through his veins, and he can hear the intricate harmonies most can't. He loves to have everyone together. He likes projects and keeps a creative vision, never getting caught up in the details. MS has never slowed him down in that way.

That said, his top priority in life is being a disciple of Jesus Christ, providing for and loving his family, and sharing the gospel with anyone willing to listen. He's family centered and loves to have fun. Father is faith motivated and has strength beyond his own. We have a large family, full of the typical happy and challenging events, and we are good at coming together to support each other through whatever life brings. We are always there for each other and have maintained certain family traditions over time, such as new pajamas and banana splits on Christmas Eve, or gathering together every other year for Thanksgiving.

I am grateful for my family and the faith-centered home my parents provided. Everything about my parents is founded upon faith and family. Laura and I couldn't ask for better examples and mentors in our lives.

From Alex

My father inspired me to learn web design and development. After I earned a bachelor's degree in digital media with an emphasis in Internet Technologies from Utah Valley University, I had the opportunity to start my career working as a product designer for The Church of Jesus Christ of Latter-day Saints. I now design mobile and web applications that are literally blessing millions of people throughout the world every day. I have worked for the church now for more than twelve years and it has been a dream come true.

I'm a planner and live life intentionally. How I use my time is important to me. Making memories with my family and improving to be a better husband, father, and man is my priority and how I try to invest it. I am detail oriented, love a good checklist, and manage my life in my calendar (my events) and a couple of apps called Due (my reminders) and Things (my tasks).

I don't want to go back to Branson—I agree with some of my brothers, it wasn't Missouri, it was Misery. I have never been comfortable performing. At the same time, I feel that it has helped me be successful by learning to do hard things that make me stretch and push me outside of my comfort zone. I liked the small town feel of Fairview, it was quiet and peaceful; it did grow on me. I love the country, but I love the city too—I like a happy medium.

My parents' example motivates me, the way they approach Father's disease, and each other. I wasn't yet born when Father came down with multiple sclerosis, so I have never known anything different. When it comes to caring for my father with his MS, I have never once seen Mother complain or get frustrated. I have only seen her do what she does best, love and care for him. I am grateful for her love and devotion to each of us, especially my father. The way Father handles MS, inspires me as I deal with my own health issues.

Mother is always prepared every Sunday afternoon not knowing how many kids and grandkids might show up for dinner. She is always ready, has her door open to us, and can throw together an amazing meal that is enough to feed an army.

Father is always producing—always creating, always at the computer. I think it was and is, his creative outlet. Even with MS he still does what he loves. He taught me how the internet worked, how to use Adobe Dreamweaver and got me into web design and development. He purchased a lot of domains and had a blog, the-family.com.

I loved watching him record his ideas, projects, and songs on the computer. One of his many hobbies was creating websites. I remember the first time he showed me how to use dial-up internet and Netscape Navigator. It inspired me to learn more about technology and leverage my creative talents.

One day Father pulled me aside and expressed how much he cared about me. He told me, "Alex, I hope you truly know how much I love you. You mean more to me than you will ever know, but I'll always love your mother more."

He is completely faithful, protective, and devoted to Mother in all things. I am grateful for how completely he loves and cherishes all of us, but mostly how he cares for her. I have learned that the best way I can care for and protect my own kids is to love, protect, and cherish my wife, their mother.

As I grew older, I served my mission in the Georgia Atlanta North Mission. I knew I wanted technology to be part of my career and to do what my father loved.

Jessie and I were married October 20, 2011, and have four children. I am most proud of being a husband and father. I don't like being in the public eye, and prefer to live more privately, close to the mountains where we have a good blend of country and city. We have a trailer and love to go camping with our family. I'm proud of my kids, but I don't put our pictures on social media—I prefer to keep our lives private.

My wife, Jessie adds, "Alan and Suzanne are great examples of prioritizing each other and their marriage. Their examples of loyalty and commitment have been a blessing in our own lives.

From Tyler

Like my brothers, I grew up on the stage. My first shows began when we moved to Branson in 1992 to perform at our Family Theater. Initially, Alex and I had small parts alongside our brothers, but after performing daily for several years, we began taking on more diverse roles.

Our time in Branson prepared us for our national tours of *Joseph and the Amazing Technicolor Dreamcoat*, where Alex and I were cast as the "Masters of the Dream Choir." Traveling and performing across the country with my brothers were pivotal moments in my youth, ultimately shaping my future as a musician.

After the tours ended, Alex and I were the only ones left at home. With my brothers going to college and starting families, my parents decided to move from the ranch to Orem, Utah. That same year, Alex started playing guitar and suggested I pick up the bass so we could jam together. That Christmas, my parents changed my life by giving me my first bass. I was instantly obsessed. Soon after, Alex and I started our own band, Set In Stone, eventually recruiting our cousins, Jason and Eric (Jay's sons) to join. We played all around Utah, but the band eventually fizzled out when Alex left on a mission for the church.

That didn't stop me from performing. I continued playing around Utah Valley with different groups throughout high school. In 2008, I joined a band called Desert Noises.

We immediately clicked, signed to a local record label, and released our first full-length album. After a couple of years of regional and West Coast tours, we decided to commit to touring full-time. We started booking our own tours, took out a loan for a minivan, and began touring non-stop across the country.

After years of touring and releasing a few records, we moved to

Nashville in 2015 to continue riding the wave we had found ourselves on.

Moving to Nashville was the best decision of my life. Once we moved, I started playing with anyone and everyone I could, not only with Desert Noises but also as a "Hired Gun" for other bands. This gave me the opportunity to share the stage, both nationally and internationally, with some of my favorite artists, such as Metallica, the Lumineers, Cage the Elephant, and Modest Mouse.

I've performed at some of the biggest festivals in the country, like Austin City Limits, Bonnaroo, and Lollapalooza, as well as some of the most notable venues, including the Hollywood Bowl, Merriweather Post Pavilion, and Chicago Theater. Ironically enough, backstage at the Chicago Theater, there are murals commemorating some of the more notable shows that have played there. One mural was from 1996 when my Uncle Donny was there with *Joseph*, and I found his signature, 'Donny Osmond

1996.' I signed my name, 'Tyler Osmond 2016,' right next to it. It felt pretty amazing to perform on the same iconic stage as him, 20 years later.

My move to Nashville didn't just change my life musically; it changed everything when I met my wife, Kate. She moved to Nashville from Houston in 2007 and built her own life and career here. Thankfully, our paths collided. We started dating in 2019 and married in 2023.

In February 2024, our lives were completely transformed when we welcomed our son, Ace—my parents' thirtieth grandchild—into the world. Together, we've never been happier, and I personally want to thank my parents for that. They've been perfect examples of responsibility, patience, and unconditional love. We didn't have a "normal" childhood, but I wouldn't trade it for anything. Kate, Ace, and I are still living in Nashville, proud to be part of my parents' legacy.

GIVING BACK

MY PARENTS, George and Olive Osmond taught us to always give back and bless others' lives. As our success grew, my parents started their first charity—an organization to help the hearing-impaired. Since they had raised two deaf children of their own, Virl and Tom, they knew how much help was needed in that community.

From that beginning foundation, the Osmond charitable reach grew into something globally helping millions.

George and Olive in Hawaii

The Children's Miracle Network (CMN)

Joe Lake and Mick Shannon from the March of Dimes, along with my sister Marie and actor John Schneider (*The Dukes of Hazzard*) had the idea to start the Children's Miracle Network Telethon, a program to raise money for children's hospitals, but lacked the financial means and a studio to produce it.

Marie loves to help children. She and John Schneider started The Children's Miracle Network.

Marie sent Mick and Joe to our home to tell us about the concept and to see if the Osmond Family would support them by allowing CMN to use our name as well as The Osmond Televisions Studios to originate their telethon. Suzanne and I liked the idea but needed to present it to our entire family for consideration. The family unanimously agreed to give their support.

We volunteered our time and talents and gave CMN the use of our new studios free of charge. CMN hadn't yet created a 501c3 non-profit, so we met with our board of directors which allowed them to use our Osmond Foundation and Osmond name to begin.

Mick Shannon, Marie, Joe Lake, John Schneider

Prior to the kickoff of the LIVE broadcast, we hosted the sponsors and celebrities for a luncheon at our home on Osmond Lane.

The commitment made by every Osmond was that, at our concert performances, we would reach out to local TV stations, children's hospitals and corporations to come to our shows as our guests, where we told them about our telethon idea and asked (sometimes begged) them to carry the telethon on their local TV stations benefiting their local children's hospital.

The first year we raised over four million dollars, and our continual growth eventually led to where one hundred percent of the money raised stayed with local hospitals. It was a true win-win. Eventually the telethon was moved to Disneyland, then Disney World where our sons, The Osmond Second Generation, served as youth Chairmen for CMN and performed for several years.

As of today, The Children's Miracle Network has raised an astounding nine billion dollars for sick children in local children's hospitals. Corporations and sponsors love it, television stations and media love it, and, best of all, the parents of those children who are helped, love it the most. Through the vision of just a few, supported by hard work and generous giving, a true miracle was created.

Furthering CMN's mission, John Bishop, Rand O'Donnel (Chairman of the Children's Miracle Network), and I helped create a program that was welcomed by the Premier of China, Li Peng and President George HW Bush.

Through CMN's one hundred and seventy hospitals, we donated essential equipment, such as CT Scanners and X-ray machines, to China through the Chinese CCTF Charity. In addition, we helped them create a cause marketing program where they selected Poster Children (orphans) to be put on postage stamps, and the government apportioned a fraction of that income to be placed in a reserve so orphans could be treated at their hospitals. Through this program, over one million children have received critical care, something we are especially proud of.

The announcement of this great venture was celebrated with

the Premier of China at a special dinner hosted at the Great Hall of the People in a ceremony that was televised to five hundred million people. It was the first ever simulcast between the US and Chinese governments.

One Heart oneheart.org

In 1994, Suzanne and I started our own charity called One Heart Inc.—a non-profit foundation for strengthening the family—the basic unit of society. I also acquired **thefamily.com** and published a newsletter for several years with the goal to help strengthen families around the world. I wrote a song for *One Heart* called, 'World of Giving.' "Except men have charity they are nothing."

A CHARITY FOR ORPHANS

Through One Heart Inc., we awarded 'The Family Award' to recognize individuals and companies who gave and did much to help strengthen and keep families together. We have given awards to Faith Hill and Tim McGraw, Martina McBride, and Paul McCartney, among others, for their examples in strengthening the family.

While helping many families with various needs, our friends John and Elaine Bishop approached us about getting *One Heart* to support orphans, which we embraced. Suzanne and I currently work through the Royal Families organization to support orphanages around the world. We have helped build schools, provide supplies, food, clothing and money for orphanages in Mexico, El Salvador, Ecuador, China, Africa, Spain, Russia and Sao Tome.

Our **warmingfamilies.org**, a subsidiary of One Heart Inc., was created for children in need of housing and clothing. We secured the support of Michele Casper of 'Lands' End,' who gave us yarn for a thousand volunteer knitters, who helped coordinate the making of at least ten thousand knitted caps, mittens, blankets, etc.

Deseret Industries Humanitarian Services then volunteered to help distribute the items around to those in need. We gave many items to children of American Indian Services, to hospitals and homeless shelters.

Alan at children's hospital

Former Prince of Ethiopia being honored in Salt Lake City with the staff of One Heart

At the Great Wall of China with John Bishop and One Heart staff members

My parents, George and Olive Osmond wanted to do all they could to help our deaf brothers Virl and Tom. They started the original Osmond Foundation to help other hearing-impaired children.

With **deaf.net**, another subsidiary of One Heart Inc., we promoted the donation of used hearing aids and later 'Starkey' who joined us and Olive Osmond's Hearing Fund, in getting hearing aids to many thousands of hearing-impaired children.

Helping Our Community

SCERA, a historic non-profit landmark in Orem, Utah, was established in 1933. When it turned fifty years old, then President Norm Nielsen directed the building of a large amphitheater in the SCERA Park. They wanted to attract crowds to the new facility and celebrate its golden anniversary, so they asked my brothers and me, the Osmonds, to perform at the inaugural concert in 1984. As our gift to the community, we donated our time and talents at no charge. Thousands filled the park and helped launch one of the most popular entertainment centers in Utah.

In 1987 Suzanne and I, along with friends Jim and Collette Lindahl, were concerned about our children starting junior high school and felt that their educational opportunities could be improved, so we started our own school called Ivy Hall Academy. The first year there were only thirteen seventh-grade students, with two teachers. The school still exists today and has expanded to two hundred and fifty plus students with classes from pre-school to twelfth grade.

Helping Our Fellow Performers

In the early 1990s, a talented good friend, David Brewer, taught me how to write and program html code and to design websites. He also showed me how to acquire various URL's. I acquired ninety-seven different URL's, including alanosmond.com, osmond.com, osmond.org, osmond.net, osmond.net, and the ones we needed for our various charitable organizations. We were living in Branson, Missouri, where several celebrities had their own theaters. Most of them didn't see the need for a URL in the future, but I did. I told them it would help their theater business and that, "someday, you will thank me." So, I created and gave many of them their own URL's. Our goal was to 'make a difference for good in the world.' Many of them expressed their gratitude later when they were able to use them for their websites.

FILMS, DOCUMENTARIES, AND OTHER PRODUCTIONS ABOUT THE OSMONDS

THROUGHOUT THE YEARS, the fascination about the Osmond family has spurred multiple documentaries and other productions. As the leader and spokesman of the Osmonds, I have learned that in today's world, many questions we are asked may be 'baited' or 'leading,' to put us on the spot, in order to create an attention-getting headline; while others are sincere in desiring to know more about our lives, beliefs, actions and thinking. After an interview is taped, there is no guarantee what they choose to use. As a family, we've always tried hard to 'shoot straight' and be honest and sincere in how we respond, then we never have to worry about any conflicting stories.

I also like to give purpose and reasons as to 'why' we did what we did. But the proof in what we say can be verified by how we live our lives. It reminds me of a favorite poem:

I'd rather see a sermon than hear one any day.

I'd rather one would walk with me than merely point the way.

The eye's a better pupil more willing than the ear.

Fine council is confusing but example always clear.

And the best of all the preachers is the one who lives his creed.

For to 'see' good put in action, is what everybody needs."

I hope you'll enjoy watching these various videos and truly 'see' the good we tried to be—'The Way We Were,' and still are.

In 1982, my sister, Marie starred in *Side by Side, The True Story of the Osmond Family*, a TV movie about Father, Mother, and all of us children. Mother helped write and produce the show and Marie played the role of our mother, Olive Osmond.

Other productions, many of which can be found on YouTube, include:

- *The Osmonds* – 1972 ABC-TV Saturday morning cartoon series
- *On Tour with The Osmonds* – 1973 documentary of UK Tour
- *The Osmond Family Christmas Album* – 1976
- *Inside the Osmonds* – 2001 ABC-TV Movie
- *Being The Osmonds* – 2003 UK documentary featuring the Osmond Brothers)
- *Oprah – Osmond Family Reunion* – November 9, 2007
- *The Osmonds: Family, Faith, and Fame* – 2023 KSL
- *The Last Chapter* – Osmond Brothers' last show together
- *At Home with The Osmonds Second Generation* – Parts One, Two, and Three
- *Alan Osmond One Way Ticket Announcement*
- *and many more…!*

OSMONDS
THE PLAN

FULL DESCRIPTION AND LYRICS
OF *THE PLAN* ALBUM

War In Heaven

(A battle before this world that was over Free Agency)

We lived before this world was as spirit children of God, created spiritually male or female before we were created naturally (flesh and bones) upon the face of the earth. [Moses 3:5] and dwelt with our Heavenly Parents nearest to the planet Kolob, which is set nigh unto the throne of God, to govern all those planets which belong to the same order as that upon which thou standest (the earth). (Abraham 3:9)

Heavenly Father's Plan of Life was presented to us, and Jesus was chosen to be our Savior. We wrote the song as though it was sung by Jesus: "Let me take care of you and keep an eye on you," with the glory being given to the Father. Satan then stepped forward saying how he would be our savior and make sure we all returned back home, set to music as though he sang: "Gonna tame ya, make you mind!" There arose what was deemed a War in Heaven where a third part of the hosts of heaven followed Satan and kept not their first estate, denying them of getting natural bodies and were cast down to earth. Fighting over Free Agency is what the War in Heaven was all about. Remember? We were all there!

This musical expression of *The War in Heaven* was well arranged and orchestrated by Tommy Oliver, as an instrumental only.

Traffic in My Mind

(Who Am I? Why am I here? Where am I going?)

These three questions are probably the most asked about life and religion.

This song was written and likened to someone who was driving on a busy highway with much traffic, confusion in their mind, and trying to determine which road to follow. Just like in one's mind in answering these questions, we sang, addressing those three questions. It had a hard driving guitar riff that "drove" the message home.

Before The Beginning

(We lived as spirit children of God in Heaven)

This song expresses our belief that we lived a premortal life with bodies of spirits before this world was. As we sang, "we called it 'Home' but didn't stay. We knew that we would leave one day and cry" . . . followed by the sound of "a slap on a baby's behind" (as doctors used to do), getting the baby to start breathing . . . representing life on earth as a child. It sings of how we were taught and introduced to The Plan of Life before we were born and that we came here to get a mortal body of flesh and bones, as sung: "Ever since we came to be, with *The Plan* we learned to see, we alone would guide our destiny."

In the preexistence, we had our Free Agency and the power to choose between following either Jesus or Satan. God had chosen Jesus, and we chose to come to this world with Jesus as our Savior and Redeemer.

Movie Man

(Your Conscience – Thoughts – Works)

Have you ever done something wrong, thinking that no one was watching, or that no one will ever know that you did it? Well, someone is watching. This song refers to that someone who is watching as *The Movie Man!* He's not only filming you, but he's recording your thoughts, too!

It's your conscience! As the Scriptures indicate, God knows all things. Even our very thoughts! All things will be remembered coming judgment day, and they will be made known from the housetops. . . on TV maybe?

What about judgment day? As we sang: "You're in living color it's your picture show. Even what you are thinking, everyone will know. That's the day you'll have to take the stand, the Movie Man."

Let Me In

(Repentance)

Have you ever made a mistake? Left the one you loved, thinking you could live without him/her? Only to realize that you can't get him/her out of your mind.

Only then realizing that you "really need her, and promise to never leave her, begging her please" . . . to let you in her arms again; that you'll never go away. Because you love her!

Well, this makes a great love song. But it was actually written about Jesus!

A song about repentance. That . . . you're sorry you left Him and want to be back in His arms again. It's about Forgiveness! A most important part of becoming all you can be.

One Way Ticket to Anywhere

(Works Free Agency with the Power to Choose)

With Free Agency, we can choose to be more than what we are, but what we want to become! This song represents life's journey as a "One Way Ticket to Anywhere, There's no place you can't go! So, hold on baby don't let go!" No, No! We MUST endure to the end in order to receive our reward of a higher heaven.

Are You Up There?

(God – Faith – Testimony)

This is a song I wrote, but I really didn't. You see, I had some special help from my *Ghost Writer*, the *Holy Ghost*, and received inspiration from on high. I was sitting up in my bed late one night, working on *The Plan* album, determined to write down what I was feeling about my Heavenly Father and answering the question that many people ask today, Is there really a God?

I spent several hours pondering and praying, trying to listen to that still small voice of the spirit from within me, and to express what that warm feeling was that I was having inside me. About two o'clock that morning, it all started coming to me very quickly; I wrote on my notepad as fast as I could, the lyrics, notes, and chords, as they came to me. I didn't stop writing until it was finished, and when we recorded it, we never changed a single thing. In answer to the question, Are you up there?

Yes, He is.

It's Alright

(Works – Free Agency – The Power to Choose)

Everyone was taught God's plan of happiness before we were born on earth, and we will have the chance to hear about the Gospel of Jesus Christ again. Our test in life is to see what we will choose, truth and light or wickedness and darkness, and also who we will choose to follow and serve, either Jesus or Satan. Our works decide our exaltation; to which kingdom of heaven we will go to at the resurrection; the telestial like unto the stars, the terrestrial like unto the moon, or celestial like unto the sun. If we cannot live the higher truths or light, we cannot go to the highest heaven of light and truth where God is: the Celestial. And when we learn something that is true, we should choose to add it to what we believe until we have a fulness of truth and light. God created you and me to become all that we can be, and Jesus is 'The Way' to make it happen. The Holy Ghost will lead you, if you listen, and will tell you the truth of all things. You can't do it alone but must be married eternally to another and to be 'as one' as husband (male) and wife (female). You have to want it, and the ONLY one stopping you is 'YOU'! As we sang, "Some find, some will never see, others throw it away. Alright! It's ALRIGHT!" Why?

Because, whatever we choose in life, there's a place for us in the 'Many Mansions' in the heavens above. (John 14:2, 1 Corinthians 15:40–42, D&C 76:50–119), or in outer darkness below. We have free agency, and God wants us to be happy.

Mirror, Mirror

(Reflection – Reality – in 5/4 Time)

A reflective song whereas we look in a mirror to evaluate what we look like, inside as well as outside, . . .who we are and what we end up being as a person. Liking what you see or not, and in asking how I became this way. Sometimes we tap dance through life in dealing with this!

Darlin'

(True Love and Marriage)

Marriage between a man and a woman is ordained of God, and the family is central to the Creator's plan for the eternal destiny of His children. When a man and woman marry and then have their marriage sealed or bound together in The House of the Lord (the temple) for time and for all eternity, (not until "death do you part") and have their children sealed to them, also. Only then can their marriage and family be together forever. That's also true about your deceased ancestors. ..."For we without them and they without us cannot be made perfect." (D&C 128:15,18)

This song of true love is about the one you love and how blessed you are knowing that because you've had your marriage sealed together for time and for all eternity, there is nothing we can't do.

The Last Days

(How things will be before Jesus returns again)

Not even the angels in heaven know when Jesus will return again in the last days, but prophecy in the scriptures talks of certain things that will precede Jesus's return and what would exist in the last days.

The message of the song expresses the conditions of the world in the last days. As we sang: "That's what they said, someday it would be, Now just look around, if that's what we see, it's got to be the last days!"

Have you watched the news lately? :-)

Goin' Home

(Death – A Graduation – Returning back Home)

Have you ever wondered what happens after we die? The gospel of Jesus Christ clearly teaches that life on earth is not all there is. Our spirit bodies existed before we were born and will continue to live after we die. After death, our spirits go to the spirit world or spirit prison to await the judgement day and our resurrection. The gospel of Jesus Christ is also taught in the spirit world. Because every soul is precious to God, Jesus Christ provided a way to salvation for those who died without an opportunity to receive the gospel.

Exaltation is eternal life; the kind of life God lives. He lives in great glory and is a Creator. We can become like our Heavenly Father & Heavenly Mother. Learn How: comeuntochrist.org.

If we prove faithful to the Lord and make sacred covenants in the temple, and keep them, we will live in the highest degree of glory in the Celestial Kingdom of Heaven with our Heavenly Father and Mother in eternal families. Exaltation is the greatest gift that Heavenly Father can give his children. (D&C 14:7) '*What a Plan!*'

All songs composed, written, and played by The Osmonds: Alan Osmond, Merrill Osmond, Wayne Osmond.

Produced by Alan Osmond-Recorded at Kolob Studios, Los Angeles, California-Engineer Ed Greene, arranged by Tommy Oliver.

SIDE 1

1. War In Heaven 1:38

2. Traffic In My Mind 3:00

Vignette: Don't Take It to Easy 0:57

3. Before The Beginning 3:39

Vignette: It's All Up To You 0:27

4. Movie Man 3:20

Vignette: I'm Sorry 0:19

5. Let Me In 3:38

6. One Way Ticket To Anywhere 3:08

SIDE 2

1. Are You Up There? 4:32

2. It's Alright 2:36

3. Mirror, Mirror 2:25

4. Darlin' 3:10

5. The Last Days 3:04

6. Goin' Home 2:29

Listen to *The Plan* for FREE!

SIDE ONE

War In Heaven (Instrumental) 1.41 *

1. Traffic In My Mind 3:55

I've got traffic in my mind yeah
Don't know which road to follow
I've got traffic in my mind yeah
I'm all alone flying solo
I've got questions looking at me
Answers trying to find me
Everybody telling me what they don't know
I've got traffic in my mind yeah
Don't know which road to follow.

I see blind men leading blind men
And telling us how to make it
I get better answers watching
Some little kid trying to fake it
So, tell me who am I?
Why am I here?
Where in heaven's name am I going?
I've got traffic in my mind, yeah
Don't know which road to follow.

So, tell me who am I?
Why am I here?
Where in heaven's name am I going?
I've got traffic in my mind, yeah
Don't know which road to follow.
Which road should I follow?
Don't know which road to follow.

Vignette: Don't Take It Too Easy

Don't take it too easy
Don't take it too easy
Gonna take you for a ride
Don't take it too easy
A place where nothing hides
Don't take it too easy
Come on and step inside
Don't take it too easy
Gonna take you for a ride
Don't take it too easy
Gonna take you for a ride
Don't take it too easy
Don't take it too easy
Don't take it too easy.

2. Before The Beginning 4.06 *

Before the beginning we were living
Oh, so far away from here
And we called it home but didn't stay
We knew that we could leave one day and cry
Before the beginning we were willing
To lay aside whom we had been
And take a chance to slip away
Or make it back to home one day, what for
Ever since we came to be
With the plan we've learned to see
We alone would guide our destiny
In the beginning we'd be living
As we would be, he once was
To look at him, to look at me
And think some day like him I'll be, what more

Ever since we came to be
With the plan we learned to see
We control infinity, what more
What more

Vignette: It's All Up To You
We are what we were and will be what we do
We're all on our own, yes it's all up to you
To learn what is false and to do what is true
It's what you've always wanted to do.

3. Movie Man 3.36

Why did you do it, you should not make your mother cry
I'd say you blew it, and yes he gave you one more try
Yet you laugh and you smile try to run away
Don't you know what you do you might regret someday
Cause there's one who has eyes on your evil ways
The movie man
Why do you do it, you're in for a big surprise
Oh, I never knew it, but honey there's no telling lies
You're in living color, it's your picture show
Even what you're thinking everyone will know
That the day you'll have to take the stand
The movie man
You're in living color, it's your picture show
Even what you're thinking everyone will know
That's the day you'll have to take the stand
The movie man
Why did you do it, you should not make your mother cry

Vignette: I'm Sorry
Please don't let me see you cry. Let me say I'm sorry. So sorry. Oh yes, I'm sorry.

4. Darlin' 3.11 **

Darlin', I look into your eyes
And see what words could never tell
Darlin' you've made me understand
The me I thought I knew so well
Like an angel sent from up above
You came and touched my life with love
Oh, Darlin' I'd love to make you mine, I would
Darlin' each time I look at you
I see a missing part of me
Darlin' if you will walk with me
We'll step towards eternity
And when the world is finally through
I'll still be ever loving you
Oh, Darlin' there is no end if I'm with you
Oh, Darlin' there's really nothing we can't do

5. The Last Days 3.01 *

Nations take up their battle stations
Patrons of zodiac revelations
Lustations breaking family relations
Litigation allowing shoot up sensations
That's what they said, someday it would be
Now just look around if that's what we see
It's gotta be the last days
Gotta be the last days.
People living lives of confusion
Millions caught up in revolution
Cities lost in their own pollution
Question, what is the Constitution
That's what they said, someday it would be

Now just look around if that's what we see
It's gotta be the last days
Gotta be the last days
That's what they said, someday it would be
Now just look around if that's what we see
It's gotta be the last days
Last days, it's gotta be the last days
It's gotta be the last days
It's gotta be the last days
It's gotta be the last days
It's gotta be the last days
It's gotta be the last days
It's gotta be the last days

6. Goin' Home 2:31 (*including "Don't take it too easy"*)

I'm a track star, I gotta run far
And I'm ready to go
It's a long, long road and I gotta make it on my own
Everybody's gaining on me
Trying to slow me down
But if I'm gonna make it gotta fight, fight, fight all day
And night, and day, alright
Goin' home, goin' home, goin' home
I gotta make it gonna make it alright
Goin' home, goin' home, goin' home
If it takes me the rest of my life
I'm a space man, from a different land
I've gotta get back home
I've been gone so long that I'm feeling like a useless man
Everybody's looking at me
Trying to help me down

ABOUT THE AUTHOR

Like songs, scripts aren't written; they're re-written:

ALAN RALPH OSMOND is the third oldest of eight boys and one girl. His love of music, and sharp ear to hear harmonies, was instrumental in starting The Osmond Brothers Barbershop Quartet which gradually moved into pop, where they rose to stardom. At the age of eight Alan became their leader and for six decades, guided the singing sensation now known as the Osmonds to worldwide OSMONDMANIA.

Alan plays a variety of musical instruments, writes poetry, and has penned and produced over two hundred original songs. Together with his siblings, they accumulated sales of over 100 million records. He was Executive Producer of *Donny & Marie* and was over Osmond Studios. Alan directed a SESAC award video, as well as many other music videos. He helped create and produce Ronald Reagan's Opening Inauguration Ceremonies in 1981 which led to the creation of 'Stadium of Fire,' an annual Fireworks Celebrity Extravaganza for God, Family, Freedom and Country, featuring top name celebrities and visually thrilling entertainment.

He served in the military for six years earning top awards in marksmanship, overall testing, and was voted 'Outstanding Trainee.'

Alan faced a devastating diagnosis of MS in his thirties which eventually ended his performing career, but not his spirit. "I may have MS, but MS does not have me," is a phrase you'll often hear him declare.

Alan and his eternal love, Suzanne Pinegar recently celebrated their 50th Wedding Anniversary. They have been blessed with eight sons who began at very young ages to follow in their father's footsteps, singing and performing as the Osmonds Second Generation. Living at the foot of the beautiful Utah Wasatch Mountains, their family is their greatest treasure as their sons add grandchildren to the ever-expanding Osmond posterity.

Alan, spiritually driven and exercising devout faith in all areas of his life, has served as a temple ordinance worker for fifteen years in the Church of Jesus Christ of Latter-day Saints.

Olive D. Osmond wrote Alan
a note on her death bed.

(Alan served as Leader of their musical family.)

"There is no limit
in the good you can do if you
don't care who gets the credit."